# M. TVLLI CICERONIS

## PRO M. CAELIO

### ORATIO

EDITED WITH TEXT, INTRODUCTION, AND
COMMENTARY BY

## R. G. AUSTIN

THIRD EDITION

CLARENDON PRESS · OXFORD

Oxford University Press, Great Clarendon Street, Oxford OX2 6DP

Oxford New York
Athens Auckland Bangkok Bogota Bombay
Buenos Aires Calcutta Cape Town Dar es Salaam
Delhi Florence Hong Kong Istanbul Karachi
Kuala Lumpur Madras Madrid Melbourne
Mexico City Nairobi Paris Singapore
Taipei Tokyo Toronto
and associated companies in
Berlin Ibadan

Oxford is a trade mark of Oxford University Press

Published in the United States by
Oxford University Press Inc., New York

British Library Cataloguing in Publication Data
Data available

Library of Congress Cataloging in Publication Data
M. Tulli Ciceronis Pro M. Caelio oratio.
1. Caelis Rufus, Marcus. I. Austin, R. G.
(Roland Gregory), 1901–1974. II. Title.
PA6279.C18 1988 875'.01 87-34985
ISBN 0-19-814062-2

7 9 10 8

Printed in Great Britain on acid-free paper by
J. W. Arrowsmith Ltd., Bristol

# PREFACE

In this third edition of my commentary on the *pro Caelio*, I have corrected some errors of statement and translation, and Appendix III has been rewritten. The additional notes contain both new matter and comments on passages where my previous treatment was unsatisfactory. The text remains Clark's, but I am grateful to the Delegates of the Clarendon Press for allowing me to make one very important change: I have admitted to the text in § 5 the emendation which most modern scholars, I believe, would now accept as providing valid evidence for the birthplace of Caelius Rufus. This has necessitated certain adjustments in the relevant notes, and also the revision of Appendix II.

I must thank Mr. J. P. V. D. Balsdon, of Exeter College, for pointing out some historical slips. Mr. William M. Calder III, of Concord, Massachusetts, sent me some helpful comments and parallels. My debt to Professor W. S. Watt, of the University of Aberdeen, is again deep: my added material owes much to the way in which he laid an unerring finger on points that I had previously left either untouched or hopefully vague.

R. G. A.

*Liverpool*
*March 1959*

# CONTENTS

INTRODUCTION . . . . . v

THE MANUSCRIPTS . . . . . xvii

SELECTION OF READINGS FROM *OX. PAP.* X. 1251
(*Π*) . . . . . . . xxii

COLLATION OF THE OXFORD AND THE TEUB-
NER TEXT . . . . . . xxiv

BIBLIOGRAPHY . . . . . xxviii

SIGLA . . . . . . . xxxii

TEXT . . . . . . . I

COMMENTARY . . . . . 41

APPENDIXES
    I. Date of Caelius' birth . . . 144
    II. Place of Caelius' birth . . . 146
    III. Caelius and Catullus . . . 148
    IV. Date of delivery of the *pro Caelio* . . 151
    V. The charges . . . . 152
    VI. The prosecutors . . . . 154
    VII. The case against Antonius in 59 B.C. . . 158
    VIII. Note on the composition of the speech . 159

ADDITIONAL NOTES . . . . 162

INDEXES . . . . . 176

# INTRODUCTION

## LIFE OF CAELIUS

M. CAELIUS RUFUS was born, according to Pliny (*N.H.* vii. 165), on 28 May 82 B.C.; the date has been disputed, but the evidence from this speech suggests that Pliny has been wrongly discredited (see Appendix I). His birthplace cannot be definitely ascertained, since our only information comes from a corrupt passage in § 5 of the *pro Caelio*; it is, however, most probable that he was born at Interamnia in the territory of Picenum, the modern Teramo (see Appendix II).

We learn from Cicero that Caelius' father was a Roman knight who had possessions in Africa. His economical mode of life was apparently turned against the son in this trial; but the truth seems to be that the latter did not receive an allowance adequate to his ideas,[1] and was accustomed to behave in a manner unsuited to his position. After the young Caelius had assumed the *toga virilis* his father took him to Rome and put him in the charge of Cicero and Crassus. His aptness as a pupil may be illustrated by Cicero's remark in later years (*ad Fam.* ii. 8. 1) πολιτικώτερον *enim te adhuc neminem cognovi*, and by his ultimate attainments as an orator. This *tirocinium fori* lasted from 66 to 63, when Caelius broke away from his tutelage and became entangled with Catiline.[2] There is nothing to prove that he actually joined the conspiracy, although, as Cicero finds it necessary to give an elaborate vindication of this period of his life, his reputation must have suffered severely. At the end of 62 or early in 61 he travelled to Africa in the *cohors* of Q. Pompeius Rufus the proconsul, no doubt influenced in his choice by the presence there of his father's

---

[1] Cf. Vell. Pat. ii. 68 'peior illi res familiaris quam mens erat', and see § 3 note.
[2] Cf. Boissier, *Cicéron et ses amis*, p. 170 'le passage était brusque, mais Caelius ne s'est jamais donné la peine de ménager les transitions'.

property. He seems to have made an energetic and successful aide-de-camp.[1]

On returning to Rome in 60, Caelius formally entered public life by prosecuting C. Antonius Hybrida, Cicero's colleague as consul in 63.[2] Antonius was strongly suspected of Catilinarian leanings; but he was a trimmer, and as such unpopular on both sides. After his year in office he had scandalously and ingloriously mismanaged the province of Macedonia. The trial took place in March 59 and Antonius was condemned. Cicero was displeased at the attack and dejected by the result, for he defended Antonius himself. Although he was never on good terms with his colleague, he probably felt it necessary to defend him, as officially at least Antonius had commanded the army which defeated the Catilinarians at Pistoria; the verdict naturally cast an indirect slur on himself.

This success at once made Caelius a notable. Emancipated from Cicero and dissatisfied with living quietly at home with his father, he rented a house from P. Clodius in the fashionable quarter of the Palatine (see § 17, note), near the centre of affairs in Rome. It was also near Clodia. At this time she was about 36 years of age, and lately widowed. For the moment Caelius became her chief favourite; Cicero paints a vivid picture of the scenes from high life in which the two were concerned—concert-parties, garden-parties, river-picnics, banquets, both at Rome and at Baiae. If Caelius is actually the Rufus whom Catullus upbraids as his supplanter in Lesbia's affections (Appendix III) we have personal evidence of a unique nature to show how supreme he reigned. The intimacy lasted about two years; Caelius then grew tired, and there was a disastrous quarrel. As Boissier remarks (p. 184), 'Clodia qui, comme on l'a vu, prenait ordinairement les avances, n'était pas habituée

---

[1] For the date see Wieschhölter, *De M. Caelio Rufo oratore*, pp. 12 f.

[2] See Appendix VII. Antonius went into exile at Cephallenia, where he became a great personage (Strabo x. 2. 13 τὴν ὅλην νῆσον ὑπήκοον ἔσχεν ὡς ἴδιον κτῆμα). The trial was held on the day of Clodius' transference to the plebs (*de domo* 41; cf. Wieschhölter, p. 16).

à ce dénoûment'. Just as she had broken Catullus, so she
hoped to punish Caelius. But he was made of stronger stuff,
and Clodia's fierce resentment showed itself in her connexion
with the present case.

At the beginning of 56 Caelius brought a charge of *ambitus*
against L. Calpurnius Bestia, the father of L. Sempronius
Atratinus (Appendix VI, p. 154). Cicero defended him, and
the case was heard on 11 February. Bestia was acquitted, and
must have begun a new candidature for office, as Caelius
promptly instituted fresh proceedings against him.[1] No reason
is stated for Caelius' animosity; Bestia had at one time some
connexion with Catiline (Appendix VI, p. 156), and Caelius
may have prosecuted him to avert similar suspicion from himself, a motive which had possibly been behind his previous
accusation of Antonius. His anxiety for success points to some
imperative need to rehabilitate himself.[2] However, the second
accusation never took shape, for the young Atratinus intervened to save his father, and prosecuted Caelius himself for
*vis*, supported by L. Herennius Balbus and P. Clodius.
Caelius spoke in his own defence, probably first. A few objectionable expressions are extant from his speech, notably his
nickname for Clodia 'quadrantaria Clytaemnestra';[3] he termed
one of his opponents (probably Atratinus) 'Pelia cincinnatus
(see § 18, note),[4] and mockingly alleged that Atratinus' speech
was written for him by his master Plotius Gallus, 'a barley-
blown rhetorician' ('hordearius rhetor').[5] Caelius in fact shows
himself here, as usual, a master of gibes and flouts and jeers;
his remarks, akin as they are to the spirit of Catullus' lampoons,

[1] Cf. Heinze, *Hermes* lx, p. 195, note 2.
[2] Cf. § 76 'ut iste interpositus sermo deliciarum desidiaeque moreretur
. . . nomen amici mei de ambitu detulit'.
[3] Quintil. viii. 6. 53; cf. ibid. 'in triclinio Coam, in cubiculo Nolam'.
[4] Quintil. i. 5. 61.
[5] Suet. *Rhet.* 2 (cf. Tyrrell and Purser, *Correspondence of Cicero* iii,
p. xlv); for a suggestion that Gallus was a democrat and that in common
with other *Latini rhetores* he was forbidden to teach for political reasons
see Gwynn, *Roman Education*, pp. 63 f.

INTRODUCTION

point to the existence of a circle of wits who would understand
and relish such allusions (cf. also *ad Att.* i. 18. 3). Crassus
spoke second,[1] and Cicero last,[2] according to his favourite
practice (*Brut.* 190, *Orat.* 130). The trial was held on 3–4 April
56 B.C. (see Appendix IV, and § 1, note); the charges are discussed in Appendix V.[3] Whatever the secret history, it is clear
that the actual indictment was formal, and that Clodia was the
real driving force behind it; society reasons prompted the case,
and the issue was the social disappearance of either Clodia or
·Caelius. The accused was acquitted, and except for a reference to another attack on him by the Clodii two years later
(*Q.F.* ii. 11. 2) we hear no more of his enemies in connexion
with him. Clodia herself vanishes from sight, a fact which
shows significantly enough the social importance of the trial.
Caelius did not proceed with his new prosecution of Bestia;
he probably dropped it out of respect for Cicero.[4]

Caelius could now follow his political career. The question
of his quaestorship is discussed in Appendix I. In 52 he was
tribune, and naturally championed Milo in the disturbances
of that year. He enabled Milo to hold a *contio ad populum*
in the disorders consequent upon the burning of the Curia after
Clodius' murder, but the meeting was attacked and Caelius
and Milo fled (*Mil.* 91; Appian, *B.C.* ii. 22). Then, when
Clodius' supporters demanded an examination under torture
of Milo's slaves, Caelius made a counter-demand against those

[1] Cf. Heinze, p. 199; in view of the covert attack upon Pompey afforded
by the case, Crassus' position is interesting; for at this time his relations
with Pompey were certainly strained, and the latter seems to have suspected Crassus of helping Clodius against him (*Q.F.* ii. 3. 4).
[2] I cannot believe Humbert's theory that Cicero did not speak last but
took only a minor part and left Rome before the case was ended; it is
entirely based on an unnecessary misinterpretation of Quintil. iv. 2. 27.
[3] For an ingenious reconstruction of the political setting of the trial,
see Tenney Frank, *Catullus and Horace*, p. 79.
[4] Cf. Heinze, p. 195, note 2; van Wageningen groundlessly assumes
that it was brought into court. The identification of Atratinus' father with
Bestia shows that the first prosecution took place in 56, not the end of 57
as stated by van Wageningen, following Wieschhölter and others.

of Clodius (Ascon., p. 30 KS, but the text is doubtful). Finally
Caelius violently opposed Pompey's bills *de vi* and *de ambitu*,
as amounting to a *privilegium* aimed at Milo; Pompey grew
angry and threatened force (Ascon., pp. 31, 32). Caelius had
to yield, and a beginning of his estrangement from Pompey
had been made. He continued to help Milo;[1] among other
things, he and Cicero defended Saufeius, the leader of the
gang which murdered Clodius, and secured his acquittal by
one vote (Ascon., p. 48).

This anti-Pompeian tendency continued. At the beginning
of 51 Caelius brought a charge, presumably for *vis*,[2] against his
colleague as tribune in 52, Q. Pompeius Rufus; this man was
Sulla's grandson (Ascon., p. 28; Dio Cassius xl. 45) and had
been prominent in the obstructionist tactics which helped
Pompey to his sole consulship. He had inflamed the people
by exciting them against Milo, and more especially by insinuat-
ing that the latter was plotting against Pompey's life.[3] Caelius
made another of his savage attacks, and Rufus was condemned
(Val. Max. iv. 2. 7); he went to Bauli in Campania, where he
lived in great poverty (*ad Fam.* viii. 1. 4). An odd story shows
that Caelius was not devoid of a certain sense of sportsman-
ship. Rufus' mother refused to restore to him some property
of his that she held, and he appealed to Caelius for aid. Caelius
took the matter up with his usual impetuosity, and succeeded
in getting the estate restored (Val. Max., loc. cit.).

This same year came the event which has made Caelius far
more than a name to us. Cicero went to Cilicia as governor,
and before leaving Rome arranged that Caelius should be his

[1] Ascon., p. 48; see *Mil.* 91 for a panegyric, and cf. *Brut.* 273 'talis
tribunus pl. fuit ut nemo contra civium perditorum popularem turbulen-
tamque dementiam a senatu et a bonorum causa steterit constantius'.

[2] There is no actual evidence either for the ground or for the matter of
the charge brought by Caelius. For the date see Clark's *pro Milone*,
pp. 129 ff.

[3] Dio Cassius xl. 49, Ascon., pp. 33, 45 'Q. Pompeius Rufus ... dixerat
in contione . . . : "Milo dedit quem in curia cremaretis, dabit quem in
Capitolio sepeliatis." ' Later it was rumoured that he had murdered
Cicero on the latter's journey to his province (*ad Fam.* viii. 1. 4).

home correspondent (*ad Fam.* viii. 1. 1). The body of letters preserved (*ad Fam.* viii) does much to illustrate his character. He appears as a light-hearted and amusing informant, cynical perhaps, yet with an acute penetration of the political position, as might be expected from what we know of his personal history. His style[1] is one of the most interesting in Latin literature, vivid, dramatic, elliptical, familiar, and the whole collection is particularly valuable as exemplifying the type of writing fashionable among the bright young men of the day, besides expressing the writer's personality in a way that nothing else could do. All the gossip of Rome is to be found here—all Caelius' own quarrels and those of others; and encroaching everywhere is the steady tide of civil war. As curule aedile for the year 50, Caelius was anxious to distinguish himself, and we find him pestering Cicero for a supply of Cilician panthers and for subscriptions from the province. Cicero, however, refused both requests. In his official capacity Caelius made an important reform in connexion with the city's water-supply. The *aquarii* had long been in the habit of allowing shopkeepers and private citizens to draw free water from the public supplies by means of side-pipes. Caelius stopped the nuisance by an informed and vigorous speech, which in later days received emphatic praise from the expert Frontinus.[2] He himself merely tells Cicero in his careless way 'nisi ego cum tabernariis et aquariis pugnarem, veternus civitatem occupasset' (*ad Fam.* viii. 6. 4). Another frequent topic is a quarrel with the censor Appius Claudius Pulcher, who had refused Caelius a loan of money. We also hear of a successful defence of M. Tuccius, accused under the lex Plotia *de vi* (*ad Fam.* viii. 8. 1).

[1] See Tyrrell and Purser, *Correspondence of Cicero* iii, pp. cviii f., F. Becher, *Über den Sprachgebrauch des M. Caelius* (Nordhausen, 1888), F. Burg, *De M. Caelii Rufi genere dicendi* (Leipzig, 1888), F. Antoine, *Lettres de Caelius à Cicéron* (Paris, 1894), pp. 51 ff.

[2] Frontin. *de aqu.* 75 'cuius rei causa est fraus aquariorum, quos aquas ex ductibus publicis in privatorum usus derivare deprehendimus ... ac de vitiis eiusmodi nec plura nec melius dici possunt quam a Caelio Rufo dicta sunt in ea contione, cui titulus est "de aquis" '

All else, however, is overshadowed by the one absorbing topic of the day: should Caesar be allowed to stand for the consulship in absence?[1] A man such as Caelius could at once see the trend of events, and these letters to Cicero, with their detail and penetration, constitute invaluable evidence for the inner history of the political crisis which led directly to the civil war. More than this, they reveal the psychology of a shrewd young Roman when confronted with such a crisis. Caelius had always inclined to the politically spectacular. In his youth he had chafed at Cicero's guardianship, and his restiveness nearly proved his undoing, leading as it did to the connexion with Catiline. But with that flair for politics which he showed even then, he escaped, before it was too late, without lasting damage. Probably at that time he dallied with the idea of supporting Pompey, then apparently at the height of his power on his return from the East. This attitude is reflected later (56) in the curiously persistent charges brought against him of complicity in the murder of Dio; for it is hardly possible not to see in this an attempt by Pompey's enemies to injure him through Caelius.[2] But Caelius must have realized, earlier than most men, that Caesar, not Pompey, was to dominate future politics, and this, coupled with his hostility to Clodius, led him to his violence in 52. After this his leanings were increasingly and naturally towards Caesar. He had already withdrawn his opposition to the 'law of the ten tribunes' which permitted Caesar to stand for the consulship while retaining command of the army; Cicero himself, oddly enough, urged him to this course.[3] Moreover, some of the events of 51–50, in themselves

[1] See G. R. Elton, 'The Terminal Date of Caesar's Gallic Proconsulate', *JRS* xxxvi, 1946, pp. 18 ff., for recent views on the problems involved.

[2] See §§ 23, 51, 78, notes; the acquittal of Sex. Clodius in March 56 was also a blow at Pompey (§ 78). Dio Cassius, however (xxxviii. 10), implies that Cicero held Caesar responsible for the accusation brought against Antonius. If so, Caelius must have been feeling his way towards Caesar as early as 59.

[3] *ad Att.* vii. 1. 4 (cf. *ad Fam.* vi. 6. 5), Caes. *B.C.* i. 32, Suet. *Iul.* 28; see Denniston on *Phil.* ii. 24, where Cicero gives a different account of his

petty, made his position still more definite. His quarrel with Appius Claudius made him look for support from the other censor, Piso Caesoninus, a Caesarian; and the breach with Pompey was widened by yet another quarrel, this time with L. Domitius Ahenobarbus. In fact a politician of Caelius' calibre could easily analyse Pompey: in *ad Fam*. viii. 1 (51 B.C.) he sums him up thus: 'solet aliud sentire et loqui, neque tantum valere ingenio ut non adpareat quid cupiat.'

In September 50 B.C. Caelius wrote a reasoned letter to Cicero (*ad Fam*. viii. 14) giving as his opinion that in such a civil crisis, so long as no recourse is had to arms, men ought *honestiorem sequi partem*, but when war breaks out openly, *firmiorem*. He adds that the safer side is the better. Pompey, in his view, would have the support of the senate and those *qui res iudicant*, while those living in fear or despair would join Caesar, who had an incomparably better army. To this realization of Caesar's strength must be ascribed Caelius' ultimate decision to join him, far more than to his own lack of means and hopes of *novae tabulae*. Nor could Pompey's personal character have attracted him as compared with Caesar's, though that would probably not have stood in his way had the position of the two leaders been reversed.

On the kalends of January 49 Scipio made his proposal that Caesar should be declared a public enemy if he refused to dismiss his army by a given date (Caes. *B.C.* i. 2). Caelius had already defined his position by supporting Calidius' proposal that Pompey should go off to Spain, his province, and so avoid war (ibid.); and now, on Scipio's motion, he took his decision: he and Curio voted against it and soon after joined Caesar.[1] His new leader sent him to quell a revolt at

conduct. Pompey's law *de iure magistratuum* apparently withdrew this privilege (52), but it was granted again in an appended clause of doubtful validity.

[1] Dio Cassius xli. 3; cf. Caes. *B.C.* i. 5 ff.; they accompanied the tribunes Antonius and Cassius. Caesar was then at Ravenna, waiting for news, and met Caelius at Ariminum.

Intimilium in Liguria, a command which did not seem to him to be of sufficient importance (*ad Fam.* viii. 15), while this early discontent was reinforced by his concern at Caesar's clemency. He already began to see that Caesar's way was not his. However, in April he went to Spain with Caesar, after writing a letter to Cicero (*ad Fam.* viii. 16),[1] urging him not to leave Italy for Pompey's camp but to remain neutral—of course with no effect. His time in Spain made him more and more dissatisfied, and he appears to have been revolving some mysterious plans.[2] His self-conceit and volatile restiveness were at last to bring about his fall. In 48 Caesar had him appointed praetor peregrinus (Caes. *B.C.* iii. 20, Dio Cassius xlii. 22); but the urban praetorship was given to C. Trebonius, and that too by nomination and not by lot. Caelius was not the man to be entrusted with financial administration of the sort then needed (cf. Caes. *B.C.* iii. 1), and Trebonius was a man of sound judgement and proved loyalty. Caelius himself did not see this, and his furious anger is reflected in the letters (cf. *ad Fam.* viii. 17). He began to interfere with Trebonius, and his attempt to pass the most radical measures caused a riot in which Trebonius was driven off his tribunal (Caes. *B.C.* iii. 20 f., Dio Cassius xlii. 22–25; cf. Quintil. vi. 3. 25). However, the consul Servilius and the Senate used a force of Caesarian soldiers, who happened to be in the city, to protect Trebonius, and a motion was carried deposing Caelius from his office.

Caelius left Rome, pretending that he was going to put his case before Caesar. In reality he went off to join Milo, who was still at large, in an attempt to raise southern Italy in revolt against him. But his wild proposals were unacceptable to the majority of the inhabitants, and he could only get together a rabble of slaves and gladiators. In a scuffle at Thurii, 48 B.C., Caelius met his death at the hands of Caesarian troops.[3]

---

[1] Cicero's reply is in *ad Fam.* ii. 16, cf. *ad Att.* x. 9. Caelius had asked Caesar to write also to Cicero, urging the same course; Caesar's letter is extant (*ad Att.* x. 8 b).    [2] Cf. *ad Att.* x. 12 a, 14, 15, 16.

[3] The accounts of Caesar and Dio differ. Caelius had sent a message

# INTRODUCTION

In Marcus Caelius Rufus we see one of the most notable members of the 'younger set' at Rome in his day. He owes his repute not to the chance vagaries of history, but to a personality which distinguished him from his companions and made him the friend of a famous man and the enemy of an infamous woman. As a man he was passionate,[1] vivacious, with a strong[2] if sometimes schoolboyish[3] sense of humour, a handsome young man and a dandy,[4] one of the three most skilled dancers of his time.[5] As a politician he was an opportunist and a cynic, too impetuous for any really consistent and far-sighted policy in spite of his singular sensitiveness to the current trend of politics,[6] too egoistic ever to be dependable, and too independent ever to satisfy his egoism. As an orator he ranked among the first by universal consent;[7] he spoke with much power, though he was better at attack than defence (cf. Cicero's remark, quoted by Quintil. vi. 3. 69, that he had 'bonam dextram, malam sinistram'), and was capable of a vitriolic invective notable even in that age when abuse was a part of polite education. His style did not please everyone; Cicero says of it (*Brut.* 273) 'antiquam eius actionem multum tamen et splendida et grandis et eadem in primis faceta et perurbana commendabat oratio', but Tacitus censures his harshness, his archaisms, and his vulgarity;[8] his qualities are admirably illustrated

to Milo, then in exile at Massilia, to meet him; Caesar states that they actually met, Dio that Milo was killed in Apulia before any meeting could take place. Dio adds that Milo left Massilia of his own accord, not at Caelius' suggestion. Cf. van Wageningen's note (p. xvi); Wieschhölter, p. 49; Wegehaupt, *M. Caelius Rufus*, p. 20.

[1] § 76, Sen. *de ira* iii. 8. 6.     [2] See the correspondence *passim*.
[3] Cf. Quintil. vi. 3. 25.                              [4] §§ 6, 36, 77.
[5] Macrob. iii. 14. 15: a disreputable claim. Clodia too was noted as being 'studiosa saltandi profusius et immoderatius quam matronam deceret' (Schol. Bob. ad Cic. *Sest.* 116).     [6] Cf. *ad Fam.* ii. 8. 1.
[7] Cf. the frequent references in Quintil. (i. 5. 61 and 6. 29, iv. 2. 123, vi. 3. 39 and 41, viii. 6. 53, ix. 3. 58, x. 1. 115, xii. 10. 11).
[8] *Dial.* 21 'sordes autem reliquae verborum et hians compositio et inconditi sensus redolent antiquitatem; nec quenquam adeo antiquarium puto, ut Caelium ex ea parte laudet qua antiquus est' (cf. ibid. 18, 25). Quintil. x. 2. 25 mentions his 'asperitas', and instancing his archaisms

INTRODUCTION

by the famous fragment of his speech against Antonius
preserved by Quintilian.[1] As a correspondent, though on his
own confession[2] he was both dilatory and irregular, he was a
writer of peculiar interest and charm, quick to seize upon the
vital points at issue, an amusing and amused observer of other
men, again with an odd harsh style all his own. In him is to be
seen a clear picture of a brilliant young Roman whose exceptional talents were forced by the very decadence of the period
to do him disservice; possibly, according to modern standards
of morality, he is an unscrupulous, unattractive, and even dangerous figure, yet very certainly he is a tragic one—it is only
necessary to read the *Brutus* to realize how the declining years
of the Republic brought honour to degradation and brilliance
to decay. He should rather be judged by the spirit of his
generation; and with all his faults, and they were many, he is a
man whose very exuberant vitality lends him charm and
fascination for all who realize that the Romans were human
like ourselves.[3] One instinctively couples him with his rival
Catullus, to whom in some ways he was closely akin in temper.
Not the least testimony to him is the friendship which Cicero
felt for him even when separated by widely divergent politics;
and a fair-minded critic will endorse the penetrating judgement of Quintilian, who saw in Caelius (x. 1. 115) 'dignus vir

remarks (i. 6. 42) 'nec [quisquam ferat] *parricidatum*, quod in Caelio vix
tolerabile videtur'.
    [1] iv. 2. 123 'namque ipsum offendunt temulento sopore profligatum,
totis praecordiis stertentem, ructuosos spiritus geminare, praeclarasque
contubernales ab omnibus spondis transversas incubare et reliquas circum-
iacere passim; quae tamen exanimatae terrore, hostium adventu percepto,
excitare Antonium conabantur, nomen inclamabant, frustra a cervicibus
tollebant, blandius alia ad aurem invocabat, vehementius etiam nonnulla
feriebat; quarum cum omnium vocem tactumque noscitaret proximae
cuiusque collum amplexu petebat, neque dormire excitatus neque vigilare
ebrius poterat, sed semisomno sopore inter manus centurionum concubina-
rumque iactabatur.'
    [2] *ad Fam.* viii. 1. 1 'ad litteras scribendas, ut tu nosti, pigerrimo'.
    [3] Cf. Val. Max. iv. 2. 7 'Caeli vero Rufi ut vita inquinata, ita miseri-
cordia . . . probanda'; Vell. Pat. ii. 68 'M. Caelius vir eloquio animoque
Curioni simillimus, sed in utroque perfectior, nec minus ingeniose
nequam'.

XV

cui et mens melior et vita longior contigisset'. Boissier's chapter on him in *Cicéron et ses amis* is both sympathetic and just, and there is an admirable sketch of his career and character in the introduction to the third volume of Tyrrell and Purser's *Correspondence of Cicero*. The fragments of his speeches, with *testimonia*, are conveniently collected by H. Malcovati, in *Oratorum Romanorum Fragmenta* (2nd edition, Turin, 1955), pp. 480–9.

# THE MANUSCRIPTS

THE main tradition of the *pro Caelio* is contained in (*a*) *Codex Parisinus* 7794 (ninth century), and (*b*) the variants, marginalia, etc., added by a second hand in *Codex Parisinus* 14749, which, together with certain excerpts made by Bartolommeo da Montepulciano in *Codex Laurentianus* LIV. 5, represent the text of the lost *Codex Cluniacensis* of Poggio ( ? eighth century). A considerable portion of the speech is contained in an Oxyrhynchus papyrus (fifth century); and there are some fragments in two palimpsests, the Taurinensis (fourth century) and the Ambrosianus (fifth century), for which see Clark, *Descent of Manuscripts*, pp. 138 ff. and 153 ff.

(1) *Cod. Par.* 7794 (*P*) contains also the *Orationes post reditum, de domo, de haruspicum responsis, pro Sestio, in Vatinium, de provinciis consularibus, pro Balbo*; see Clark, op. cit., pp. 266 ff., Klotz, preface to the Teubner Cicero, vol. vii (1919), pp. vi, xxi f., xxxviii f., Halm in *Rh. Mus.* ix, 1854, pp. 321 ff.; Chatelain, *Paléographie des classiques latins* (Paris, 1884–92), has a facsimile of fol. 73 of this MS., from § 9 to § 11 of the *pro Caelio*.

There are three later MSS. which were once thought to be derived from *P* (see Halm, loc. cit.): these are the *Gemblacensis* (*g*), now Bruxellensis 5345 (twelfth century), *Erfurtensis* (*e*), now Berol. 252 (twelfth–thirteenth century), and *Harleianus* 4927 (*h*) (twelfth century). A. Klotz showed, however, that *g* and *e* are derived not from *P*, but from a lost MS. which had the same archetype as *P*, while *h* is mainly derived from *P*, with some admixture from *Σ* (for which see below); see his preface *passim*, and *Rh. Mus.* lxvii, 1912, pp. 358 ff. Clark was ultimately convinced by Klotz's argument (op. cit., pp. 270 ff.).

For his Oxford text Clark also used two fifteenth-century MSS., *Cod. S. Marci* 255 (*b*) and *Cod. Laur.* (*Gadd.*) xc sup. 69 (ψ), the former being the earlier; see his *Anecdota Oxoniensia*, Classical Series, part x (1905), pp. xlvii ff.

(2) Our knowledge of the *Cluniacensis* is due to Clark (cf. Klotz, preface to vol. viii of the Teubner Cicero, 1918, pp. iii f., vol. vii, p. xxxiv). The testimony of this MS. may be dated not later than the eighth century; I summarize here the fascinating story of its partial reconstruction by Clark (*An. Ox.* x).

Poggio obtained this MS. from the Abbey of Cluni, in Burgundy, in 1413 or 1414. It contained the *pro Cluentio*, the *pro Roscio Amerino*, and the *pro Murena* (these two latter being previously unknown); Poggio himself states this, in a letter to Niccolo Niccoli, and he implies that it contained other speeches also (see *An. Ox.*, p. iii). Clark first showed which these others were: (*a*) by identifying Poggio's MS. with that denoted by an entry (496) in the twelfth-century catalogue at Cluni, he deduced that the *pro Milone* was included in Poggio's MS.; (*b*) he showed that the excerpts from certain speeches of Cicero in *Cod. Laur.* LIV. 5 were made by Poggio's friend Bartolommeo da Montepulciano, and were all taken from one MS., which must have been the Cluni MS.; these excerpts belong not only to the four speeches already named, but to the *pro Caelio* as well, so that this speech must also have been contained in the *Cluniacensis*.

It was therefore established (see *An. Ox.*, p. lxiii) that as early as the eleventh century there was a MS. at Cluni containing the *pro Cluentio*, *pro Roscio*, *pro Murena*, *pro Milone*, and *pro Caelio*. Clark next showed (*An. Ox.*, pp. xi ff.; *Descent of MSS.*, p. 266) that at the beginning of the fifteenth century this MS., then very illegible, was used by the French scribes who made the *Codex S. Victoris* (*Par. Lat.* 14749). The *pro Roscio* and the *pro Murena*, being known from no other source, were transcribed in full and very faithfully; where the original was illegible or corrupt, a blank was left which was filled later by a second hand with an exact facsimile

## THE MANUSCRIPTS

of what the scribe found before him. The three other speeches were not transcribed in full, but extracts were made in the form of supralineal variants, marginalia, and supplements, which were added to a text taken from a vulgar source; in the case of the *pro Caelio*, this source was descended from *P* (see Peterson, *CQ* iv, 1910, p. 168; Clark, *Descent of MSS.*, p. 24).

These marginalia, etc., agree throughout with the excerpts made in *Cod. Laur.* LIV. 5 by Bartolommeo, and they have a close affinity with the two palimpsests already mentioned. They preserve certain readings known from ancient writers on rhetoric or grammar (§§ 8, 31, 32, 50; see *An. Ox.*, p. xxx), confirm many conjectures made by various scholars (six by Madvig, §§ 41, 43, 45, 46, 58, 61), and vindicate certain passages originally omitted in *P* and added by a later hand, which had previously been regarded as interpolations (§§ 24, 35, 49, 50, 52; see *An. Ox.*, pp. xxxiii f.; *Descent of MSS.*, pp. 267 ff.). Clark denotes these supplements, marginalia, etc. (now brought back from the fifteenth century to at least the eighth) in *Par. Lat.* 14749 by the symbol $\Sigma$ (Klotz uses V); a beautiful facsimile page in *An. Ox.* shows two of the passages where Madvig's conjectures are confirmed. The early date of their origin is shown by the fact that they are not affected by the Carolingian spelling-reforms (*An. Ox.*, pp. xvii ff.), and may perhaps go back even earlier than the eighth century. Some of the readings preserved in $\Sigma$ percolated down through various MSS. (notably *S*, the fifteenth-century *Codex Monacensis* 15734; see *An. Ox.*, p. v) to the early editors of Cicero, such as Gulielmius and especially Lambinus (*An. Ox.*, p. xxxi; cf. notes on 24. 19, 35. 6), but their authoritative origin was not recognized.

The new evidence from the Cluniacensis necessitated a complete revision of the text of the *pro Caelio*; this was done by Clark in his Oxford Text of 1905 (second impression, 1908).

(3) A fifth-century papyrus ($\Pi$) from Oxyrhynchus (Grenfell and Hunt, x. 1251, published in 1914) contains a great

part of two consecutive leaves from the *pro Caelio* (§ 26. 23 [-*tio illa silves*]*tris* . . . § 55. 16 *nefa*]*ri*[*o*] *dic*[*itur*), which belonged to the same MS. as *Ox. Pap.* 1097, a papyrus containing fragments of the *pro lege Manilia* and the *in Verrem* II. i. It is heterogeneous in character (G.–H., p. 143); its affinities are now with Σ (some of these passages are of special interest), now with *P* (cf. *Descent of MSS.*, p. 268); its independent readings are unimportant. Klotz discusses its features in *BPhW* 1914, cols. 956 ff.; in spite of its disappointing evidence for the text, it is of some significance as indicating that the two traditions of Σ and *P*, which were evidently separated early (cf. Klotz in *Rh. Mus.* lxvii, 1912, p. 373; Teubner, vol. vii, preface, p. xxxiv), had already undergone a fusion (note 29. 2, *habet* Π¹Σ, *habeat* Π²*P*); its relations with *P* are on the whole closer than those with Σ; its ultimate importance is cultural, since it shows that Cicero was being read in Egypt in the fifth century. Klotz used the papyrus in his Teubner text of 1915; a selection of its readings is given below (pp. xxii f.).

————

Albert Curtis Clark died on 5 February 1937. His work on the 'Vetus Cluniacensis' was perhaps his most notable achievement; its significance for the *pro Caelio* is at once seen by comparing his text with those of earlier scholars[1] (e.g. Müller or Vollgraff), and still further evident from the important paper of Klotz in *Rh. Mus.* lxvii, 1912, pp. 358 ff. Klotz's own text bears witness to Clark's acumen on every page, even though in many passages he differs from the Oxford text[2] and returns

[1] Some earlier notes make odd reading now; thus Bake (*Schol. Hypomn.* iii, pp. 301–2) remarks of Madvig's conjecture in § 45, now confirmed by Σ, 'nec aptum per se et otiosum est', and Vollgraff censures it as 'rhetoribus et magistellis quam Tullio Cicerone aliquanto digniorem'; Halm thought the supplement in § 35, confirmed by Σ, a 'pannus intolerabilis'; see also my note on 8. 8, and Orelli on 52. 15.
[2] See Schönberger, *Tulliana*, for a careful examination of the characteristic features of Σ, with some strictures on the reliance that Clark placed upon it; Klotz often disagrees with his disparagement of the Cluniacensis.

to Müller's reading (in a number of these he has the evidence of *Π*, which was not available to Clark). I am glad of this opportunity of reminding a generation for whom Clark is necessarily a now distant name, of the debt which Oxford scholarship and the whole world of classical learning owes to him. In this edition of the *pro Caelio* his text is reproduced without change, except at 5. 1 (see Appendix II), but I have not always found myself able to accept his readings in preference to those of Klotz and others, and I have tried to record the more important of such differences.

# SELECTION OF READINGS FROM
## *OX. PAP.* X. 1251 (*Π*)

### 1. *Agreements with Σ against P*

27. 5 probem; 29. 28 et copiose;[1] 30. 19 talia; 30. 22 nullae (v. edd.); 35. 6–7 facis . . . arguis;[1] 35. 13 praeceps; 39. 20 ut; 39. 23 suae vitae; 43. 23 libet; 44. 3 quoniam; 45. 18 atqui; 46. 4 est paene; 46. 5 labor offendit; 47. 12 nihilne . . . nihilne; 54. 15 elaborata.

The editors of *Π* infer that its archetype agreed with *Σ* in reading *modo facimus non* at 45. 24; they think that *Π* probably agreed with *Σ* in adding *sed etiam . . . meretrix* at 49. 9.[1]

### 2. *Agreements with P against Σ*

27. 1 lenior; 30. 11 magnam ne; 31. 5 sed; 33. 6 familiaris huic; 36. 4 parasti; 37. 21 disce;[1] 38. 13 sustentaret ( ? —v. edd.); 40. 14 aliqua; 41. 19 dicendi; 44. 2 iam; 45. 14 vestra prudentia est; 47. 6 hic; 47. 9 in hac; 53. 23 erat; 53. 5 illa.

*Note*: 29. 2 habet *Π*[1] (so *Σ*), habeat *Π*[2] (so *P*), the *a* being added supralineally. 29. 27 *om.* ipsa (?); 33. 27 *om.* qui (?); 42. 17 *om.* et (?); 43. 19 *om.* quidem (?); 44. 8 hae deliciae (?); 52. 15 ceterum (?).

### 3. *Agreements with T*

39. 20 ut; 42. 2 putaverunt; 42. 4 aliqui ludus; 54. 27 locisque; 55. 7 L. Luc(c)ei testimonium.

*Note*: 39. 22 haec *Π* (but *ha-* appears to be a correction from *in*; v. edd.): in hac *T*.

### 4. *Divergences from T*

38. 1 quisque; 39. 17 igitur est; 39. 2 convivia (? —v. edd.); 39. 5 illos fuisse; 40. 14 aliqua; 54. 22 *om.* illis (? —v. edd.); 55. 6 percipite atque (? —v. edd.).

### 5. *Other affinities*

27. 8 si licet *ΠP*: scilicet *codd. recent.*; 27. 9 qui . . . fuerit *Donatus*: *om. ΠP*; 30. 7 de praevarica[tione *Π* (v. edd.), depraevaricatione *e*:

---

[1] Cf. Clark, *Descent of MSS.*, p. 268.

deprecari vacationem *P*; 32. 19 cum ea *ΠP*: *om*. Quintil.; 35. 10 acta *Πge*: actas *P*; 36. 18 his igitur tuis *ΠP²ge*: his igitur *P¹*; 37. 16 quid velim *Π* (? —v. edd.): egone quid velim *P*; 42. 16 rei publicae *Πge*: reique publicae *P*; 45. 20 disputo *ΠP²ge*: disputato *P¹*, disputavi *Σ*; 51. 5 L. Luc(c)ei *ΠP²ge*: L. *om*. *ΣP¹*.

*Note*: 31. 1 *potuit* (so *P*) has been changed from *voluit* by the original hand.

## 6. *Independent readings*

28. 19 eruant (*evertant*); 29. 24 confociat (*deficiat, deficiet*); 32. 7 virtute (*prudentia*); 33. 23 mallet (*malit*); 37. 17 nequaquam velis (*nequiquam velim*); 37. 21 decede (*dide*, v. Kl. ad loc.); 38. 26 cessisse (*decessisse*); 38. 1 ista maledicta (*tam maledica*); 46. 4 etiam familiar⟨i⟩um (*familiarium*); 52. 11 in rem (*ob rem Σ*; *ad rem P*).

Other variations are due to omissions and to alteration of the word-order: note 28. 14 *bonam frugem*, which is the better order (see commentary).

# COLLATION OF THE OXFORD AND THE TEUBNER TEXT

| *Oxford* (Clark, 1905 and 1908) | *Teubner* (Klotz, 1915) |
|---|---|
| 1. 2 consuetudinisque | consuetudinis |
| 12 adulescentem | adulescentem nobilem |
| 14 Atratini ipsius | [Atratini] illius |
| 3. 9 causa et | causa |
| 13 etiam sine mea oratione tacitus | et sine mea oratione et tacitus |
| 16 hi | ii |
| 18 summam hodieque | summamque hodie |
| 4. 20 equitis autem Romani | equitis Romani autem |
| 6. 12 ad hominum famam | [ad hominum famam] |
| 14 demanavit | dimanavit |
| 23 notet | ut notet |
| 8. 9 omnes | homines |
| 13 quis est qui huic | qui isti |
| 14 etiam si | etiam |
| 9. 19 quoad | quod (*sed vide praef., p. lxviii*) |
| 10. 12 annus, causam | annus * * * causam |
| 11. 28 iam | is iam |
| 12. 11 *atque* | ⟨et⟩ |
| 14. 2 facilitatis | facultatis |
| 5 bonis | etiam bonis |
| 15. 14 impudicitiae | pudicitiae |
| 16. 28 sese | se |
| 5 cupiditas | cupiditatis |
| 18. 17 in | iam in |
| et ex | ex |
| 1 mihi quidem | quidem mihi |
| 6 hanc Palatinam Medeam migrationemque hanc | hanc migrationem Palatinamque Medeam huic |
| 19. 22 esse solum | solum esse |
| 21. 7 hoc esse | esse hoc |
| 13 iam | nam |
| 24. 20 qui cum | cum |
| 21 habitabat | habitabat is |
| 22 Dio, erat | fuerat |
| 25. 5 leniter accederet | leviter accideret |
| 27. 1 etiam | et ea |

| *Oxford* (Clark, 1905 and 1908) | *Teubner* (Klotz, 1915) |
|---|---|
| 27. 8 si licet | scilicet |
| 9 qui in hortis fuerit | [qui in hortis fuerit] |
| 28. 13 dedidissent | dedissent |
| 14 frugem bonam | bonam frugem |
| 29. 27 vitia ista | vitia |
| 2 habeat | habet |
| 6 ita ut oportet | ut oportet ita |
| 30. 9 si qua est | si quaest |
| 11 tamen ne | ne |
| 22 nullae | nulla |
| 31. 2 clam attulit | attulit |
| 32. 8 Caelio | M. Caelio |
| 16 fratrem | fratre |
| 33. 27 et qui | et |
| 6 familiaris | familiaris huic |
| 34. 9 non proavum non *abavum* non atavum | proavum ⟨abavum⟩ atavum |
| 36. 18 igitur | igitur tuis |
| 22 cubitabat | cubitavit |
| 4 paratos | parasti |
| 37. 15 ferrei sunt isti patres | ferrei . . . patres *post* velim (*infra*, 17) |
| 16 quid | egone quid |
| 18 vix ferendi | ferrei sunt isti patres, vix ferendi |
| 21 dissice | disice |
| 22 *tibi* licet | licebit |
| tibi dolebit, *non mihi* | tibi dolebit |
| 38. 1 praesertim in | in |
| 7 Caeli | fili |
| 13 sustineret | sustentaret |
| 39. 21 quis | qui |
| 2 convivium delectaret | convivia delectarent |
| nihil | ⟨qui⟩ nihil |
| 42. 4 aliqui ludus | aliquid |
| 6 vera | severa |
| 43. 19 multi quidem | multi |
| 21 defervissent | deferbuissent |
| 44. 8 deliciae | hae deliciae |
| 10 impeditumve | impeditumque |
| 45. 22 desiderio | desidia |
| 46. 4 paene est | est paene |
| 47. 7 sese | se |
| dedidisset | dedisset |

| *Oxford* (Clark, 1905 and 1908) | *Teubner* (Klotz, 1915) |
|---|---|
| 47. 9 hac in | in hac |
| 48. 26 ipsam | iam |
| 1 tantum | totum |
| 52. 11 ob | ad |
| 53. 5 alia | illa |
| 54. 20 a M. Caelio | [a M. Caelio] |
| 21 neque tulisset | ⟨auditum⟩ [neque tulisset] |
| 55. 7 recita. L. LVCCEI TESTI-MONIVM | recita L. Luccei testimonium. ⟨TESTIMONIUM L. LUCCEI⟩ |
| 56. 24 dare vellet | vellet dare |
| 57. 9 is | hic |
| 58. 25 dominae esse | esse dominae |
| 59. 22 mori | emori |
| 60. 26 tonantem | conantem |
| 61. 5 paratum sit | sit paratum |
| 7 constitutum | [constitutum] pactum |
| 62. 19 his | iis |
| 22 deinde | dein |
| 64. 9 ad hoc | hoc |
| 65. 17 vocarent | revocarent |
| 66. 4 reperietur | reperitur |
| 6 iudices testis | testis iudices |
| 67. 11 conlocatos | locatos |
| quem ad modum | quonam modo |
| 15 quem | quam |
| 68. 8 rem tute | tu rem te |
| 69. 15 est factum | est |
| 70. 22 causa iudices | iudices causa |
| 1 libidines et | libidinosae |
| 71. 3 o stultitiam! stultitiamne | o stultitiamne |
| 5 audetis | audetisne |
| 9 Vettiano | [Vettiano] |
| 72. 17 disciplinae dedita | dedita disciplinae |
| 18 instruimur | instituimur |
| 21 vellet, eis | velitis, is |
| 73. 2 provincialis non | provincialis * * * non |
| 75. 19 eius mulieris | mulieris |
| 25 eiecit | erexit (*sed vide praef., p. lxi*) |
| 76. 29 repugnante me | repugnante |
| 77. 13 effervisse | efferbuisse |
| 16 deferverint | deferbuerint |
| 18 bonarum | ⟨studiosum⟩ bonarum (*sed vide praef., p. lxi*) |

| *Oxford* (Clark, 1905 and 1908) | *Teubner* (Klotz, 1915) |
|---|---|
| 78. 24 cum | quod |
| 5 hominem . . . inquinatum *post* vidistis | hominem . . . inquinatum *post* incendit (*infra*, 9) |
| 11 ad inflammandam | inflammandam |
| 12 ea | hac |
| 14 fratre et | [fratre] |
| 80. 1 aluisse vos | aluisse |

# BIBLIOGRAPHY

*Note*: Some abbreviated references are shown in square brackets. References to periodicals in the Commentary follow the system of *L'Année Philologique*.

## I. EDITIONS

BORNECQUE, H. Cicéron, Discours pour Sestius, etc. Paris (Garnier), n.d. (with translation).

CLARK, A. C. M. T. Ciceronis Orationes pro Sex. Roscio, etc. Oxford [1905, new impr. 1908]. [Cl.]

GRAEVIUS, J. G. M. T. Ciceronis Orationes (Variorum edition), vol. iii, part i. Amsterdam, 1699.

KLOTZ, A., and SCHOELL, F. M. T. Ciceronis scripta, vol. vii, Leipzig (Teubner), 1919. NOTE: this volume contains the very important *preface*; the *text* of the *pro Caelio* is given unchanged from that published separately in 1915 (fasc. 23), ed. A. Klotz. [Kl.]

LABRIOLLE, P. DE. Cicéron pro Caelio. Paris, 'Les Cours de Sorbonne' [1937] (with translation).

LONG, G. Ciceronis Orationes, vol. iv. London, 1858.

MAGGI, A. Cicerone, Orazione pro Marco Caelio. Milan, 1936.

MÜLLER, C. F. W. Ciceronis scripta ii. 3. Leipzig (Teubner), 1904. [Müll.]

ORELLI, J. C. Ciceronis orationes pro M. Caelio, pro Sestio. Zürich, 1832.

VOLLGRAFF, J. C. Ciceronis oratio pro M. Caelio. Leiden, 1887.

WAGENINGEN, J. VAN. Ciceronis oratio pro M. Caelio. Groningen, 1908. [W.]

## II. TEXTUAL CRITICISM AND GENERAL COMMENT

BAEHRENS, E. Ad Ciceronis Caelianam (*Revue de Philologie* viii, 1884, pp. 33–54).

BAKE, J. De emendanda Ciceronis oratione pro Caelio (*Scholica Hypomnemata* iii, pp. 266–310). Leiden, 1844.

# BIBLIOGRAPHY

BARWES, C. Quaestionum Tullianarum specimen primum ad Caelianam orationem spectans. Göttingen, 1868.

BUSCHE, K. *Berliner Philologische Wochenschrift* 1917, cols. 1387–8 (a review of Klotz's text).

CIACERI, E. Il Processo di M. Celio Rufo e l'Arringa di Cicerone (*Atti della Reale Accademia di Archeologia, Lettere e Belle Arti di Napoli* NS, xi, 1929–30, pp. 1–24).

CLARK, A. C. Anecdota Oxoniensia, Classical Series, x. Oxford, 1905. [An. Ox.]

—— The Descent of Manuscripts. Oxford, 1918.

DAMSTÉ, P. H. Ad Ciceronis orationem pro M. Caelio annotatiunculae criticae (*Mnemosyne* NS, xxxvi, 1908, pp. 119–25).

DREXLER, H. Zu Ciceros Rede pro Caelio (*Nachrichten von der Akademie der Wissenschaften in Göttingen*, Phil.-Hist. Kl., 1944, pp. 1–32). (Equivalent to a partial commentary.)

FRANCKEN, C. M. Ciceronis Oratio pro Caelio (*Mnemosyne* NS, viii, 1880, pp. 201–29). [Fra.]

GRENFELL, B. P., and HUNT, A. S. Oxyrhynchus Papyri x, pp. 142–61. London, 1914.

HALM, K. Interpolationen in Ciceronischen Reden aus dem Codex Par. 7794 (*Rheinisches Museum* ix, 1854, pp. 321–50).

HEINZE, R. Ciceros Rede pro Caelio (*Hermes* lx, 1925, pp. 193–258). (A very valuable paper, equivalent to a commentary.) [H.]

HELLER, J. L. Cicero *Pro Caelio* 55 (*Classical Philology* xxix, 1934, pp. 141–3).

HOUSMAN, A. E. Ciceroniana (*Journal of Philology* xxxii, 1913, pp. 261–9).

HUMBERT, J. Les Plaidoyers écrits et les plaidoiries réelles de Cicéron. Paris, 1925.

KARSTEN, H. T. Spicilegium Criticum. Leiden, 1881.

KAYSER, C. L. *Heidelberger Jahrbücher der Literatur* 1870, pp. 417–29 (a review of Oetling and Wrampelmeyer).

KLOTZ, A. Zur Kritik einiger Ciceronischer Reden (*Rheinisches Museum* NF, lxvii, 1912, pp. 358–90).

—— Der neue Ciceropapyrus (*Berliner Philologische Wochenschrift* 1914, cols. 955–8).

MADVIG, J. N. Opuscula Academica, pp. 304–32 (2nd edition). Copenhagen, 1887.

NORDEN, E. Aus Ciceros Werkstatt (*Sitzungsberichte der preussischen Akademie der Wissenschaften* 1913, pp. 2–32).

# BIBLIOGRAPHY

OETLING, W. Librorum manuscriptorum qui Ciceronis orationem pro Caelio continent, qualis sit conditio, examinatur. Göttingen, 1868.

OPPERSKALSKI, T. De Ciceronis orationum retractatione quaestiones selectae. Greifswald, 1914.

PETERSON, W. Cicero's *Post Reditum* and other speeches (*Classical Quarterly* iv, 1910, pp. 167–77).

PLUYGERS, W. G. Lectiones Tullianae (*Mnemosyne* x, 1861, pp. 97–112, and NS, ix, 1881, pp. 141 f.).

REITZENSTEIN, R. Zu Ciceros Rede für Caelius (*Nachrichten von der Gesellschaft der Wissenschaften zu Göttingen*, Phil.-Hist. Kl., 1925, pp. 25–32).

SCHÖLL, F. Die Interpolationen der Ciceronischen Caeliana (*Rheinisches Museum* NF, xxxv, 1880, pp. 543–63).

SCHÖNBERGER, J. K. Tulliana. Augsburg, 1911. [Schönb.]

—— Mitteilungen zu Cic. *Cael.* 24 (*Philologische Wochenschrift* 1933, col. 1104).

SCHWARZ, H. Coniectanea critica in Ciceronis orationes. Hirschberg, 1883.

SYDOW, R. Kritische Beiträge zu Cicero (*Hermes* lxv, 1930, pp. 319–21).

—— Kritische Beiträge zu Ciceros Reden (*Rheinisches Museum* NF, xci, 1942, pp. 353–65).

WRAMPELMEYER, H. Librorum manuscriptorum qui Ciceronis orationes pro Sestio et pro Caelio continent, ratio qualis sit, demonstratur. Detmold, 1868.

## III. BIOGRAPHICAL, HISTORICAL, AND LEGAL

ANTOINE, F. Lettres de Caelius à Cicéron. Paris, 1894.

BOISSIER, G. Cicéron et ses amis. Paris, 1865 (13th edition, 1905).

COUSIN, J. Lex Lutatia de Vi (*Revue historique de Droit français et étranger* 1943, pp. 88–94).

DRUMANN, W., and GRÖBE, P. Geschichte Roms (2nd edition). Leipzig, 1899–1929.

FRANK, TENNEY. Catullus and Horace. Oxford (Blackwell), 1928.

GREENIDGE, A. H. J. The Legal Procedure of Cicero's Time. Oxford, 1901. [LP]

—— Roman Public Life. London, 1901.

# BIBLIOGRAPHY

GRÖBE, P. Das Geburtsjahr und die Heimath des M. Caelius Rufus (*Hermes* xxxvi, 1901, pp. 612–14).

HERMANN, C. F. Disputatio de lege Lutatia. Göttingen, 1844.

HOUGH, J. N. The *Lex Lutatia* and the *Lex Plautia de Vi* (*American Journal of Philology* li, 1930, pp. 135–47).

KLERK, J. Dissertatio Literaria et Juridica de M. Tullii Ciceronis Oratione pro M. Coelio. Leiden, 1825.

MÜNZER, F. Pauly-Wissowa, Realencyclopädie iii, cols. 1266 ff. (s.v. *Caelius*, no. 35).

—— Aus dem Leben des M. Caelius Rufus (*Hermes* xliv, 1909, pp. 135–42).

TYRRELL, R. Y., and PURSER, L. C. The Correspondence of Cicero, vol. iii (2nd edition). Dublin, 1914.

WEGEHAUPT, W. M. Caelius Rufus. Breslau, 1878.

WEIHMAYR, W. Ueber Lex Plautia de Vi und Lex Lutatia. Augsburg, 1888.

WIESCHHÖLTER, H. De M. Caelio Rufo oratore. Leipzig, 1886.

ZELLMER, W. De Lege Plautia quae fuit de Vi. Rostock, 1875.


## IV. GRAMMAR, STYLE, ETC.

KREBS, J. P., and SCHMALZ, J. H. Antibarbarus der lateinischen Sprache, 7th edition. Basel, 1905–7. [Krebs]

KÜHNER, R. Ausführliche Grammatik der lateinischen Sprache, 2nd edition, revised by F. Holzweissig and C. Stegmann. Hanover, 1912–14. [K.]

LANDGRAF, G. Kommentar zu Ciceros Rede pro Sex. Roscio Amerino, 2nd edition. Leipzig, 1914.

LAURAND, L. Études sur le style des discours de Cicéron (vols. i and ii, 4th edition; vol. iii, 3rd edition). Paris, 1931–6. [Laur.]

LEBRETON, J. Études sur la langue et la grammaire de Cicéron. Paris, 1901. [Lebr.]

LEUMANN, M., and HOFMANN, J. B. Lateinische Grammatik (5th edition of Stolz-Schmalz). Munich, 1928. [L.-H.]

LÖFSTEDT, E. Syntactica. Lund, 1933–42.

—— Vermischte Studien zur lateinischen Sprachkunde und Syntax. Lund, 1936.

—— Coniectanea i. Uppsala, 1950.

NÄGELSBACH, K. F. Lateinische Stilistik. 9th edition, Nürnberg, 1905. [N.]

# BIBLIOGRAPHY

NISBET, R. G.  M. T. Ciceronis de domo sua oratio. Oxford, 1939.

NORDEN, E.  Die antike Kunstprosa. Leipzig, 1909.

OTTO, A.  Die Sprichwörter und sprichwörtlichen Redensarten der Römer. Leipzig, 1890. [Otto]

PARZINGER, P.  Beiträge zur Kenntnis der Entwicklung des Ciceronischen Stils. Landshut, 1912.

SEYFFERT, M., and MÜLLER, C. F. W.  M. Tullii Ciceronis Laelius, 2nd edition. Leipzig, 1876. [S.-M.]

ZILLINGER, W.  Cicero und die altrömischen Dichter. Würzburg, 1911.

(For further bibliographical material, see Additional Notes, p. 162.)

# SIGLA

$A$ = Palimpsestus Ambrosianus (*continens* §§ 71-75 Caeserni . . . infelici)

$T$ = Palimpsestus Taurinensis (*continens* §§ 38-42 quisque . . . curam rei, §§ 54-56 -dis illis . . . Caelio, §§ 66-69 -lus exitus . . . miramur si)

$\Pi$ = Ox. Pap. x. 1251

$\Sigma$ = m. 2 in cod. Paris. 14749

$B$ = Excerpta Bartolomaei de Montepolitiano

$P$ = cod. Paris. 7794, saecl. ix

$e$ = cod. Erfurtensis, nunc Berol. 252, saecl. xii/xiii

$g$ = cod. Gemblacensis, nunc Bruxellensis 5345, saecl. xii

$h$ = cod. Harleianus 4927, saecl. xii

$b$ = cod. S. Marci 255, saecl. xv

$\psi$ = cod. Laur. (Gadd.) xc sup. 69, saecl. xv

$\pi$ = codd. *egh*

$\delta$ = codd. *bψ*

# M. TVLLI CICERONIS
## PRO M. CAELIO ORATIO

Sɪ quis, iudices, forte nunc adsit ignarus legum iudi- <sup>ɪ</sup>
ciorum consuetudinisque nostrae, miretur profecto quae sit
tanta atrocitas huiusce causae, quod diebus festis ludisque
publicis, omnibus forensibus negotiis intermissis, unum hoc
5 iudicium exerceatur, nec dubitet quin tanti facinoris reus
arguatur ut eo neglecto civitas stare non possit. Idem cum
audiat esse legem quae de seditiosis consceleratisque civibus
qui armati senatum obsederint, magistratibus vim attulerint,
rem publicam oppugnarint cotidie quaeri iubeat : legem non
10 improbet, crimen quod versetur in iudicio requirat; cum
audiat nullum facinus, nullam audaciam, nullam vim in
iudicium vocari, sed adulescentem inlustri ingenio, industria,
gratia accusari ab eius filio quem ipse in iudicium et vocet et
vocarit, oppugnari autem opibus meretriciis : Atratini ipsius
15 pietatem non reprehendat, libidinem muliebrem compri-
mendam putet, vos laboriosos existimet quibus otiosis ne in
communi quidem otio liceat esse. Etenim si attendere 2
diligenter atque existimare vere de omni hac causa volue-
ritis, sic constituetis, iudices, nec descensurum quemquam
20 ad hanc accusationem fuisse cui utrum vellet liceret nec,
cum descendisset, quicquam habiturum spei fuisse, nisi
alicuius intolerabili libidine et nimis acerbo odio niteretur.

---

2 consuetudinisque ΣB : consuetudinis *cett.*      3 quod] quia ΣB
6 arguatur] accusatus ΣB      8 magistratibus ΣBπδ : *om. P*      12
adulescentem nobilem ΣB      14 Atratini ipsius *scripsi* : Atratini illius
BPπδ : illius *Muretus*      15 libidinem muliebrem ΣB : muliebrem
libidinem *cett.*      18 atque Σ : *om. Pπδ* : et *Angelius*

Sed ego Atratino, humanissimo atque optimo adulescenti,
meo necessario, ignosco, qui habet excusationem vel pie-
tatis vel necessitatis vel aetatis.   Si voluit accusare, pietati
tribuo, si iussus est, necessitati, si speravit aliquid, pueritiae.
Ceteris non modo nihil ignoscendum sed etiam acriter est 5
resistendum.

**2**
**3**      Ac mihi quidem videtur, iudices, hic introitus defensionis
adulescentiae M. Caeli maxime convenire, ut ad ea quae
accusatores deformandi huius causa et detrahendae spoli-
andaeque dignitatis gratia dixerunt primum respondeam. 10
Obiectus est pater varie, quod aut parum splendidus ipse
aut parum pie tractatus a filio diceretur.   De dignitate
M. Caelius notis ac maioribus natu etiam sine mea oratione
tacitus facile ipse respondet ; quibus autem propter senectutem, quod iam diu minus in foro nobiscumque versatur, 15
non aeque est cognitus, hi sic habeant, quaecumque in
equite Romano dignitas esse possit, quae certe potest esse
maxima, eam semper in M. Caelio habitam esse summam
hodieque haberi non solum a suis sed etiam ab omnibus
**4** quibus potuerit aliqua de causa esse notus.   Equitis autem 20
Romani esse filium criminis loco poni ab accusatoribus
neque his iudicantibus oportuit neque defendentibus nobis.
Nam quod de pietate dixistis, est ista quidem nostra existimatio sed iudicium certe parentis.   Quid nos opinemur
audietis ex iuratis ; quid parentes sentiant lacrimae matris 25
incredibilisque maeror, squalor patris et˙ haec praesens
**5** maestitia quam cernitis luctusque declarat.   Nam quod est
obiectum municipibus esse adulescentem non probatum

---

5 nihil *om.* Σ      9 causa et *Bake* : causae Σ : causa *Pπδ*      13
M. Σ, *Lambinus* : *om. Pπδ*      etiam sine . . . tacitus *ed. R* : et sine
. . . tacitus Σ: et sine . . . et tacitus *Pnδ*      14 respondit Σ*b²ψ*
18 summam hodieque Σ*P¹ψ²* : summamque hodie *P²πδ*      20 autem
Romani *Quintil.* xi. 1. 28 : Romani autem *Pπδ*      21 criminessloco
*P¹* : criminis in loco *coni. Halm* (*contra Quintil.*)      23 ista quidem
Σ, *Lambinus* : quidem ista *Pπδ*      vestra *b, Halm*

suis, nemini umquam praesenti Praetuttiani maiores honores habuerunt, iudices, quam absenti M. Caelio; quem
et absentem in amplissimum ordinem cooptarunt et ea non
petenti detulerunt quae multis petentibus denegarunt.
5 Idemque nunc lectissimos viros et nostri ordinis et equites
Romanos cum legatione ad hoc iudicium et cum gravissima
atque ornatissima laudatione miserunt.    Videor mihi iecisse
fundamenta defensionis meae, quae firmissima sunt si ni-
tuntur iudicio suorum.    Neque enim vobis satis commen-
10 data huius aetas esse posset, si non modo parenti, tali viro,
verum etiam municipio tam inlustri ac tam gravi displiceret.
Equidem, ut ad me revertar, ab his fontibus profluxi ad $\frac{3}{6}$
hominum famam, et meus hic forensis labor vitaeque ratio
demanavit ad existimationem hominum paulo latius com-
15 mendatione ac iudicio meorum.

Nam quod obiectum est de pudicitia quodque omnium
accusatorum non criminibus sed vocibus maledictisque
celebratum est, id numquam tam acerbe feret M. Caelius
ut eum paeniteat non deformem esse natum.    Sunt enim
20 ista maledicta pervolgata in omnis quorum in adulescentia
forma et species fuit liberalis.    Sed aliud est male dicere,
aliud accusare.    Accusatio crimen desiderat, rem ut definiat,
hominem notet, argumento probet, teste confirmet; maledictio autem nihil habet propositi praeter contumeliam;
25 quae si petulantius iactatur, convicium, si facetius, urbanitas
nominatur.    Quam quidem partem accusationis admiratus 7
sum et moleste tuli potissimum esse Atratino datam.    Neque
enim decebat neque aetas illa postulabat neque, id quod

1 Praetut(t)iani *Gruter* (*cf. Plin. N. H.* iii. 13–14): Praestutiani $\Sigma$:
praetoriani (-tori- $P^2$ *in ras.*) $P\pi\delta$: Puteolani *Beroaldus* (*cf. Val. Max.*
ix. 3. 8): Tusculani *Baiter* (*cf. C.I.L.* xiv. 2622)    2 iudices $\Sigma$:
om. $P\pi\delta$    quam] per $\Sigma$    7 iecisse *ex* legisse P: egisse *Halm*
14 demanavit $\Sigma B$: dimanavit $P\pi\delta$ ($\H{a}\pi a\xi$ $\lambda\epsilon\gamma$.)    20 in] per $\Sigma$
21 fuit forma et species $\Sigma$    23 hominem $\Sigma B$: hominem ut $P\pi\delta$:
nomine ut *Manutius*    25 iaciatur *Muretus*

3

animum advertere poteratis, pudor patiebatur optimi adulescentis in tali illum oratione versari. Vellem aliquis ex
vobis robustioribus hunc male dicendi locum suscepisset ;
aliquanto liberius et fortius et magis more nostro refuta-
remus istam male dicendi licentiam. Tecum, Atratine, 5
agam lenius, quod et pudor tuus moderatur orationi meae
et meum erga te parentemque tuum beneficium tueri debeo.

8 Illud tamen te esse admonitum volo, primum ut qualis es
talem te omnes esse existiment, ut quantum a rerum turpitudine abes tantum te a verborum libertate seiungas ; 10
deinde ut ea in alterum ne dicas quae, cum tibi falso
responsa sint, erubescas. Quis est enim cui via ista non
pateat, quis est qui huic aetati atque isti dignitati non
possit quam velit petulanter, etiam si sine ulla suspicione, at
non sine argumento male dicere ? Sed istarum partium 15
culpa est eorum qui te agere voluerunt ; laus pudoris tui,
quod ea te invitum dicere videbamus, ingeni, quod ornate
4
politeque dixisti. Verum ad istam omnem orationem
9
brevis est defensio. Nam quoad aetas M. Caeli dare potuit
isti suspicioni locum, fuit primum ipsius pudore, deinde 20
etiam patris diligentia disciplinaque munita. Qui ut huic
togam virilem dedit—nihil dicam hoc loco de me ; tantum
sit quantum vos existimatis ; hoc dicam, hunc a patre continuo ad me esse deductum—nemo hunc M. Caelium in
illo aetatis flore vidit nisi aut cum patre aut mecum aut in 25
M. Crassi castissima domo cum artibus honestissimis
erudiretur. ⌉

1 animum advertere Σ (*cf. Clu.* § 1) : animadvertere *Pπδ*    2
aliquis Σπδ : aliqui *P*    6 lenius agam Σ*B*    tuus *om.* Σ*B*    7
meum *om.* Σ*B*    debet Σ    8 ut Σ, *Lambinus* : *om. Pπδ*    9
te omnes esse (se) Σ : te *Pπδ* : te esse omnes *Klotz*    13 quis est
Σ : *om. Pπδ*    huic aetati atque isti (huic *Agroetius*) dignitati Σ,
*Agroetius* (*K. vit.* 118) : isti aetati *Pbh* : isti aetati atque etiam isti
dignitati *cett.*    15 non sine ullo Σ    18 omnem *om.* Σ    19
potuit isti Σ, *Naugerius* : potuisti *Pe* : potuit *cett.*    22 togam virilem Σ : virilem togam *Pπδ*    23 existimetis *Ernesti*

Nam quod Catilinae familiaritas obiecta Caelio est, longe 10
ab ista suspicione abhorrere debet.  Hoc enim adulescente
scitis consulatum mecum petisse Catilinam.  Ad quem si
accessit aut si a me discessit umquam—quamquam multi
5 boni adulescentes illi homini nequam atque improbo stu-
duerunt—tum existimetur Caelius Catilinae nimium familiaris fuisse.  At enim postea scimus et vidimus esse hunc
in illius etiam amicis.  Quis negat?  Sed ego illud tempus
aetatis quod ipsum sua sponte infirmum, aliorum autem
10 libidine infestum est, id hoc loco defendo.  Fuit adsiduus
mecum praetore me ; non noverat Catilinam ; Africam tum
praetor ille obtinebat.  Secutus est tum annus, causam de
pecuniis repetundis Catilina dixit.  Mecum erat hic ; illi
ne advocatus quidem venit umquam.  Deinceps fuit annus
15 quo ego consulatum petivi ; petebat Catilina mecum.  Numquam ad illum accessit, a me numquam recessit.  Tot igitur **5**
annos versatus in foro sine suspicione, sine infamia, studuit $_{11}$
Catilinae iterum petenti.  Quem ergo ad finem putas custo-
diendam illam aetatem fuisse ?  Nobis quidem olim annus
20 erat unus ad cohibendum bracchium toga constitutus, et ut
exercitatione ludoque campestri tunicati uteremur, eademque
erat, si statim merere stipendia coeperamus, castrensis ratio ac
militaris.  Qua in aetate nisi qui se ipse sua gravitate et castimonia et cum disciplina domestica tum etiam naturali
25 quodam bono defenderet, quoquo modo a suis custoditus
esset, tamen infamiam veram effugere non poterat.  Sed qui
prima illa initia aetatis integra atque inviolata praestitisset, de
eius fama ac pudicitia, cum iam sese conroboravisset ac vir
inter viros esset, nemo loquebatur.  At studuit Catilinae, cum 12

4 si a] si Σ      6 tum Σ, *Angelius* : tamen Pπδ      8 etiam Σ :
om. Pπδ      neget Σ      9 autem ΣB : om. Pπδ      10 libidini Σ,
*Ascens.* 3 *in mg.*      12 tum annus Σ : annus Pπδ : annus cum
*Garatoni*      22 merere ΣB : mereri Pπδ      25 defenderet (-rit *h*)
πδ : defenderat P      27 illa prima Σ      28 ac] et Σ      iam sese Σ :
is iam se Pπδ : iam se *Vollgraf*      29 at *Francken* : ac Σ : om. Pπδ

iam aliquot annos esset in foro, Caelius. Et multi hoc
idem ex omni ordine atque ex omni aetate fecerunt. Habuit
enim ille, sicuti meminisse vos arbitror, permulta maxi-
marum non expressa signa sed adumbrata virtutum. Vte-
batur hominibus improbis multis ; et quidem optimis se 5
viris deditum esse simulabat. Erant apud illum inlecebrae
libidinum multae ; erant etiam industriae quidam stimuli
ac laboris. Flagrabant vitia libidinis apud illum ; vigebant
etiam studia rei militaris. Neque ego umquam fuisse tale
monstrum in terris ullum puto, tam ex contrariis diversisque 10
*atque* inter se pugnantibus naturae studiis cupiditatibusque
**6** conflatum. Quis clarioribus viris quodam tempore iucun-
13 dior, quis turpioribus coniunctior? quis civis meliorum
partium aliquando, quis taetrior hostis huic civitati ? quis
in voluptatibus inquinatior, quis in laboribus patientior ? 15
quis in rapacitate avarior, quis in largitione effusior ? Illa
vero, iudices, in illo homine admirabilia fuerunt, comprehendere multos amicitia, tueri obsequio, cum omnibus com-
municare quod habebat, servire temporibus suorum omnium
pecunia, gratia, labore corporis, scelere etiam, si opus esset, 20
et audacia, versare suam naturam et regere ad tempus atque
huc et illuc torquere ac flectere, cum tristibus severe, cum
remissis iucunde, cum senibus graviter, cum iuventute
comiter, cum facinerosis audaciter, cum libidinosis luxu-
14 riose vivere. Hac ille tam varia multiplicique natura cum 25
omnis omnibus ex terris homines improbos audacisque
conlegerat, tum etiam multos fortis viros et bonos specie
quadam virtutis adsimulatae tenebat. Neque umquam ex

2 ordine omni Σ        6 simulaverat Σ        8 illum] eum Σ
11 atque *Lambinus* : *om. P*πδ : *et unus det.*        12 quodam tempore]
quondam Σ (*contra Frontonem, ad Anton.* ii. 6)        13 turpioribus
viris Σ        17 admirabilia Σ : mirabilia *P*πδ        20 corporibus Σ
esset et Σ*b²ψ²* : esset (*ante ras. P*) *cett.*        22 ac] et Σ        24
audaciter Σ*Beg* : audacter *Ph*        26 ex omnibus Σ        28 quadam
rei p. adsimulatam Σ        neque] ne Σ

illo delendi huius imperi tam consceleratus impetus exsti-
tisset, nisi tot vitiorum tanta immanitas quibusdam facilitatis et patientiae radicibus niteretur. Qua re ista condicio,
iudices, respuatur, nec Catilinae familiaritatis crimen haereat.
5 Est enim commune cum multis et cum quibusdam bonis.
Me ipsum, me, inquam, quondam paene ille decepit, cum
et civis mihi bonus et optimi cuiusque cupidus et firmus
amicus ac fidelis videretur; cuius ego facinora oculis prius
quam opinione, manibus ante quam suspicione deprendi.
10 Cuius in magnis catervis amicorum si fuit etiam Caelius,
magis est ut ipse moleste ferat errasse se, sicuti non numquam in eodem homine me quoque erroris mei paenitet,
quam ut istius amicitiae crimen reformidet.

Itaque a maledictis impudicitiae ad coniurationis invidiam **7**
15 oratio est vestra delapsa. Posuistis enim, atque id tamen
titubanter et strictim, coniurationis hunc propter amicitiam
Catilinae participem fuisse; in quo non modo crimen non
haerebat sed vix diserti adulescentis cohaerebat oratio.
Qui enim tantus furor in Caelio, quod tantum aut in moribus
20 naturaque volnus aut in re atque fortuna? ubi denique est
in ista suspicione Caeli nomen auditum? Nimium multa
de re minime dubia loquor; hoc tamen dico. Non modo
si socius coniurationis, sed nisi inimicissimus istius sceleris
fuisset, numquam coniurationis accusatione adulescentiam
25 suam potissimum commendare voluisset. Quod haud scio 16
an de ambitu et de criminibus istis sodalium ac sequestrium,
quoniam huc incidi, similiter respondendum putem. Numquam enim tam Caelius amens fuisset ut, si sese isto
infinito ambitu commaculasset, ambitus alterum accusaret,

2 facultatis *Madvig*    5 quibusdam Σ : quibusdam etiam *Pπδ*
(*cf. Zielinski p.* 77)    13 ipsius Σ    14 impudicitiae Σ, *Garatoni*
*ex Quintil.* iv. 2. 27 : pudicitiae *Pπδ*    15 oratio delapsa est Σ
16 propter amicitiam hunc Σ    22 tamen *Pπδ* : tantum *Lambinus*
26 sequestrum *B*    28 si sese *scripsi* : ses se Σ : si se *Pπδ*

7

neque eius facti in altero suspicionem quaereret cuius ipse
sibi perpetuam licentiam optaret, nec, si sibi semel periculum
ambitus subeundum putaret, ipse alterum iterum ambitus
crimine arcesseret.  Quod quamquam nec sapienter et me
invito facit, tamen est eius modi cupiditas ut magis insectari 5
alterius innocentiam quam de se timide cogitare videatur.

17   Nam quod aes alienum obiectum est, sumptus reprehensi,
.tabulae flagitatae, videte quam pauca respondeam.  Tabulas
qui in patris potestate est nullas conficit.  Versuram numquam omnino fecit ullam.  Sumptus unius generis obiectus 10
est, habitationis ; triginta milibus dixistis habitare.  Nunc
demum intellego P. Clodi insulam esse venalem, cuius
hic in aediculis habitat decem, ut opinor, milibus.  Vos
autem dum illi placere voltis, ad tempus eius mendacium
vestrum accommodavistis.                               15

18   Reprehendistis a patre quod semigrarit.  Quod quidem
in hac aetate minime reprendendum est.  Qui cum et ex
publica causa iam esset mihi quidem molestam, sibi tamen
gloriosam victoriam consecutus et per aetatem magistratus
petere posset, non modo permittente patre sed etiam 20
suadente ab eo semigravit et, cum domus patris a foro
longe abesset, quo facilius et nostras domus obire et ipse
a suis coli posset, conduxit in Palatio non magno domum.

8 Quo loco possum dicere id quod vir clarissimus, M. Crassus,
cum de adventu regis Ptolemaei quereretur, paulo ante 25
dixit :

      Vtinam ne in nemore Pelio—

    5 cupiditas *b'ψ²* : cupiditatis Σ : cupidus (-idinis *g*) *cett.* : *del. Lam-
binus*     9 est] sit Σ     confecit *ed. R*     11 dixistis] eum
*add. Pπδ, ego delevi (clausulae gratia)*     12 demum ‖ ‖ ‖ *P* : demum,
iudices *Halm*     14 eius] eris Σ : *num* eri ?     15 vestrum]
*sequuntur in Peg verba* renuerit qui unguenta § 27 *usque ad* inanes
metus § 36     17 in hac Σ, *Lambinus* : iam in hac *Pπδ*     ex
publica causa Σ*b²ψ²*, *Francken* : et (*om.* et *π*) ex rei p. causa *Pπδ*
21-22 et cum … abesset] cum … abesset, et *Schwartz*     23 posset
Σ*P⁵bg²ψ* : possit *cett.*

    8

Ac longius mihi quidem contexere hoc carmen liceret:

Nam numquam era errans

hanc molestiam nobis exhiberet

Medea animo aegro, amore saevo saucia.

5 Sic enim, iudices, reperietis quod, cum ad id loci venero, ostendam, hanc Palatinam Medeam migrationemque hanc adulescenti causam sive malorum omnium sive potius sermonum fuisse.

Quam ob rem illa quae ex accusatorum oratione prae- 19
10 muniri iam et fingi intellegebam, fretus vestra prudentia, iudices, non pertimesco. Aiebant enim fore testem senatorem qui se pontificiis comitiis pulsatum a Caelio diceret. A quo quaeram, si prodierit, primum cur statim nihil egerit, deinde, si id queri quam agere maluerit, cur productus
15 a vobis potius quam ipse per se, cur tanto post potius quam continuo queri maluerit. Si mihi ad haec acute arguteque responderit, tum quaeram denique ex quo iste fonte senator emanet. Nam si ipse orietur et nascetur ex sese, fortasse, ut soleo, commovebor; sin autem est rivolus arcessitus
20 et ductus ab ipso capite accusationis vestrae, laetabor, cum tanta gratia tantisque opibus accusatio vestra nitatur, unum senatorem esse solum qui vobis gratificari vellet inventum.

DE TESTE FVFIO.

Nec tamen illud genus alterum nocturnorum testium per- 20
25 horresco. Est enim dictum ab illis fore qui dicerent uxores suas a cena redeuntis attrectatas esse a Caelio. Graves erunt homines qui hoc iurati dicere audebunt, cum sit eis con-

---

1 mihi quidem Σ: quidem mihi Pπδ      6 migrationemque hanc *scripsi* : migrationemque huic Pπδ : eamque migrationem huic *Kayser*
11 aiebant] ‖aiebant (-i- *m. 2 in ras.*) P : iaciebant Σ      17 quo iste
bʲψ : quote Pˡ*eg* : quoto P²bh : quo g²      19 arcessitus Σ: accersitus *cett.*      22 esse solum Σ: solum esse Pπδ      23 DE TESTE FVFIO
Σ, *om.* Pπδ (*cf. Mur.* 57)      24 tamen] tantum ψ¹      perhorresco
Σ: pertimesco Pπδ      25 suas uxores Σ (*contra Severian., Rhet. M. p.* 369)      27 audeant bψ²

fitendum numquam se ne congressu quidem et constituto
9 coepisse de tantis iniuriis experiri. Sed totum genus
oppugnationis huius, iudices, et iam prospicitis animis et,
cum inferetur, propulsare debebitis. Non enim ab isdem
accusatur M. Caelius a quibus oppugnatur ; palam in eum 5
21 tela iaciuntur, clam subministrantur. [Neque ego id dico
ut invidiosum sit in eos quibus gloriosum etiam hoc esse
debet. Funguntur officio, defendunt suos, faciunt quod
viri fortissimi solent ; laesi dolent, irati efferuntur, pugnant
lacessiti. Sed vestrae sapientiae tamen est, iudices, non, si 10
causa iusta est viris fortibus oppugnandi M. Caelium, ideo
vobis quoque causam putare esse iustam alieno dolori
potius quam vestrae fidei consulendi. Iam quae sit multi-
tudo in foro, quae genera, quae studia, quae varietas
hominum videtis. Ex hac copia quam multos esse arbitra- 15
mini qui hominibus potentibus, gratiosis, disertis, cum
aliquid eos velle arbitrentur, ultro se offerre soleant, operam
22 navare, testimonium polliceri ? Hoc ex genere si qui se in
hoc iudicium forte proiecerint, excluditote eorum cupiditatem,
iudices, sapientia vestra, ut eodem tempore et huius saluti 20
et religioni vestrae et contra periculosas hominum potentias
condicioni omnium civium providisse videamini. Equidem
vos abducam a testibus neque huius iudici veritatem quae
mutari nullo modo potest in voluntate testium conlocari
sinam quae facillime fingi, nullo negotio flecti ac detorqueri 25
potest. Argumentis agemus, signis luce omni clarioribus
crimina refellemus ; res cum re, causa cum causa, ratio cum
ratione pugnabit.]

10
23     Itaque illam partem causae facile patior graviter et ornate

2 coepisse Σ*egδ* : caedisse *Ph*    4 debebitis propulsare Σ    6
administrantur Σ    ego id Σ : id ego *Pπδ* : eo id *Schütz*    7 esse
hoc Σ    12 vobis quoque Σ, *Garatoni* : vobis quoque vos *Pπδ* :
vos quoque *ed. R*    13 consulendi. Iam *scripsi* : consulendum Σ :
consulendi (-i *add. m.* 2) . . . *P* : consulendi *πδ*    15 vidistis Σ
25 fingi *gψ*[1] : effingi *Pehbψ*[2]

a M. Crasso peroratam de seditionibus Neapolitanis, de
Alexandrinorum pulsatione Puteolana, de bonis Pallae.
Vellem dictum esset ab eodem etiam de Dione.  De quo
ipso tamen quid est quod exspectetis?  quod is qui fecit
5 aut non timet aut etiam fatetur; est enim rex; qui autem
dictus est adiutor fuisse et conscius, P. Asicius, iudicio est
liberatus.  Quod igitur est eius modi crimen ut qui commisit
non neget, qui negavit absolutus sit, id hic pertimescat qui
non modo a facti verum etiam a conscientiae suspicione
10 afuit?  Et, si Asicio causa plus profuit quam nocuit invidia,
huic oberit maledictum tuum qui istius facti non modo
suspicione sed ne infamia quidem est aspersus?  At prae- 24
varicatione est Asicius liberatus.  Perfacile est isti loco
respondere, mihi praesertim a quo illa causa defensa est.
15 Sed Caelius optimam causam Asici esse arbitratur; cuicuimodi autem sit, a sua putat esse seiunctam.  Neque solum
Caelius sed etiam adulescentes humanissimi et doctissimi,
rectissimis studiis atque optimis artibus praediti, Titus
Gaiusque Coponii qui ex omnibus maxime Dionis mortem
20 doluerunt, qui cum doctrinae studio atque humanitatis tum
etiam hospitio Dionis tenebantur.  Habitabat apud Titum,
ut audistis, Dio, erat ei cognitus Alexandriae.  Quid aut
hic aut summo splendore praeditus frater eius de M. Caelio
existimet ex ipsis, si producti erunt, audietis.  Ergo haec 25
25 removeantur, ut aliquando, in quibus causa nititur, ad ea
veniamus.

---

2 Paliae Σ      3 vellem vellem Σ        9 facti *Naugerius* : facto
*Pπδ*      10 causa *Pπδ* : in causa *Müller* : *fort.* ea        11 maledictum tuum Σ : tuum maledictum *Pπδ*       13 est] sit Σ        15
cuicuimodi *Ant. Augustinus* : cuiusmodi *Pπδ*        16 esse Σ, *edd.*
*VR* : eius esse *Pπδ*       19-20 Coponii ... doluerunt Σ*b²ψ²* (*de Coponiis*
*cf. Balb.* § 53) : *om. P in lac., sine lac.* πδ        20-22 qui cum ... erat
*om. P¹ in lac.*      20 qui cum doctrinae studio Σ*b²ψ²* : omni cum (*om.*
cum *eg*) doctrina *P²πδ*       21 apud Titum Σ : is apud L. Lucceium *P²πδ*
22 Dio erat Σ : fuerat ei *P²πδ*       25 removeantur Σ, *ed. Mediol.* ·
removentur *Pπδ*

11 Animadverti enim, iudices, audiri a vobis meum familiarem,
L. Herennium, perattente. In quo etsi magna ex parte
ingenio eius et dicendi genere quodam tenebamini, tamen
non numquam verebar ne illa subtiliter ad criminandum
inducta oratio ad animos vestros sensim ac leniter accederet. 5
Dixit enim multa de luxurie, multa de libidine, multa de
vitiis iuventutis, multa de moribus et, qui in reliqua vita
mitis esset et in hac suavitate humanitatis qua prope iam
delectantur omnes versari periucunde soleret, fuit in hac
causa pertristis quidam patruus, censor, magister; obiurgavit 10
M. Caelium, sicut neminem umquam parens; multa de
incontinentia intemperantiaque disseruit. Quid quaeritis,
iudices? ignoscebam vobis attente audientibus, propterea
quod egomet tam triste illud, tam asperum genus orationis
26 horrebam. Ac prima pars fuit illa quae me minus movebat, 15
fuisse meo necessario Bestiae Caelium familiarem, cenasse
apud eum, ventitasse domum, studuisse praeturae. Non
me haec movent quae perspicue falsa sunt; etenim eos
una cenasse dixit qui aut absunt aut quibus necesse est
idem dicere. Neque vero illud me commovet quod sibi in 20
Lupercis sodalem esse Caelium dixit. Fera quaedam
sodalitas et plane pastoricia atque agrestis germanorum
Lupercorum, quorum coitio illa silvestris ante est instituta
quam humanitas atque leges, si quidem non modo nomina
deferunt inter se sodales sed etiam commemorant sodali- 25
tatem in accusando, ut ne quis id forte nesciat timere
27 videantur! Sed haec omitto; ad illa quae me magis
moverunt respondeo.

---

4 subtilis et ad *B*      5 ad animos ... accederet] animos ...
accenderet *h*    7 et qui Σ*g*² : ut qui *cett.*    10 quidam *om.* Σ    14
illud tam Σ : illud et tam *Pπδ*    20 idem dicere *P²πδ* : idem d.....*P*¹
21 esse sodalem Σ    22 pastoricia *BP²πδ* : pa ...... *P*¹ : pasto-
ralis *coni. Halm*      26 ne quis *P*¹ : ne quis si Σ: ne si quis *P²πδ*
27 videantur *Abram* : videatur *Pπδ*    omitto Σ : omittam *Pπδ*    28
respondebo *b²ψ*

Deliciarum obiurgatio fuit longa, etiam lenior, plusque
disputationis habuit quam atrocitatis, quo etiam audita est
attentius.  Nam P. Clodius, amicus meus, cum se gravissime
vehementissimeque iactaret et omnia inflammatus ageret
5 tristissimis verbis, voce maxima, tametsi probabam eius
eloquentiam, tamen non pertimescebam ; aliquot enim in
causis eum videram frustra litigantem.  Tibi autem, Balbe,
respondeo primum precario, si licet, si fas est defendi a me
eum qui nullum convivium renuerit, qui in hortis fuerit, qui
10 unguenta sumpserit, qui Baias viderit.  Equidem multos et $\overset{12}{\phantom{x}}$
$\overset{\phantom{x}}{28}$
vidi in hac civitate et audivi, non modo qui primoribus labris
gustassent genus hoc vitae et extremis, ut dicitur, digitis
attigissent sed qui totam adulescentiam voluptatibus dedidissent, emersisse aliquando et se ad frugem bonam, ut
15 dicitur, recepisse gravisque homines atque inlustris fuisse.
Datur enim concessu omnium huic aliqui ludus aetati, et
ipsa natura profundit adulescentiae cupiditates.  Quae si
ita erumpunt ut nullius vitam labefactent, nullius domum
evertant, faciles et tolerabiles haberi solent.  Sed tu mihi 29
20 videbare ex communi infamia iuventutis aliquam invidiam
Caelio velle conflare.  Itaque omne illud silentium quod est
orationi tributum tuae fuit ob eam causam quod uno reo
proposito de multorum vitiis cogitabamus.  Facile est
accusare luxuriem.  Dies iam me deficiat, si quae dici in
25 eam sententiam possunt coner expromere ; de corruptelis,
de adulteriis, de protervitate, de sumptibus immensa oratio
est.  Vt tibi reum neminem sed vitia ista proponas, res
tamen ipsa et copiose et graviter accusari potest.  Sed

1 etiam *scripsi* : et ea *P*πδ : et eo *Kayser*      alienior Σ (*fort.* et a
causa alienior)      4 inflammatus] *fort.* inflatius      5 probem Σ
8 respondebo *Donatus ad Ter. Hecyram* iv. 1. 30      9 renuerit *h*δ :
reminierit *P* : inierit Σ*eg*      qui . . . fuerit *Donatus* : *om. P*πδ      13
dedidissent *Ascens.* (3) *mg.* : dedissent *P*πδ      24 deficiat *P*,
*Ernesti* : deficiet πδ      25 possint *Ernesti*      coner] -er *add. P*² *in
ras.*      27 ista *scripsi* : ipsa Σ : *om. P*πδ      28 et copiose Σ,
*Naugerius* (2) : *om. P*πδ

vestrae sapientiae, iudices, est non abduci ab reo nec, quos
aculeos habeat severitas gravitasque vestra, cum eos accusator
erexerit in rem, in vitia, in mores, in tempora, emittere in
hominem et in reum, cum is non suo crimine sed multorum
30 vitio sit in quoddam odium iniustum vocatus.   Itaque ego 5
severitati tuae ita ut oportet respondere non audeo.   Erat
enim meum deprecari vacationem adulescentiae veniamque
petere.   Non, inquam, audeo; perfugiis nihil utor aetatis,
concessa omnibus iura dimitto ; tantum peto ut, si qua est
invidia communis hoc tempore aeris alieni, petulantiae, 10
libidinum iuventutis, quam video esse magnam, tamen ne
huic aliena peccata, ne aetatis ac temporum vitia noceant.
Atque ego idem qui haec postulo quin criminibus quae in
hunc proprie conferuntur diligentissime respondeam non
recuso.                                                    15

13  Sunt autem duo crimina, auri et veneni ; in quibus una
atque eadem persona versatur.   Aurum sumptum a Clodia,
venenum quaesitum quod Clodiae daretur, ut dicitur.   Omnia
sunt alia non crimina sed maledicta, iurgi petulantis magis
quam publicae quaestionis.   ' Adulter, impudicus, sequester ' 20
convicium est, non accusatio.   Nullum est enim fundamentum horum criminum, nullae sedes ; voces sunt con-
tumeliosae temere ab irato accusatore nullo auctore emissae.
31 Horum duorum criminum video auctorem, video fontem,
video certum nomen et caput.   Auro opus fuit ; sumpsit 25
a Clodia, sumpsit sine teste, habuit quamdiu voluit.   Maximum video signum cuiusdam egregiae familiaritatis.   Necare

---

1 iudices est] est *in ras. hab. P*: est, iudices. *Halm*          2 habet
Σ          5 ego Σ : *om. Pπδ*          6 ita ut oportet Σ : ut oportet ita
*Pπδ*          8 nihil Σ : non *Pπδ*          9 si quae *Halm*          11 tamen
*Wrampelmeyer* : tam Σ : *om. Pπδ*          18 ut Σ : *om. Pπδ (cf. Zielinski
p. 207)*          somnia Σ          19 alia] talia Σ : illa *Ernesti*          22
nullae Σ : nulla *Pπδ*          23 ab irato accusatore] arbitratu accusatoris
$b^2\psi$          24 auctorem vid°o fontem Σ : fontem video auctorem *Pπδ*
27 necare $b^1g^i\psi$ : negare *Pπb²*

14

eandem voluit ; quaesivit venenum, sollicitavit servos,
potionem paravit, locum constituit, clam attulit. Magnum
rursus odium video cum crudelissimo discidio exstitisse.
Res est omnis in hac causa nobis, iudices, cum Clodia,
5 muliere non solum nobili verum etiam nota ; de qua ego
nihil dicam nisi depellendi criminis causa. Sed intellegis 32
pro tua praestanti prudentia, Cn. Domiti, cum hac sola rem
esse nobis. Quae si se aurum Caelio commodasse non
dicit, si venenum ab hoc sibi paratum esse non arguit,
10 petulanter facimus, si matrem familias secus quam matro-
narum sanctitas postulat nominamus. Sin ista muliere
remota nec crimen ullum nec opes ad oppugnandum M.
Caelium illis relinquuntur, quid est aliud quod nos patroni
facere debeamus, nisi ut eos qui insectantur repellamus ?
15 Quod quidem facerem vehementius, nisi intercederent mihi
inimicitiae cum istius mulieris viro—fratrem volui dicere ;
semper hic erro. Nunc agam modice nec longius progrediar
quam me mea fides et causa ipsa coget : nec enim muliebris
umquam inimicitias mihi gerendas putavi, praesertim cum
20 ea quam omnes semper amicam omnium potius quam
cuiusquam inimicam putaverunt.

Sed tamen ex ipsa quaeram prius utrum me secum ¹⁴
severe et graviter et prisce agere malit, an remisse et leniter ³³
et urbane. Si illo austero more ac modo, aliquis mihi ab
25 inferis excitandus est ex barbatis illis, non hac barbula qua
ista delectatur sed illa horrida quam in statuis antiquis
atque imaginibus videmus, qui obiurget mulierem et qui

1 servos, potionem *Bährens* : quos potuit *Pπδ*    2 clam attulit
*scripsi* : quam *ante* locum *hab.* Σ : *om. Pπδ*    5 nobili verum Σ,
*Quintil.* ix. 4. 97 : nobili sed (nobi . . . . . .*P¹) Pπδ*    12 M. Σ : *om.
Pπδ*    16 fratrem Σ*Bb²*, *Claud. Sac.* (*K.* vi. 468) : fratre *Pπδ*,
*Rufinian.* (*Rhet. M.* 40)    18 cogit Σ*b²*    nec Σ : neque *Pπδ*
19 mihi inimicitias Σ    cum ea *om. Quintil.* ix. 2. 99    20 semper
*om. Quintil.*    24 si *Ernesti* : sin *BPπδ* : si enim *Bährens*    25
hac barbula] ex barbula illa Σ*B*    26 sed illa Σ*B* : sed ex illa *cett.*
27 et qui Σ : et *Pπδ*

pro me loquatur ne mihi ista forte suscenseat. Exsistat
igitur ex hac ipsa familia aliquis ac potissimum Caecus ille ;
minimum enim dolorem capiet qui istam non videbit. Qui
profecto, si exstiterit, sic aget ac sic loquetur : ' Mulier,
quid tibi cum Caelio, quid cum homine adulescentulo, quid 5
cum alieno ? Cur aut tam familiaris fuisti ut aurum com-
modares, aut tam inimica ut venenum timeres ? Non
patrem tuum videras, non patruum, non avum, non proavum,
34 non *abavum, non* atavum audieras consules fuisse ; non
denique modo te Q. Metelli matrimonium tenuisse sciebas, 10
clarissimi ac fortissimi viri patriaeque amantissimi, qui simul
ac pedem limine extulerat, omnis prope civis virtute, gloria,
dignitate superabat ? Cum ex amplissimo genere in familiam
clarissimam nupsisses, cur tibi Caelius tam coniunctus fuit ?
cognatus, adfinis, viri tui familiaris ? Nihil eorum. Quid 15
igitur fuit nisi quaedam temeritas ac libido ? Nonne te, si
nostrae imagines viriles non commovebant, ne progenies
quidem mea, Q. illa Claudia, aemulam domesticae laudis
in gloria muliebri esse admonebat, non virgo illa Vestalis
Claudia quae patrem complexa triumphantem ab inimico 20
tribuno plebei de curru detrahi passa non est ? Cur te
fraterna vitia potius quam bona paterna et avita et usque
a nobis cum in viris tum etiam in feminis repetita moverunt ?
Ideone ego pacem Pyrrhi diremi ut tu amorum turpissi-
morum cotidie foedera ferires, ideo aquam adduxi ut ea tu 25
inceste uterere, ideo viam munivi ut eam tu alienis viris
comitata celebrares ? '
35   Sed quid ego, iudices, ita gravem personam induxi ut

15
35

6 familiaris *Severian.* (*Rhet. M.* 360) : famil. huius ΣB : famil. huic
Pπδ   accommodares ΣB   8 non proavum ΣB : proavum *cett.*
9 non abavum, non atavum *scripsi* (*cf. Nipperdey, Leges Ann. p.* 42) :
non atavum non ΣB : atavum *cett.*   15 eorum] horum b¹, *Ernesti*
17 ne *et* quidem *om.* B   23 ‖ moverunt (mov- *m. 2 in ras.*) P :
*fort.* commoverunt   28 introduxi *Quintil.* ix. 2. 60   ut Σ · ut
et Pπδ : ut etiam *Wesenberg*

16

verear ne se idem Appius repente convertat et Caelium
incipiat accusare illa sua gravitate censoria? Sed videro
hoc posterius atque ita, iudices, ut vel severissimis discepta-
toribus M. Caeli vitam me probaturum esse confidam.   Tu
5 vero, mulier—iam enim ipse tecum nulla persona introducta
loquor—si ea quae facis, quae dicis, quae insimulas, quae
moliris, quae arguis, probare cogitas, rationem tantae familiaritatis, tantae consuetudinis, tantae coniunctionis reddas
atque exponas necesse est.   Accusatores quidem libidines,
10 amores, adulteria, Baias, actas, convivia, comissationes,
cantus, symphonias, navigia iactant, idemque significant
nihil se te invita dicere.   Quae tu quoniam mente nescio
qua effrenata atque praecipiti in forum deferri iudiciumque
voluisti, aut diluas oportet ac falsa esse doceas aut nihil
15 neque crimini tuo neque testimonio credendum esse fateare.

Sin autem urbanius me agere mavis, sic agam tecum. 36
Removebo illum senem durum ac paene agrestem; ex his
igitur sumam aliquem ac potissimum minimum fratrem qui
est in isto genere urbanissimus; qui te amat plurimum, qui
20 propter nescio quam, credo, timiditatem et nocturnos
quosdam inanis metus tecum semper pusio cum maiore
sorore cubitabat.   Eum putato tecum loqui: 'Quid tu-
multuaris, soror? quid insanis?

Quid clamorem exorsa verbis parvam rem magnam facis?

25 Vicinum adulescentulum aspexisti; candor huius te et pro-
ceritas, voltus oculique pepulerunt; saepius videre voluisti;
fuisti non numquam in isdem hortis; vis nobilis mulier

3 ut vel Σ: vel (om. g) Pπδ    6 loquar Σ    6–7 facis . . . arguis
(quae ante moliris om. b²: quae insimulas om. ψ²) Σb²ψ²: om. P¹:
facis, quae dicis, quae in sororem tuam moliris, quae argumenta P²πδ
10 actas P: acta πδ    13 praeceps Σ    14 ac Halm: aut Pπδ
17 illum illum Σ    his igitur P¹: his igitur tuis P²πδ: istis tuis
Madvig    22 cubitabat Quintil. viii. 3. 22: cubitavit Pπδ    24
clamorem Ribbeck: clamore Pπδ    26 pepulerunt Σπδ: perpulerunt
P    27 vis P¹, Madvig: visa P²πδ

17

illum filium familias patre parco ac tenaci habere tuis copiis
devinctum.  Non potes ; calcitrat, respuit, repellit, non
putat tua dona esse tanti.  Confer te alio.  Habes hortos
ad Tiberim ac diligenter eo loco paratos quo omnis iuventus
natandi causa venit ; hinc licet condiciones cotidie legas ; 5
cur huic qui te spernit molesta es ? '

**16**
**37** Redeo nunc ad te, Caeli, vicissim ac mihi auctoritatem
patriam severitatemque suscipio.  Sed dubito quem patrem
potissimum sumam, Caecilianumne aliquem vehementem
atque durum :                                                                    10

Nunc enim demum mi animus ardet, nunc meum cor
cumulatur ira

aut illum :

O infelix, o sceleste !

Ferrei sunt isti patres :                                                         15

Egone quid dicam, quid velim ? quae tu omnia
Tuis foedis factis facis ut nequiquam velim,

vix ferendi.  Diceret talis pater : ' Cur te in istam vicini-
tatem meretriciam contulisti ? cur inlecebris cognitis non
refugisti ? '                                                                     20

Cur alienam ullam mulierem nosti ? Dide ac dissice ;
Per me *tibi* licet.  Si egebis, tibi dolebit, *non mihi.*
Mihi sat est qui aetatis quod relicuom est oblectem
meae.

38 Huic tristi ac derecto seni responderet Caelius se nulla 25
cupiditate inductum de via decessisse.  Quid signi ? Nulli
sumptus, nulla iactura, nulla versura.  At fuit fama.  Quotus

---

2 potest Σ : potes ‖ *P*    repellit Σ*B* : *om. cett.*    3 esse dona
Σ    4 paratos Σ*B* : parasti *P* : praeparasti πδ    11 demum mi
*Ribbeck* : demum mihi *P*πδ : mihi demum *B*    12 ira] cura *B*    16
quid velim *Spengel* : egone quid velim *P*πδ    21 alienam *om.* Σ
dissice Σ, *Puteanus* : disce *P*πδ    22 tibi *Francken* : *om. P*πδ    non
mihi *Francken* : *om. P*πδ    25 se nulla . . . in tam *om. P*[1] *in* 4
*versuum lac.*

quisque istam effugere potest, praesertim in tam maledica
civitate? Vicinum eius mulieris miraris male audisse cuius
frater germanus sermones iniquorum effugere non potuit?
Leni vero et clementi patre cuius modi ille est :

5    Fores ecfregit, restituentur ; discidit
     Vestem, resarcietur,

Caeli causa est expeditissima. Quid enim esset in quo se
non facile defenderet? Nihil iam in istam mulierem dico ;
sed, si esset aliqua dissimilis istius quae se omnibus per-
10 volgaret, quae haberet palam decretum semper aliquem,
cuius in hortos, domum, Baias iure suo libidines omnium
commearent, quae etiam aleret adulescentis et parsimoniam
patrum suis sumptibus sustineret ; si vidua libere, proterva
petulanter, dives effuse, libidinosa meretricio more viveret,
15 adulterum ego putarem si quis hanc paulo liberius salutasset?
     Dicet aliquis : 'Haec igitur est tua disciplina? sic tu ¹⁷₃₉
instituis adulescentis? ob hanc causam tibi hunc puerum
parens commendavit et tradidit, ut in amore atque in volupta-
20 tibus adulescentiam suam conlocaret, et ut hanc tu vitam
atque haec studia defenderes?' Ego, si quis, iudices, hoc
robore animi atque hac indole virtutis ac continentiae fuit
ut respueret omnis voluptates omnemque vitae suae cursum
in labore corporis atque in animi contentione conficeret,

---

1 quisque *BP²πδ* : quisque est qui *T*    effugere potest, praesertim
*scripsi* : praesertim effugere potest *ΣB* : effugere potest (*ante* 12 *litt.
lac. P²*) *cett.* : effugere possit *Halm*    4 patre *Schwarz* : patri
*Pπδ*    5 ecfregit *Müller* : etfregit *P¹* : effregit *P²πδ*    7 Caelii
*Angelius* : filii *PTπδ*    10 decretum] *fort.* devinctum (*cf.* § 36)
13 sustineret *Σ* (*cf. Liv.* xxxix. 9. 6) : sustentaret *cett.*    15 quis]
qui *Quintil.* viii. 4. 1    17 est igitur *T* (*contra Quintil.* ix. 2. 15)
discipulina *Σ* (*cf. Rep.* ii. 19)    18 parens tibi hunc puerum *Σ*
19 amoribus *Σ*    20 ut *TΣ* : om. *Pπδ*    21 si quis *Σg* : si quid *TB* :
si qui *cett.* (*variant codd. Quintil.*)    22 ac *BPπδ, Quintil.* : ad (*ex
adq.*) *T* : atque *Halm*    23 suae vitae *ΣB*    24 atque in]
atque *ΣB*

19

quem non quies, non remissio, non aequalium studia, non
ludi, non convivium delectaret, nihil in vita expetendum
putaret nisi quod esset cum laude et cum dignitate coniunctum, hunc mea sententia divinis quibusdam bonis
instructum atque ornatum puto. Ex hoc genere illos fuisse 5
arbitror Camillos, Fabricios, Curios, omnisque eos qui haec
40 ex minimis tanta fecerunt. Verum haec genera virtutum
non solum in moribus nostris sed vix iam in libris repe-
riuntur. Chartae quoque quae illam pristinam severitatem
continebant obsoleverunt; neque solum apud nos qui hanc 10
sectam rationemque vitae re magis quam verbis secuti
sumus sed etiam apud Graecos, doctissimos homines,
quibus, cum facere non possent, loqui tamen et scribere
honeste et magnifice licebat, alia quaedam mutatis Graeciae
41 temporibus praecepta exstiterunt. Itaque alii voluptatis 15
causa omnia sapientes facere dixerunt, neque ab hac
orationis turpitudine eruditi homines refugerunt; alii cum
voluptate dignitatem coniungendam putaverunt, ut res
maxime inter se repugnantis dicendi facultate coniungerent;
illud unum derectum iter ad laudem cum labore qui proba- 20
verunt, prope soli iam in scholis sunt relicti. Multa enim
nobis blandimenta natura ipsa genuit quibus sopita virtus
coniveret interdum; multas vias adulescentiae lubricas
ostendit quibus illa insistere aut ingredi sine casu aliquo ac
prolapsione vix posset; multarum rerum iucundissimarum 25
varietatem dedit qua non modo haec aetas sed etiam
42 iam conroborata caperetur. Quam ob rem si quem forte
inveneritis qui aspernetur oculis pulchritudinem rerum, non
odore ullo, non tactu, non sapore capiatur, excludat auribus

---

2 convivium *TB* : convivia *Pπδ*     delectaret *scripsi* : delectarent
*codd.*     qui nihil *Halm*     6 Fabricios *ante* fuisse *hab. T*     Furios
*B*     14 alia *TΣg²* : aliqua *Pπδ*     16 nec ab Σ     19 dicendi]
verborum Σ     23 interdum Σ, *Madvig* : et interdum *cett.*     24
ac *TB* : aut *Pπδ*

omnem suavitatem, huic homini ego fortasse et pauci deos
propitios, plerique autem iratos putabunt.   Ergo haec 18
deserta via et inculta atque interclusa iam frondibus et
virgultis relinquatur.   Detur aliqui ludus aetati ; sit adule-
5 scentia liberior ; non omnia voluptatibus denegentur ; non
semper superet vera illa et derecta ratio ; vincat aliquando
cupiditas voluptasque rationem, dum modo illa in hoc
genere praescriptio moderatioque teneatur.   Parcat iuventus
pudicitiae suae, ne spoliet alienam, ne effundat patrimonium,
10 ne faenore trucidetur, ne incurrat in alterius domum atque
familiam, ne probrum castis, labem integris, infamiam bonis
inferat, ne quem vi terreat, ne intersit insidiis, scelere
careat.   Postremo cum paruerit voluptatibus, dederit aliquid
temporis ad ludum aetatis atque ad inanis hasce adulescentiae
15 cupiditates, revocet se aliquando ad curam rei domesticae,
rei forensis reique publicae, ut ea quae ratione antea non
perspexerat satietate abiecisse et experiendo contempsisse
videatur.

Ac multi quidem et nostra et patrum maiorumque me- 43
20 moria, iudices, summi homines et clarissimi cives fuerunt
quorum, cum adulescentiae cupiditates defervissent, eximiae
virtutes firmata iam aetate exstiterunt.   Ex quibus neminem
mihi libet nominare ; vosmet vobiscum recordamini.   Nolo
enim cuiusquam fortis atque inlustris viri ne minimum
25 quidem erratum cum maxima laude coniungere.   Quod si
facere vellem, multi a me summi atque ornatissimi viri
praedicarentur quorum partim nimia libertas in adulescentia,
partim profusa luxuries, magnitudo aeris alieni, sumptus,
libidines nominarentur, quae multis postea virtutibus obtecta

2 putaverunt *T*   3 et virg.] ac virg. Σ   4 aliqui ludus *T* : aliquid
*P*πδ   5 voluptatibus] cupiditatibus Σ   6 superent Σ   et] ac Σ
derecta Σ*P* : directa πδ   via et ratio Σ   11 familiam Σ : famam *cett.*
17 et Σ : *om. P*πδ   19 quidem Σ : *om. P*πδ   21 deferv.]
deferuu- *P¹* : deseru- Σ   23 libet Σ, *Madvig* : liquet *P* : necesse
est πδ   28 profluxa Σ   29 obiecta Σ

21

19
44 adulescentiae qui vellet excusatione defenderet.  At vero
in M. Caelio—dicam enim iam confidentius de studiis eius
honestis, quoniam audeo quaedam fretus vestra sapientia
libere confiteri—nulla luxuries reperietur, nulli sumptus,
nullum aes alienum, nulla conviviorum ac lustrorum libido. 5
Quod quidem vitium ventris et gurgitis non modo non
minuit aetas hominibus sed etiam auget.   Amores autem
et deliciae quae vocantur, quae firmiore animo praeditis
diutius molestae non solent esse—mature enim et celeriter
deflorescunt—numquam hunc occupatum impeditumve te- 10
45 nuerunt.   Audistis cum pro se diceret, audistis antea cum
accusaret—defendendi haec causa, non gloriandi loquor—
genus orationis, facultatem, copiam sententiarum atque verborum, quae vestra prudentia est, perspexistis.   Atque in eo
non solum ingenium elucere eius videbatis, quod saepe, 15
etiam si industria non alitur, valet tamen ipsum suis viribus,
sed inerat, nisi me propter benivolentiam forte fallebat, ratio
et bonis artibus instituta et cura et vigiliis elaborata.   Atqui
scitote, iudices, eas cupiditates quae obiciuntur Caelio
atque haec studia de quibus disputo non facile in eodem 20
homine esse posse.   Fieri enim non potest ut animus libidini
deditus, amore, desiderio, cupiditate, saepe nimia copia,
inopia etiam non numquam impeditus hoc quicquid est
quod nos facimus in dicendo, quoquo modo facimus, non
46 modo agendo verum etiam cogitando possit sustinere.   An 25
vos aliam causam esse ullam putatis cur in tantis praemiis
eloquentiae, tanta voluptate dicendi, tanta laude, tanta

2 iam] hoc Σ      3 quoniam Σ, *Muretus* : quondam *Pπδ*      5
lustrorum] stuprorum Σ      6 gutturis *ed. R*      8 deliciae Σ : hae
deliciae *Pπδ*      firmo ingenio Σ      10 impeditumve *scripsi* : ne
impeditum que Σ : impeditumque *Pπδ*      12 loquor Σ, *Naugerius* :
eloquor *Pπδ*      14 quae vestrae si prudentiae Σ : *fort.* quae vestra
est prudentia      18 atqui Σ, *Lambinus* : atque *Pπδ*      20 dis-
puto] disputavi Σ : disputato *Pλ*      24 modo facimus non Σ, *suppl.*
*Madvig* : *om. Pπδ*

22

**gratia,** tanto honore, tam sint pauci semperque fuerint qui
in hoc labore versentur? Obterendae sunt omnes voluptates,
relinquenda studia delectationis, ludus, iocus, convivium,
sermo paene est familiarium deserendus. Qua re in hoc
5 genere labor offendit homines a studioque deterret, non
quo aut ingenia deficiant aut doctrina puerilis. An hic, si 47
sese isti vitae dedidisset, consularem hominem admodum
adulescens in iudicium vocavisset? hic, si laborem fugeret,
si obstrictus voluptatibus teneretur, hac in acie cotidie
10 versaretur, appeteret inimicitias, in iudicium vocaret, subiret
periculum capitis, ipse inspectante populo Romano tot iam
mensis aut de salute aut de gloria dimicaret? ⌈Nihilne 20
igitur illa vicinitas redolet, nihilne hominum fama, nihil
Baiae denique ipsae loquuntur? Illae vero non loquuntur
15 solum verum etiam personant, huc unius mulieris libidinem
esse prolapsam ut ea non modo solitudinem ac tenebras
atque haec flagitiorum integumenta non quaerat sed in
turpissimis rebus frequentissima celebritate et clarissima
luce laetetur.⌋

20 Verum si quis est qui etiam meretriciis amoribus inter- 48
dictum iuventuti putet, est ille quidem valde severus—negare
non possum—sed abhorret non modo ab huius saeculi
licentia verum etiam a maiorum consuetudine atque concessis. Quando enim hoc non factitatum est, quando repre-
25 hensum, quando non permissum, quando denique fuit ut
quod licet non liceret? Hic ego ipsam rem definiam,

---

4 est paene Σ    5 labor offendit homines Σ, *Madvig*: labore
fiendi homines *P*: labor confitendi homines *eg*: homines a labore
studioque discendi *bhψ²*    6 hic *om.* Σ (*contra Arusian. K.* vii.
465)    7 dedidisset *Arusian.* (*s.v.* dedo): dedisset *mei*    9
hac in Σ: in hac *Pπδ*    11 capitis, ipse *Ph*: capitis, ipso *ed. R*:
capitis ipse, *Halm*    tot iam Σ, *Lambinus*: tot t ‖ *P*: tot *πδ*
12 nihilne... nihilne Σ: nihil... nihil *Pπδ*    18 rebus] viris Σ
22 huius Σ*g²h*: eius *cett.*    23 concessu *Ernesti*    24 factitatum Σ,
*Lambinus*: factum *Pπδ*    26 ipsam rem definiam *Halm*: iam rem
definiam (iam rem *P²* *in ras.*) *Pπδ*: iam definiam rem Σ

23

mulierem nullam nominabo ; tantum in medio relinquam.
49 Si quae non nupta mulier domum suam patefecerit omnium
cupiditati palamque sese in meretricia vita conlocarit, virorum alienissimorum conviviis uti instituerit, si hoc in urbe,
si in hortis, si in Baiarum illa celebritate faciat, si denique 5
ita sese gerat non incessu solum sed ornatu atque comitatu,
non flagrantia oculorum, non libertate sermonum, sed etiam
complexu, osculatione, actis, navigatione, conviviis, ut non
solum meretrix sed etiam proterva meretrix procaxque
videatur : cum hac si qui adulescens forte fuerit, utrum hic 10
tibi, L. Herenni, adulter an amator, expugnare pudicitiam
50 an explere libidinem voluisse videatur? Obliviscor iam
iniurias tuas, Clodia, depono memoriam doloris mei ; quae
abs te crudeliter in meos me absente facta sunt neglego ;
ne sint haec in te dicta quae dixi. ⌐ Sed ex te ipsa requiro, 15
quoniam et crimen accusatores abs te et testem eius criminis
te ipsam dicunt se habere. Si quae mulier sit eius modi
qualem ego paulo ante descripsi, tui dissimilis, vita instituto-
que meretricio, cum hac aliquid adulescentem hominem
habuisse rationis num tibi perturpe aut perflagitiosum esse 20
videatur? Ea si tu non es, sicut ego malo, quid est quod
obiciant Caelio? Sin eam te volunt esse, quid est cur nos
crimen hoc, si tu contemnis, pertimescamus? Qua re nobis
da viam rationemque defensionis. Aut enim pudor tuus
defendet nihil a M. Caelio petulantius esse factum, aut 25
impudentia et huic et ceteris magnam ad se defendendum
facultatem dabit.⌐
21
51     Sed quoniam emersisse iam e vadis et scopulos praeter-

**3** collocaverit Σ      **4** in urbe Σ*g*²*h* : urbe *cett*.      **5** faciat
*duo dett*. : facit *P*¹ : faciet *P*²π : faceret *b*      **6** gerat Σ : geret
(gereret *b*) *P*πδ      **7** sermonum Σ : sermonis *P*πδ      **8** actis
*Ernesti* : aquis *P*πδ      **9** sed etiam proterva meretrix Σ*b*²ψ² : *om*.
*P*πδ      **13** tuas Σ, *Arusian*. (*s. v.* obliviscor), *Servius ad Aen*. ii. 148 :
*om*. *P*πδ      **24** aut enim Σ : nam aut *P*πδ      **25** esse factum *P*πδ :
factum esse Σ      **26** et ceteris magnam ad se Σ : *om*. *P*πδ      **28**
e vadis Σ, *ed. R* : evades *P*¹ : evadens *P*¹π : e vado *b*²ψ²

vecta videtur esse oratio mea, perfacilis mihi reliquus cursus
ostenditur. Duo sunt enim crimina una in muliere summorum facinorum, auri quod sumptum a Clodia dicitur, et
veneni quod eiusdem Clodiae necandae causa parasse Cae-
5 lium criminantur. Aurum sumpsit, ut dicitis, quod L.
Luccei servis daret, per quos Alexandrinus Dio qui tum
apud Lucceium habitabat necaretur. Magnum crimen vel
in legatis insidiandis vel in servis ad hospitem domini
necandum sollicitandis, plenum sceleris consilium, plenum
10 audaciae! Quo quidem in crimine primum illud requiro, 52
dixeritne Clodiae quam ob rem aurum sumeret, an non
dixerit. Si non dixit, cur dedit? Si dixit, eodem se conscientiae scelere devinxit. Tune aurum ex armario tuo
promere ausa es, tune Venerem illam tuam spoliare orna-
15 mentis, spoliatricem ceterorum, cum scires quantum ad
facinus aurum hoc quaereretur, ad necem legati, ad L. Luccei, sanctissimi hominis atque integerrimi, labem sceleris
sempiternam? Huic facinori tanto tua mens liberalis con-
scia, tua domus popularis ministra, tua denique hospitalis
20 illa Venus adiutrix esse non debuit. Vidit hoc Balbus; 53
celatam esse Clodiam dixit, atque ita Caelium ad illam
attulisse, se ad ornatum ludorum aurum quaerere. Si tam
familiaris erat Clodiae quam tu esse vis cum de libidine
eius tam multa dicis, dixit profecto quo vellet aurum; si
25 tam familiaris non erat, non dedit. Ita si verum tibi
Caelius dixit, o immoderata mulier, sciens tu aurum ad
facinus dedisti; si non est ausus dicere, non dedisti.

Quid ego nunc argumentis huic crimini, quae sunt innu- 22

1 esse ΣB: om. Pπδ    5 L. P²πδ: om. ΣP¹    8 insidiandis
ΣB: insidiantes (-is gh) Pπδ    10 requiro Σ: requiram Pπδ    11-12
quam ob ... si non om. P¹ in 1½ vers. lac.    11 ob Σδ: ad P²π
sumeret Σ: tum sumeret δ: tum iret P²π    15 ceterorum Σψ¹, Gulielmius, Madvig: ceterum cett.    16 L. Luccei bg²: L. Lucullum
Pπψ    18 sempiternam Pantagathus: sempiterni Pπδ    23
erat] fuit Σ    27 ausus Σhψ: rursus cett.

25

merabilia, resistam ? Possum dicere mores M. Caeli longissime a tanti sceleris atrocitate esse disiunctos ; minime esse
credendum homini tam ingenioso tamque prudenti non
venisse in mentem rem tanti sceleris ignotis alienisque
servis non esse credendam. Possum etiam alia et ceterorum 5
patronorum et mea consuetudine ab accusatore perquirere,
ubi sit congressus cum servis Luccei Caelius, qui ei fuerit
aditus ; si per se, qua temeritate ! si per alium, per quem ?
Possum omnis latebras suspicionum peragrare dicendo ;
non causa, non locus, non facultas, non conscius, non per- 10
ficiendi, non occultandi malefici spes, non ratio ulla, non
54 vestigium maximi facinoris reperietur. Sed haec quae sunt
oratoris propria, quae mihi non propter ingenium meum
sed propter hanc exercitationem usumque dicendi fructum
aliquem ferre potuissent, cum a me ipso elaborata proferri 15
viderentur, brevitatis causa relinquo omnia. Habeo enim,
iudices, quem vos socium vestrae religionis iurisque iurandi
facile esse patiamini, L. Lucceium, sanctissimum hominem
et gravissimum testem, qui tantum facinus in famam atque
in fortunas suas neque non audisset inlatum a M. Caelio 20
neque neglexisset neque tulisset. An ille vir illa humanitate
praeditus, illis studiis, illis artibus atque doctrina illius
ipsius periculum quem propter haec ipsa studia diligebat,
neglegere potuisset et, quod facinus in alienum hominem
intentum severe acciperet, id omisisset curare in hospitem ? 25
quod per ignotos actum si comperisset doleret, id a suis
servis temptatum esse neglegeret ? quod in agris locisve

---

5 credendam *bg²* : credendum (-u- *in ras.* P) *Pπψ*    alia Σ :
illa *Pπψ*    7 fuerit ei Σ    15 elaborata Σ, *Ant. Augustinus* :
laborata *Pπψ*    18 L. *om.* Σ    19 in famam atque in (in *om.* δ)
Σδ : infamat atque *Pπ*    20 non *om.* Σ    M. Σ*P²g* : *om.* *P¹eh*
22 illis artibus *TΣ, Lambinus* : artibus *Pπδ*    24 in *TΣh* : per *g²* :
*om. cett.*    25 intentum *T* : inlatum *Pπδ*    hospitem *T* : hospite
*Pπδ*    26 si comperisset *TΣ* : cumpetisset *Pg¹e* : comperisset *g²δ* :
cum comperisset *h*    27 servis *TΣ* : *om. Pπδ*    locisque *T*

publicis factum reprehenderet, id in urbe ac domi suae
coeptum esse leniter ferret? quod in alicuius agrestis periculo non praetermitteret, id homo eruditus in insidiis doctissimi hominis dissimulandum putaret? Sed cur diutius vos, 55
5 iudices, teneo? Ipsius iurati religionem auctoritatemque
percipite atque omnia diligenter testimoni verba cognoscite.
Recita. L. LVCCEI TESTIMONIVM. Quid exspectatis amplius?
an aliquam vocem putatis ipsam pro se causam et veritatem
posse mittere? Haec est innocentiae defensio, haec ipsius
10 causae oratio, haec una vox veritatis. In crimine ipso nulla
suspicio est, in re nihil est argumenti, in negotio quod actum
esse dicitur nullum vestigium sermonis, loci, temporis;
nemo testis, nemo conscius nominatur, totum crimen pro-
fertur ex inimica, ex infami, ex crudeli, ex facinerosa, ex
15 libidinosa domo. Domus autem illa quae temptata esse
scelere isto nefario dicitur plena est integritatis, dignitatis,
offici, religionis; ex qua domo recitatur vobis iure iurando
devincta auctoritas, ut res minime dubitanda in contentione
ponatur, utrum temeraria, procax, irata mulier finxisse
20 crimen, an gravis sapiens moderatusque vir religiose testimonium dixisse videatur.

Reliquum est igitur crimen de veneno; cuius ego nec **23**
principium invenire neque evolvere exitum possum. Quae ⁵⁶
fuit enim causa quam ob rem isti mulieri venenum dare
25 vellet Caelius? Ne aurum redderet? Num petivit? Ne
crimen haereret? Num quis obiecit? num quis denique
fecisset mentionem, si hic nullius nomen detulisset? Quin

etiam L. Herennium dicere audistis verbo se molestum non
futurum fuisse Caelio, nisi iterum eadem de re suo familiari
absoluto nomen hic detulisset. Credibile est igitur tantum
facinus nullam ob causam esse commissum? et vos non
videtis fingi sceleris maximi crimen ut alterius sceleris susci- 5
57 piendi fuisse causa videatur? Cui denique commisit, quo
adiutore usus est, quo socio, quo conscio, cui tantum
facinus, cui se, cui salutem suam credidit? Servisne mulieris? Sic enim est obiectum. Et erat tam demens is cui
vos ingenium certe tribuitis, etiam si cetera inimica oratione 10
detrahitis, ut omnis suas fortunas alienis servis committeret?
At quibus servis?—refert enim magno opere id ipsum—eisne
quos intellegebat non communi condicione servitutis uti
sed licentius liberius familiariusque cum domina vivere?
Quis enim hoc non videt, iudices, aut quis ignorat, in eius 15
modi domo in qua mater familias meretricio more vivat, in
qua nihil geratur quod foras proferendum sit, in qua inusitatae libidines, luxuries, omnia denique inaudita vitia ac
flagitia versentur, hic servos non esse servos, quibus omnia
committantur, per quos gerantur, qui versentur isdem in 20
voluptatibus, quibus occulta credantur, ad quos aliquantum
etiam ex cotidianis sumptibus ac luxurie redundet? Id
58 igitur Caelius non videbat? Si enim tam familiaris erat
mulieris quam vos voltis, istos quoque servos familiaris
dominae esse sciebat. Sin ei tanta consuetudo quanta 25
a vobis inducitur non erat, quae cum servis eius potuit

---

1 L. Σ, *Lambinus* : *om. cett.*　　2 futurum Caelio *T qui in hoc*
*verbo desinit* : fut. Caelio fuisse *Halm*　　4 nullam ob Σ : ob nullam
*Pπδ*　　6 causa Σ, *edd. VR, ante* sceleris *hab.* ψ : *om. cett.*　　9
est obiectum Σ : obiectum est ψ, *ed. R* : obiectum *cett.*　　is Σ : hic
*Pπδ*　　10 tribuistis Σ　　12 eisne *Lambinus* : eiusne Σ : hisne
*Pπδ*　　13 uti sed Σ*b²ψ²* : ut (sed *b¹*) esset *cett.*　　14 familiariusque Σ : familiarius *Pπδ*　　vivere] dere Σ　　17 inusitatae Σ : illu-
stria *Pπ* : lustra δ　　20 in *om.* Σ　　23 tam Σψ : iam *Pbh* : *om.*
*eg*　　25 dominae esse Σ*g* : esse domina ‖ esse *P* : esse dominae
*cett.*　　26 eius Σ : *om. Pπδ*

familiaritas esse tanta? Ipsius autem veneni quae ratio 24
fingitur? ubi quaesitum est, quem ad modum paratum, quo
pacto, cui, quo in loco traditum? Habuisse aiunt domi
vimque eius esse expertum in servo quodam ad eam rem
5 ipsam parato; cuius perceleri interitu esse ab hoc compro-
batum venenum. Pro di immortales! cur interdum in 59
hominum sceleribus maximis aut conivetis aut praesentis
fraudis poenas in diem reservatis? Vidi enim, vidi et
illum hausi dolorem vel acerbissimum in vita, cum Q. Me-
10 tellus abstraheretur e sinu gremioque patriae, cumque ille
vir qui se natum huic imperio putavit tertio die post quam
in curia, quam in rostris, quam in re publica floruisset, inte-
gerrima aetate, optimo habitu, maximis viribus eriperetur
indignissime bonis omnibus atque universae civitati. Quo
15 quidem tempore ille moriens, cum iam ceteris ex partibus
oppressa mens esset, extremum sensum ad memoriam rei
publicae reservabat, cum me intuens flentem significabat
interruptis ac morientibus vocibus quanta inpenderet pro-
cella mihi, quanta tempestas civitati et cum parietem saepe
20 feriens eum qui cum Q. Catulo fuerat ei communis crebro
Catulum, saepe me, saepissime rem publicam nominabat, ut
non tam se mori quam spoliari suo praesidio cum patriam
tum etiam me doleret. Quem quidem virum si nulla vis 60
repentini sceleris sustulisset, quonam modo ille furenti
25 fratri suo consularis restitisset qui consul incipientem furere
atque tonantem sua se manu interfecturum audiente senatu
dixerit? Ex hac igitur domo progressa ista mulier de
veneni celeritate dicere audebit? Nonne ipsam domum
metuet ne quam vocem eiciat, non parietes conscios, non

4 ad eam rem Σ, *Madvig*: ad eadem rem *P*[1]: ad rem *cett.*          10
e sinu *ed. R*: sinu Σ: e sinu e *P*πδ          19 mihi Σ*B*, *Orelli*: ibi *Peg*:
urbi *h*δ          22 mori *P*: emori πδ          24 ille *om.* Σ          25 fratri
suo] patrueli *add. P*πδ: *del. Orelli*          consul *Manutius*: consulem *P*πδ
26 tonantem *scripsi* (*cf. Mur.* 81): conantem *P*πδ          27 ista] illa Σ
29 eiciat *Muretus*: eieciat Σ: eliciat (-eat *P*[1]) *P*πδ (*cf. Tusc.* ii. 56)

noctem illam funestam ac luctuosam perhorrescet? Sed
revertor ad crimen; etenim haec facta illius clarissimi ac
fortissimi viri mentio et vocem meam fletu debilitavit et
mentem dolore impedivit.

**25**
**61**     Sed tamen venenum unde fuerit, quem ad modum paratum sit non dicitur. Datum esse aiunt huic P. Licinio,
pudenti adulescenti et bono, Caeli familiari; constitutum
esse cum servis ut venirent ad balneas Senias; eodem
Licinium esse venturum atque eis veneni pyxidem tradi-
turum. Hic primum illud requiro, quid attinuerit ferri in
eum locum constitutum, cur illi servi non ad Caelium
domum venerint. Si manebat tanta illa consuetudo Caeli,
tanta familiaritas cum Clodia, quid suspicionis esset si apud
Caelium mulieris servus visus esset? Sin autem iam
suberat simultas, exstincta erat consuetudo, discidium
exstiterat, hinc illae lacrimae nimirum et haec causa est
**62** omnium horum scelerum atque criminum. 'Immo' inquit
'cum servi ad dominam rem totam et maleficium Caeli
detulissent, mulier ingeniosa praecepit his ut omnia Caelio
pollicerentur; sed ut venenum, cum a Licinio traderetur,
manifesto comprehendi posset, constitui locum iussit balneas Senias, ut eo mitteret amicos qui delitiscerent, deinde
repente, cum venisset Licinius venenumque traderet, prosi-
**26** lirent hominemque comprenderent.' Quae quidem omnia,
iudices, perfacilem rationem habent reprendendi. Cur
enim potissimum balneas publicas constituerat? in quibus
non invenio quae latebra togatis hominibus esse posset.

---

1 illam $\Sigma b\psi^2$ : aliam *cett.*    2 revertor $\Sigma$ : revertar $P\pi\delta$    etenim $\Sigma$, *Gruter*: sed (set *P*) enim $P\pi\delta$    5 sit paratum $\Sigma$    6 huic
$\Sigma$, *Madvig*: hoc $P\pi\delta$    7 constitutum *Naugerius*: constitutum
pactum $\Sigma$ : constitutum factum $P\pi\delta$    10 ferri $b^1$, *ed. Mediol.* : fieri
$P\pi b^2\psi$    14 iam $\Sigma B$. *Oettling* : iam iam $P\pi\delta$    18 rem totam $\Sigma$ :
remittam $P^1$ : rem istam *cett.*    19 his ut $\Sigma$, *ed. R* : suis $P\pi\delta$    20
sed ut $\Sigma h$ : sed *cett.*    21 locum *del. Ernesti*    22 deinde $\Sigma$ :
dein $P\pi\delta$    23 venenumque $\Sigma$, *Lambinus* : venenum $P\pi\delta$    26
constituebat $\Sigma$    27 possit *edd. VR*

30

Nam si essent in vestibulo balnearum, non laterent ; sin se
in intimum conicere vellent, nec satis commode calceati
et vestiti id facere possent et fortasse non reciperentur, nisi
forte mulier potens quadrantaria illa permutatione fami-
5 liaris facta erat balneatori.   Atque equidem vehementer 63
exspectabam quinam isti viri boni testes huius manifesto
deprehensi veneni dicerentur ; nulli enim sunt adhuc nomi-
nati.   Sed non dubito quin sint pergraves, qui primum sint
talis feminae familiares, deinde eam provinciam susceperint
10 ut in balneas contruderentur, quod illa nisi a viris honestissimis ac plenissimis dignitatis, quam velit sit potens, numquam impetravisset.   Sed quid ego de dignitate istorum
testium loquor ? virtutem eorum diligentiamque cognoscite.
' In balneis delituerunt.'   Testis egregios !   ' Dein temere
15 prosiluerunt.'   Homines temperantis !   Sic enim fingitis,
cum Licinius venisset, pyxidem teneret in manu, conaretur
tradere, nondum tradidisset, tum repente evolasse istos
praeclaros testis sine nomine ; Licinium autem, cum iam
manum ad tradendam pyxidem porrexisset, retraxisse atque
20 ex illo repentino hominum impetu se in fugam coniecisse.
O magnam vim veritatis, quae contra hominum ingenia,
calliditatem, sollertiam contraque fictas omnium insidias
facile se per se ipsa defendat !   Velut haec tota fabella ²⁷
veteris et plurimarum fabularum poetriae quam est sine ⁶⁴
25 argumento, quam nullum invenire exitum potest !   Quid
enim ? isti tot viri—nam necesse est fuisse non paucos ut et
comprehendi Licinius facile posset et res multorum oculis

2 nec satis commode] quomodo Σ*B*        3 reciperentur Σδ : reci-
peretur *P*π        4 permutatione] pensitatione *Pantagathus*        familiaris coeperat esse *Quintil.* ix. 4. 64        10 conducerentur Σ
14 delituerant Σ        15 temperantes *P* : gravitati deditos πδ
fingitis Σ : fing . . . *P*¹ : fingunt *cett.*        20 ex Σ : *om. P*πδ        21
magnam vim Σ : magna vis *P*πδ        hominum *ed. V* : omnium *P*πδ
23 ipsa Σ*P*¹ψ² : ipsam *cett.*        velut] ut Σ : verum *b*¹ψ²        fabel-
larum Σ        26 non paucos fuisse Σ

31

esset testatior—cur Licinium de manibus amiserunt? Qui
minus enim Licinius comprehendi potuit cum se retraxit
ne pyxidem traderet, quam si tradidisset? Erant enim illi
positi ut comprehenderent Licinium, ut manifesto Licinius
teneretur aut cum retineret venenum aut cum tradidisset. 5
Hoc fuit totum consilium mulieris, haec istorum provincia
qui rogati sunt; quos quidem tu quam ob rem temere
prosiluisse dicas atque ante tempus non reperio. Fuerant
ad hoc rogati, fuerant ad hanc rem conlocati, ut venenum,
ut insidiae, facinus denique ipsum ut manifesto comprende- 10
65 retur. Potueruntne magis tempore prosilire quam cum
Licinius venisset, cum in manu teneret veneni pyxidem?
Quae cum iam erat tradita servis, *si* evasissent subito ex
balneis mulieris amici Liciniumque comprehendissent,
imploraret hominum fidem atque a se illam pyxidem tra- 15
ditam pernegaret. Quem quo modo illi reprehenderent?
vidisse se dicerent? Primum ad se vocarent maximi facinoris crimen; deinde id se vidisse dicerent quod quo loco
conlocati fuerant non potuissent videre. Tempore igitur
ipso se ostenderunt, cum Licinius venisset, pyxidem expe- 20
diret, manum porrigeret, venenum traderet. Mimi ergo
iam exitus, non fabulae; in quo cum clausula non invenitur,
fugit aliquis e manibus, dein scabilla concrepant, aulaeum
28 tollitur. Quaero enim cur Licinium titubantem, haesitantem,
66 cedentem, fugere conantem mulieraria manus ista de manibus 25
emiserit, cur non comprenderint, cur non ipsius confessione,
multorum oculis, facinoris denique voce tanti sceleris crimen

3 illic *g²*, *Rau*   6 istorum] est horum Σ   9 ad hoc Σ, *Lam-binus*: hoc *Ph*: enim *e*: autem *g*   11 magis ΣBP¹: meliori (me-liori magis ψ²) P²πδ   13 quae cum iam erat . . . si evas. *Ernesti*, *Müller*: quae si iam erat . . . evas. *P*πδ: quae si cum iam erat . . . evas. *Bake*   15 hominum *Angelius*: omnium *P*πδ   17 ad se vocarent *scripsi*: at revocarent Σ: ad se revocarent *P*πδ   22 iam Σ: est etiam *P*πδ: est iam *Ascens.* (3)   23 dein Σ: deinde *P*πδ 26 emiserit Σπδ: miserit *P*: amiserit *codd. Lambini*   cur non com-prehenderint Σπδ: om. *P*

expresserint. An timebant ne tot unum, valentes imbecillum, alacres perterritum superare non possent?

Nullum argumentum in re, nulla suspicio in causa, nullus
exitus criminis reperietur. Itaque haec causa ab argumentis,
5 a coniectura, ab eis signis quibus veritas inlustrari solet ad
testis tota traducta est. Quos quidem ego, iudices, testis
non modo sine ullo timore sed etiam cum aliqua spe delectationis exspecto. Praegestit animus iam videre, primum 67
lautos iuvenes mulieris beatae ac nobilis familiaris, deinde
10 fortis viros ab imperatrice in insidiis atque in praesidio
balnearum conlocatos. Ex quibus requiram quem ad modum
latuerint aut ubi, alveusne ille an equus Troianus fuerit
qui tot invictos viros muliebre bellum gerentis tulerit ac
texerit. Illud vero respondere cogam, cur tot viri ac tales
15 hunc et unum et tam imbecillum quem videtis non aut
stantem comprehenderint aut fugientem consecuti sint; qui
se numquam profecto, si in istum locum processerint, explicabunt. Quam volent in conviviis faceti, dicaces, non
numquam etiam ad vinum diserti sint, alia fori vis est, alia
20 triclini, alia subselliorum ratio, alia lectorum; non idem
iudicum comissatorumque conspectus; lux denique longe
alia est solis, alia lychnorum. Quam ob rem excutiemus
omnis istorum delicias, omnis ineptias, si prodierint. Sed
me audiant, navent aliam operam, aliam ineant gratiam, in
25 aliis se rebus ostentent, vigeant apud istam mulierem venustate, dominentur sumptibus, haereant, iaceant, deserviant;
capiti vero innocentis fortunisque parcant.

At sunt servi illi de cognatorum sententia, nobilissimorum **29**
68

4 reperitur $\Sigma g$     5 eis] illis $\Sigma$     6 testis, iudices $T\Sigma$
8 prim. (*sic*) iam videre $\Sigma B$     10 atque in] atque $\Sigma$     11 col-
locatos $T$: locatos $P\pi\delta$     quem ad modum $T$: quonam modo
$P\pi\delta$     15 quem $\Sigma$: quam *cett.*     18 quam volent $P\pi\delta$:
quam volunt $\Sigma$: quamvis $T$     22 solis alia $Bb^2\psi$; solis ac $T$: solis
et $P\pi b^1$ (*cf. Fortunatian. Rhet. M. p.* 124 aliud fori lumen est, aliud
lychnorum)     25 ostendent (-ant $\Sigma$) $T^1\Sigma$

et clarissimorum hominum, manu missi. Tandem aliquid
invenimus quod ista mulier de suorum propinquorum, fortissimorum virorum, sententia atque auctoritate fecisse
dicatur. Sed scire cupio quid habeat argumenti ista manu-
missio; in qua aut crimen est Caelio quaesitum aut quaestio 5
sublata aut multarum rerum consciis servis cum causa
praemium persolutum. 'At propinquis' inquit 'placuit.' Cur
non placeret, cum rem tute ad eos non ab aliis tibi adlatam
69 sed a te ipsa compertam deferre diceres? Hic etiam
miramur, si illam commenticiam pyxidem obscenissima sit 10
fabula consecuta? Nihil est quod in eius modi mulierem
non cadere videatur. Audita et percelebrata sermonibus
res est. Percipitis animis, iudices, iam dudum quid velim
vel potius quid nolim dicere. Quod etiam si est factum,
certe a Caelio quidem non est factum—quid enim atti- 15
nebat?—est enim ab aliquo adulescente fortasse non tam
insulso quam inverecundo. Sin autem est fictum, non illud
quidem modestum sed tamen est non infacetum mendacium; quod profecto numquam hominum sermo atque
opinio comprobasset, nisi omnia quae cum turpitudine aliqua 20
dicerentur in istam quadrare apte viderentur.

70 Dicta est a me causa, iudices, et perorata. Iam intelle-
gitis quantum iudicium sustineatis, quanta res sit commissa
vobis. De vi quaeritis. Quae lex ad imperium, ad maie-
statem, ad statum patriae, ad salutem omnium pertinet, quam 25
legem Q. Catulus armata dissensione civium rei publicae
paene extremis temporibus tulit, quaeque lex sedata illa
flamma consulatus mei fumantis reliquias coniurationis
exstinxit, hac nunc lege Caeli adulescentia non ad rei

   2 de] e Σ     6 sublata *T*Σ*b*²*ψ*², *Manutius* : sublevata *cett.*     7
inquit *T* : *om.* *P*π*δ*     8 rem tute Σ*ψ*. *ed. R* : tu (tu ‖ *P*) rem te
*cett.*     10 sit] est *Halm*     12 audita] et pervulgata *add. bh*ψ²
15 quidem Σ*ψ*¹: *om. cett.*     factum Σ*b*²*ψ*¹: *om. cett.*     16 adulescente fortasse Σ, *Francken* : fortasse adulescente *P*π*δ*     17 inverecundo Σ : non verecundo *P*π*δ*     22 iudices, causa Σ     29 hac
nunc *Halm* : hac enim *P*π*δ* : hacine *Müller*

publicae poenas sed ad mulieris libidines et delicias de- 30
poscitur. Atque hoc etiam loco M. Camurti et *C.* Caeserni 71
damnatio praedicatur. O stultitiam! stultitiamne dicam an
impudentiam singularem? Audetisne, cum ab ea muliere
5 veniatis, facere istorum hominum mentionem? audetis excitare tanti flagiti memoriam, non exstinctam illam quidem
sed repressam vetustate? Quo enim illi crimine peccatoque
perierunt? Nempe quod eiusdem mulieris dolorem et iniuriam Vettiano nefario sunt stupro persecuti. Ergo ut audi-
10 retur Vetti nomen in causa, ut illa vetus aeraria fabula
referretur, idcirco Camurti et Caeserni est causa renovata?
qui quamquam lege de vi certe non tenebantur, eo maleficio
tamen erant implicati ut ex nullius legis laqueis eximendi
viderentur. M. vero Caelius cur in hoc iudicium vocatur? 72
15 cui neque proprium quaestionis crimen obicitur nec vero
aliquod eius modi quod sit a lege seiunctum, cum vestra
severitate coniunctum. Cuius prima aetas disciplinae dedita
fuit eisque artibus quibus instruimur ad hunc usum forensem,
ad capessendam rem publicam, ad honorem, gloriam, digni-
20 tatem. Eis autem fuit amicitiis maiorum natu quorum
imitari industriam continentiamque maxime vellet, eis studiis aequalium ut eundem quem optimi ac nobilissimi
petere cursum laudis videretur. Cum autem paulum iam ro- 73
boris accessisset aetati, in Africam profectus est Q. Pompeio
25 pro consule contubernalis, castissimo homini atque omnis

---

1 libidinosae Σ: libidines et (-es et *P²* *in ras.*) *Pπδ*     2 M. *om.*
Σ     Camurii *Garatoni*     C. *Orelli*: *om. Pπδ*     3 stultitiam
stultitiamne Σ, *Naugerius*: stultitiamne *Pπδ*     5 audetis Σ:
audetisne *Pπδ*     9 sunt stupro Σπδ: sunt stupro sunt *P*: stupro
sunt *Halm*     10 aeraria Σ, *Garatoni*: afraria *Pπδ*     11 referretur Σ: reficeretur *Pπδ*: refricaretur *ed. R*     12 eo maleficio tamen *AΣδ*: et maleficio *Pπ*     13 eximendi *A*: emittendi
*Pπ*     15 crimen quaestionis *AΣ*     16 cum *AΣ*: et cum *P²π*
(cum . . . coniunctum *om. P¹*)     17 disciplinae dedita (deb. Σ) *AΣ*:
dedita disciplinis (ad disc. *P¹*) *Pπδ*     18 instruimur *AΣδ*: institui-
mur *Pπ*     20 quorum . . . vellet, iis (his) *Σbψ²*: quorum . . . velit
is *cett.*: quorum eum . . . velitis *Madvig*     21 studiis aequalium
*AΣ*: aequalium studiis *Pπδ*     25 homini *AΣB*: viro *cett.*

offici diligentissimo ⁝ in qua provincia cum res erant et
possessiones paternae, tum etiam usus quidam provincialis
non sine causa a maioribus huic aetati tributus.  Decessit
illinc Pompei iudicio probatissimus, ut ipsius testimonio
cognoscetis.  Voluit vetere instituto et eorum adulescentium 5
exemplo qui post in civitate summi viri et clarissimi cives
exstiterunt industriam suam a populo Romano ex aliqua
**31** inlustri accusatione cognosci.  Vellem alio potius eum
**74** cupiditas gloriae detulisset ; sed abiit huius tempus que-
‧ relae.  Accusavit C. Antonium, conlegam meum, cui misero 10
praeclari in rem publicam benefici memoria nihil profuit,
nocuit opinio malefici cogitati.  Postea nemini umquam
concessit aequalium plus ut in foro, plus ut in negotiis
versaretur causisque amicorum, plus ut valeret inter suos
gratia.  Quae nisi vigilantes homines, nisi sobrii, nisi in- 15
dustrii consequi non possunt, omnia labore et diligentia est
**75** consecutus.  In hoc flexu quasi aetatis—nihil enim occul-
tabo fretus humanitate ac sapientia vestra—fama adulescentis paululum haesit ad metas notitia nova eius mulieris
et infelici vicinitate et insolentia voluptatum, quae, cum 20
inclusae diutius et prima aetate compressae et constrictae
fuerunt, subito se non numquam profundunt atque eiciunt
universae.  Qua ex vita vel dicam quo ex sermone—nequaquam enim tantum erat quantum homines loquebantur—
verum ex eo quicquid erat emersit totumque se eiecit atque 25
extulit, tantumque abest ab illius familiaritatis infamia ut
eiusdem nunc ab sese inimicitias odiumque propulset.
**76** Atque ut iste interpositus sermo deliciarum desidiaeque
moreretur—fecit me invito me hercule et multum repugnante

    1 **erat** *A*Σ     3 decessit *A*Σ : discessit *P*πδ     5 et Σ : *om.*
*cett.*    6 **viri et]** viri et clarissimi viri et Σ    9 sederet huius temporis
querellam Σ    10 C. *om.* Σ*B*    12 umquam *A* : *om. P*πδ    13 ut
. . . ut *om. A*    19 paululum Σ*B* : paulum *cett.*    nova eius *scripsi* :
novae Σ : nova *P*πδ    22 eiciuntur Σ    29 **me invito meherc.**
Σ : me (*om.* me *b*) meherc. invito *P*πδ

36

me, sed tamen fecit—nomen amici mei de ambitu detulit ;
quem absolutum insequitur, revocat; nemini nostrum
obtemperat, est violentior quam vellem. Sed ego non
loquor de sapientia, quae non cadit in hanc aetatem ; de
5 impetu animi loquor, de cupiditate vincendi, de ardore
mentis ad gloriam ; quae studia in his iam aetatibus nostris
contractiora esse debent, in adulescentia vero tamquam in
herbis significant quae virtutis maturitas et quantae fruges
industriae sint futurae. Etenim semper magno ingenio
10 adulescentes refrenandi potius a gloria quam incitandi fuerunt; amputanda plura sunt illi aetati, si quidem efflorescit
ingeni laudibus, quam inserenda. Qua re, si cui nimium 77
effervisse videtur huius vel in suscipiendis vel in gerendis
inimicitiis vis, ferocitas, pertinacia, si quem etiam mini-
15 morum horum aliquid offendit, si purpurae genus, si amicorum catervae, si splendor, si nitor, iam ista deferverint,
iam aetas omnia, iam res, iam dies mitigarit.

Conservate igitur rei publicae, iudices, civem bonarum 32
artium, bonarum partium, bonorum virorum. Promitto hoc
20 vobis et rei publicae spondeo, si modo nos ipsi rei publicae
satis fecimus, numquam hunc a nostris rationibus seiunctum
fore. Quod cum fretus nostra familiaritate promitto, tum
quod durissimis se ipse legibus iam obligavit. Non enim 78
potest qui hominem consularem, cum ab eo rem publicam
25 violatam esse diceret, in iudicium vocarit ipse esse in re publica civis turbulentus ; non potest qui ambitu ne absolutum
quidem patiatur esse absolutum ipse impune umquam esse

1 me Σ : *om. Pπδ* 8 significant Σ*B*δ : significat*Pπ* 10 ad
gloriam Σ*B* 11 efflorescit] etflorescit Σ*P*¹ : florescit *P*²πδ 14
vis *del. Madvig* pertinacia Σ*bψ*³ : *om. Pπψ*¹ 15 aliquod Σ
16 deferv.] deferuu. *P* : deseru. Σ (*cf.* § 43) 17 iam res iam Σδ :
iam ista *P*² *in ras.* : iam usus iam *Rau* (*cf. Mur.* 65) 19 virorum]
morum *Weiske* : studiosum *add. Müller* (*cf. Zielinski p.* 208) 23 se
durissimis Σ iam *om.* Σ 24 cum Σ : quod *Pπ*δ 25 esse Σ,
*Lambinus* : *om. Pπ*δ ipse ēē (e *P*¹) *Pπ* : ipse Σδ 26 civis
*Pπ* : civis si Σ : civis esse δ 27 patiatur Σ, *Wesenberg* : patitur
*bψ*³ : datur (dat *g*²*ψ*¹) *cett.* absolutum esse Σ

largitor. Habet a M. Caelio res publica, iudices, duas
accusationes vel obsides periculi vel pignora voluntatis.
Qua re oro obtestorque vos, iudices, ut qua in civitate paucis
his diebus Sex. Clodius absolutus est, quem vos per biennium
aut ministrum seditionis aut ducem vidistis, hominem sine 5
re, sine fide, sine spe, sine sede, sine fortunis, ore, lingua,
manu, vita omni inquinatum, qui aedis sacras, qui censum
populi Romani, qui memoriam publicam suis manibus
incendit, qui Catuli monumentum adflixit, meam domum
diruit, mei fratris incendit, qui in Palatio atque in urbis 10
oculis servitia ad caedem et ad inflammandam urbem inci-
tavit : in ea civitate ne patiamini illum absolutum muliebri
gratia, M. Caelium libidini muliebri condonatum, ne eadem
mulier cum suo coniuge et fratre et turpissimum latronem
eripuisse et honestissimum adulescentem oppressisse videa- 15
79 tur. ⌈Quod cum huius vobis adulescentiam proposueritis,
constituitote ante oculos etiam huius miseri senectutem qui
hoc unico filio nititur, in huius spe requiescit, huius unius
casum pertimescit ; quem vos supplicem vestrae misericor-
diae, servum potestatis, abiectum non tam ad pedes quam 20
ad mores sensusque vestros, vel recordatione parentum
vestrorum vel liberorum iucunditate sustentate, ut in alterius
dolore vel pietati vel indulgentiae vestrae serviatis. Nolite,
iudices, aut hunc iam natura ipsa occidentem velle maturius
exstingui volnere vestro quam suo fato, aut hunc nunc 25
primum florescentem firmata iam stirpe virtutis tamquam
80 turbine aliquo aut subita tempestate pervertere. Conservate
parenti filium, parentem filio, ne aut senectutem iam prope
desperatam contempsisse aut adulescentiam plenam spei

---

4 est Σ, *Baiter* : sit *Pπδ*       5–7 hominem ... inquinatum *post*
incendit *hab. Pπδ, huc transposuit Garatoni*     11 ad inflammandam
*Bake* : ad flammandam Σ*B* : inflammandam *Pπ*     12 ea Σ*Bδ* : hac
*Pπ*     12–13 muliebri ... muliebri] mulieris ... mulieris Σ     14
et turp. *Bake* : si turp. Σ : turp. *Pπδ*     19 vos *om.* Σ     24 ipsa
natura Σ     25 quam Σδ : quamquam *Pπ*

maximae non modo non aluisse vos verum etiam perculisse
atque adflixisse videamini.   Quem si nobis, si suis, si rei
publicae conservatis, addictum, deditum, obstrictum vobis
ac liberis vestris habebitis omniumque huius nervorum ac
5 laborum vos potissimum, iudices, fructus uberes diutur-
nosque capietis.

1 aluisse vos (al . . . . . . . . . $P^1$) $P^2\pi\delta$ : adlevasse *Müller*      verum
$\Sigma B$ : sed *cett.* (*in lac.* $P^2$)        perfluxisse atque perpulsisse $\Sigma B$        4
vestris] servis $B$ : *fort.* servum vestris (*cf. Mart. Cap., Rhet. M. p.* 471
Caeli in omni vita servitium obstrictum vobis ac liberis vestris
habebitis)

# NOTE

Asterisks in the Commentary indicate further discussion in the Additional Notes (pp. 162 ff.). The position of an entirely new note is marked by a horizontal arrow in the margin of the page.

# COMMENTARY

**§§ 1-2. EXORDIUM.** '*You are in court on a day of public festival, to try Caelius under the* Lex de vi. *But he has committed no crime competent to this court. His accuser is nominally Atratinus; but the real attack comes from behind the scenes, the work of a woman—and a bad woman.*'

The exordium to the *pro Caelio* won the admiration of Quintilian, who often illustrates his principles from it (iv. 1. 31, 39; ix. 2. 39). Cicero makes his standpoint plain from the beginning: the formal charges are to be brushed aside, the real enemy is to be Clodia—this is what the jury are to expect throughout the speech, and it is on this that they will be asked to give their verdict. He takes his argument *ex ipsis visceribus causae*, the method that he himself recommended (*de or.* ii. 318) as proper for the exordium of a speech, by which points should be made *paene ex intima defensione deprompta* (ibid. 319), such for instance as will show his client to be *bonum virum . . . liberalem . . . calamitosum . . . misericordia dignum*, points that can tell against a *falsa criminatio* (ibid. 321); the exordium, he says, should be so closely connected with the speech to follow 'ut non tamquam citharoedi prooemium adfictum aliquid sed cohaerens cum omni corpore membrum esse videatur' (ibid. 325). It is essential to remember these Ciceronian rules here, for they throw light on his whole conduct of the case. Cf. Laur., pp. 319 ff.

§ **1. 2. profecto:** 'in my opinion'. The word expresses a personal conviction; cf. 53. 24, 67. 17, *de nat. deor.* ii. 78 'atqui necesse est, cum sint di, si modo sunt, ut profecto sunt, animantes esse', *de sen.* 84 'animus vero . . . in ea profecto loca discessit quo mihi ipsi cernebat esse veniendum'; see Landgraf on *Rosc. Am.* 30, S.–M. on *de am.* 2, Clark on *Mil.* 2.

3. **tanta . . . quod:** *quod* = *propter quod* ('in that'); Cicero is stressing the reason for the apparent *atrocitas* of the case, not its result, and so does not use *ut*; see Nisbet on *de domo* 59, and cf. *de nat. deor.* ii. 131 'illa quanta benignitas naturae, quod tam multa . . . gignit'; K. II. ii, p. 271.

**atrocitas:** this term, like *atrox vis, atrox iniuria*, was used technically of cases involving aggravated assault and personal violence, for which a heavy penalty was laid down; see *Thes. L. L.* s.v., col. 1106. 63, for examples, and cf. Jordan's introduction to *Pro Caec.*, pp. 21 ff., and his note at § 36.

**diebus festis:** a good point, showing Cicero's sympathy with the jury and arousing their resentment against the prosecution. The games were the *Ludi Megalenses*, instituted in 204 B.C. in honour of the Magna Mater, held originally on 4 April and later extended to 10 April (Livy xxix. 14, xxxiv. 54, xxxvi. 36, Warde Fowler, *Roman Festivals*, pp. 69 f., Marquardt, *Staatsverwaltung* iii, p. 480); these games, which were *scenici*, always kept their 'foreign' character (cf. *har. resp.* 24 'qui uni ludi ne verbo quidem appellantur Latino'). Cicero is speaking on 4 April (see Appendix IV).

**4. forensibus negotiis**: 'legal business'. In Silver Latin, *negotium* alone is often used to mean a court case, sometimes virtually 'trial'; see Bonnell's Lexicon to Quintilian s.v., and note especially the definition in iii. 5. 17 (in ix. 2. 68 *vera negotia* are contrasted with the imaginary cases in the schools of rhetoric; in v. 12. 13 'si negotium innocenti facit' = 'if he puts an innocent man on trial').

**6. stare non possit**: a favourite expression in such a context (*stare*, as so often, means 'stand firm', like *consistere*, ὀρθοῦσθαι); cf. *Verr.* i. 20 'ut ... populus Romanus iudicaret isto absoluto rem publicam stare non posse', *Sest.* 42 'senatum, sine quo civitas stare non posset', Quintil. iii. 8. 47 'C. Caesari suadentes regnum adfirmabimus, stare iam rem publicam nisi uno regente non posse'.

**7. legem quae ... iubeat**: Cicero's imaginary stranger would expect to find a violent and subversive political revolutionary in the dock, whereas in fact he would discover the accused to be a singularly brilliant young man who has been victimized by a society hostess.

This law is mentioned again in § 70, in similar terms, from which passage it can be dated to the disturbances of 78–77, and it is made plain there that Caelius was being tried under a revival of the law which was used to crush the Catilinarians. Sallust (*Cat.* 31) and others state that the law then invoked was the Lex Plotia *de vi*, and the other cases of *vis* known at this period were also tried under the Lex Plotia; yet Cicero's language in § 70 implies that the proceedings against Caelius were being brought under a Lex Lutatia, to which there are no other references.

J. N. Hough (see bibliography) has examined the evidence and concludes that the Lex Lutatia became void when the particular situation calling for it had passed; that in § 70 Cicero is giving the history of the law *de vi* 'regarded as a continuous heritage from the original one enacted by Catulus'; and that Caelius was in fact charged under the Lex Plotia, which was a re-enactment of Catulus' law and was passed about 65–64 B.C.

More recently the problem has been examined by J. Cousin (see bibliography); he concludes that the two were different laws cover-

COMMENTARY                    §1

ing different contingencies; that the Lex Plotia was limited to cases
of *vis contra privatos* (cf. Ascon. *in Mil.*, p. 49 KS, where it is stated
that M. Saufeius, *dux operarum Milonis*, was charged under it, the
count being 'quod loca edita occupasset et cum telo fuisset'); that
the Lex Lutatia concerned *vis contra rem publicam*, with particular
reference to *seditio*, *coniuratio*, and *iniuria legatorum*. Cousin's
paper has a wealth of bibliographical material; see also Greenidge,
*LP*, p. 424, note 6, and my own bibliography.

   9. **quaeri:** the t.t. for a judicial inquiry (cf. *quaestio, quaesitor*).
The law evidently forbade adjournment even on a feast-day
(*cotidie*).

      **legem . . . requirat:** 'while he would applaud the law, he
would look round to find a charge competent to the court'; note the
adversative asyndeton, where English would subordinate the first
clause of the pair (sometimes *quidem . . . sed* are used, both methods
corresponding to the Greek μὲν . . . δέ).*

   10. **versetur:** the subjunctive is probably consecutive; but it
might be 'reported definition', the *crimen* being only 'alleged'.
   *Crimen* is a difficult word. The meaning in Cicero is not 'crime',
but 'charge' or 'ground for charge' (for the latter sense cf. 14. 13
'ut istius amicitiae crimen reformidet', 32. 11 'sin ista muliere
remota nec crimen ullum nec opes . . . relinquuntur'). It is sometimes joined with *scelus*, as in 61. 17, where *scelus* in its context
plainly means 'alleged crime' (cf. *Mil.* 9). Certain passages have
been adduced (*Cael.* 71. 7, *Verr.* ii. 49 'quod non suis sed suorum
peccatis et criminibus prematur', *de or.* ii. 199 'in nefario crimine
atque in fraude capitali esse ponendum') to prove that it can mean
'crime' in Cicero (see *Thes. L. L.* s.v., col. 1192. 53), but 'foundation
for a charge' is possible in all three passages. The clear meaning
'crime' appears first in Livy. See Landgraf on *Rosc. Am.* 83, Reid
on *Balb.* 6, and Krebs s.v.

   11. **audaciam:** 'intemperate action'; the word derives its colour
from its context, and the uncomplimentary sense is common in
oratory. Cicero defines it (*de inv.* ii. 165) as the *vitium* which corresponds to the *virtus* of *fidentia*, and Quintilian (v. 10. 34) includes
it among such 'pessimi adfectus' as *ira, odium, metus*; it is frequently
coupled with *libido* (see below), *malitia, petulantia, amentia*.

   12. **inlustri . . . gratia:** 'of distinguished intellectual gifts, remarkable application, influential position'; cf. *Verr.* iii. 60 'summa
virtute hominem, summa industria, summa gratia'. Cicero is
anxious from the outset to show that Caelius is not worthless or
frivolous (cf. § 45); his *gratia* is the result of his *ingenium*, which he
has developed by his *industria*.

   13. **eius filio:** Atratinus; his father was L. Calpurnius Bestia

(see Appendix VI, p. 154) and Caelius was at this time preparing to prosecute him again (*et vocet et vocarit*, where *vocarit* refers to the previous trial of Bestia on 11 February of this same year).

14. **oppugnari autem:** cf. § 20 'non enim ab isdem accusatur M. Caelius a quibus oppugnatur'.

**meretriciis:** the word is deliberately used here; it is then avoided until § 38, and from § 48 onwards Cicero takes it for granted that Clodia is nothing but a *meretrix*.

**Atratini ipsius:** so Cl., for MSS. *Atratini illius*; Muretus expunged the name as a gloss, and W. and Kl. accept this; Fra. proposed *filii* (omitting *Atratini*). I cannot feel that the name is in place here, and Cl.'s emendation is made simply to bolster it up; Fra.'s conjecture seems to me now unnecessary and improbable; I should prefer to adopt Kl.'s text—*illius* is quite enough in itself to take up *ab eius filio*.

15. **pietatem:** 'sense of duty'.

**reprehendat:** the verb is one of Cicero's normal expressions for 'blame'; students seldom realize that *culpare* is a comparatively uncommon word: Cicero does not use it; it occurs in Plautus, in the Augustan poets, and in Silver Latin, but not with any degree of frequency.

**libidinem:** 'selfish passions'; the word takes its tone from its context, sometimes meaning little more than 'caprice', more often sensual passion in varying degrees. See a very interesting note in S.–M., *de am.* 19, where the meaning of *cupiditas, libido, audacia* is examined; the common aspect of all three is their egoistic quality.

→ 16. **laboriosos:** 'much-enduring'; cf. *Mil.* 5 'quid enim nobis ... laboriosius, quid magis sollicitum?', *de nat. deor.* i. 52 'hunc deum rite beatum dixerimus, vestrum vero laboriosissimum', St. Jerome, *Epp.* 125 'nihil Christiano felicius, cui promittuntur regna caelorum, nihil laboriosius, qui cotidie de vita periclitatur'; in all these passages there is a contrast between desert and reality.

**§ 2. 19. sic:** anticipatory of the accusative and infinitive clause that follows (so *hoc, illud*), a 'signpost' for hearer or reader; *sic constituetis* = 'this will be your conclusion'.

**nec ... liceret:** 'that no one would have lent himself to this prosecution if he had been permitted any choice'; *descendere* is used literally, either alone or with *in forum*, etc., as a t.t. for 'coming down' to the forum to conduct public business or to speak in the courts; it is then transferred to this use with *accusatio, causa*, etc., sometimes (as perhaps here) with an accessory idea of 'demeaning'; see *Thes. L. L.* s.v., cols. 644. 68 ff. and 649. 36 ff. For the phrase *cui utrum vellet liceret*, cf. *Verr.* iv. 16, *Vat.* 34.

**22. alicuius:** purposely vague; *cuiusdam* would have implied a particular person.

**1. adulescenti:** for this word, see B. Axelson in *Mélanges Marouzeau* (Paris, 1948), pp. 7–17; he holds that there is no ground for the traditional view that *iuvenis* denotes an older man than *adulescens*, but that the difference between them is purely stylistic; *adulescens* is the normal word for 'young man' in republican Latin, whereas *iuvenis* (which occurs twice only in Cicero's speeches, one passage being *Cael.* 67) predominates in the Augustan period. Note that in this speech Cicero uses *adulescentia* and *iuventus* indifferently, e.g. § 30.

**2. meo necessario:** cf. § 26 'meo necessario Bestiae', of Atratinus' father. Cicero is intentionally kind to his young opponent, by contrast with Herennius' severity towards Caelius (§ 25): cf. Quintil. xi. 1. 68 'aliquando etiam inferioribus praecipueque adulescentulis parcere aut videri decet. utitur hac moderatione Cicero pro Caelio contra Atratinum, ut eum non inimice corripere, sed paene patrie monere videatur; nam et nobilis et iuvenis et non iniusto dolore venerat ad accusandum.' *Pueritiae* in the next sentence suggests a smile, rather than a sneer as Manutius thought.

## §§ 3–50. PRAEMUNITIO

Normally the *exordium* would be followed by the *narratio* or 'statement of facts' (see Quintil. iv. 2); in this speech there is instead a long section devoted to clearing away a number of insinuations made by the prosecution; the actual *narratio* seems about to begin in § 30, but it is quickly side-tracked, and Cicero does not return to it until § 51, where it takes a very sketchy form and is at once merged in the *argumentatio*. One reason for this treatment is no doubt the fact that Crassus had dealt with three of the five formal counts (§ 23); another is that there was every possible danger to Caelius if Cicero had offered a formal *narratio* of the matters left to him, so he 'builds up' (*praemunire*) his position in the present manner, which would hardly surprise the jury in view of his attitude in the *exordium*.

§§ 3–5. '*I shall start by rebutting various insinuations introduced by the prosecution. Caelius' father has been mentioned slightingly, and Caelius is said to have treated him with disrespect; but he is a model Roman Knight, and his son's behaviour to him is irreproachable; this is plain to all who know the facts. Again, Caelius is said to be out of favour with his fellow townsmen—but they have sent a deputation to this court to show how much they honour him.*'

→ **3. 7. hic introitus:** 'this method of approach' (anticipatory of the *ut* clause).

**9. accusatores:** strictly speaking, there was only one *accusator* (here, Atratinus), the rest being *subscriptores* (never more than three, and here two only, L. Herennius Balbus and P. Clodius). At this period it was unusual to have no *subscriptor* (cf. *ad Fam.* viii. 8. 1), and also the custom by which the accused had one *patronus* only was now nearly obsolete (cf. *Clu.* 199). *Accusator* and *subscriptores* alike could be prosecuted for *calumnia* if they had knowingly preferred a false charge. See *Rosc. Am.* 56 ff. for an interesting picture of the general Roman attitude to prosecuting.

**deformandi . . . gratia:** 'to blacken my client and to belittle and besmirch his position'. *Gratia* here is scarcely more than a variation on *causa* (cf. *Rosc. Am.* 45 'non enim exprobrandi causa sed commonendi gratia dicam'); it means 'in the interest of', and its occasional use to denote efficient cause (instead of *propter*) is quite abnormal (cf. Sall. *Cat.* 23. 1 'quem censores senatu probri gratia moverant')—the distinction is clearly shown in Quintil. ix. 4. 144 'ne, quae eius rei gratia fecerimus, propter eam fecisse videamur'. See my note on Quintil. xii. 1. 38; *causa* is the older usage (see Wölfflin, *Archiv für lat. Lex.* i, pp. 169 ff., an interesting examination).*

**11. obiectus . . . varie:** 'his father has been brought into the case against him, in differing ways'; cf. Quintil. v. 13. 26 'obiecta est paulo liberalior vita', *Mur.* 11 'obiecta est enim Asia'.

**splendidus:** cf. *Rosc. Am.* 140 'equestrem splendorem', and Landgraf's note; the adjective is used to designate a knight (so too *insignis, illustris*), just as *amplissimus* and *amplitudo* are used to mark a senator. Under the Empire, with the reorganization of the *equites*, these non-official epithets were used to distinguish particular classes among the Order (Greenidge, *Roman Public Life*, p. 405). The prosecution cannot really have made such a point against Caelius as is implied here; Cicero has distorted some remark for his own purposes, to rouse the annoyance of the equestrian members of the jury; we know from § 36 that the elder Caelius was *parcus ac tenax*, but of course neither this nor the fact that he was an *eques* could have been held against his son. The real charge was, no doubt, that Caelius had lived above his means and station (cf. Vell. Pat. ii. 68 'quippe peior illi res familiaris quam mens erat', and see Cicero's apology for his client's loud behaviour in § 77); H. suggests (p. 206) that in accusing Antonius and Bestia he had usurped the privileges of *pueri nobiles* such as Laterensis, Torquatus, or Ser. Sulpicius (he points out that the passage in *Planc.* 31, 'pater vero etiam obesse filio debet', is not a true parallel, as there Cicero is defending his order against the *invidia* that tne elder Plancius had caused).

12. **parum pie tractatus:** Cicero returns to this in § 18.

**diceretur:** the verb of saying is itself put in the subjunctive ('alleged statement'), although the allegation is contained in *tractatus*; the idiom is a conflation of 'quod parum pie tractatus esset' and 'quod parum pie tractatus esse dicebatur'; it is common in Cicero and in Caesar, but rare in later writers. Sometimes it appears to be necessitated by the clausula (e.g. *Verr.* v. 149); the present subjunctive is less usual (so *de dom.* 93, *Lig.* 25, *de am.* 27). See L.-H., p. 701, K. II. ii, p. 200, S.-M. on *de am.* l.c., Mayor on *Phil.* ii. 7, Nisbet on *de dom.* 22; there is an interesting example in *bell. Alex.* 25 'cui subsidium nemo tulit, sive quod in ipso satis praesidii putarent esse, sive quod ipsi sibi timebant'.

13. **M. Caelius:** the elder; he owned property in Africa (§ 73), and had presumably not lived originally in Rome (§ 5), but nothing else is known of him.

**notis:** 'men who know him' (contrast *quibus ... non aeque est cognitus* below); but it is only quasi-active, for the sense 'men known by him' is still present and possible, though not so natural; cf. *Verr.* i. 19 'putabam non solum notis sed etiam ignotis probatam meam fidem esse', Phaedrus i. 11. 2 'ignotos fallit, notis est derisui'. See Krebs s.v., and cf. N., pp. 318 ff.

**etiam ... tacitus:** so Cl., following the *editio princeps* (Rome, 1471); I cannot understand why Kl. objects that with this reading *tacitus* is meaningless—Cicero says 'even without me to speak for him, he is his own silent witness'. Kl. reads, with *P*, *et sine mea oratione et tacitus* ('with silence both on my part and on his'), which is surely not so good.

14. **quibus autem:** a good example of the only way in which *autem* (like *enim, vero, igitur*) may be attached to a relative pronoun, i.e. when the pronoun is a true relative and is followed (as here) by a clause containing the subject to which it refers: when the pronoun acts as a mere connective (as in such phrases as *quibus rebus gestis, quae cum ita sint*), these particles cannot be attached, since the pronoun itself contains the idea of connexion (*quibus rebus = iis igitur rebus, iis enim rebus*, etc.).

16. **habeant ... habitam ... haberi:** the Romans did not mind such repetitions (cf. 53. 3); see my note on Quintil. xii. 1. 41 (cf. id. x. 1. 7); S.-M. (on *de am.* 40) give a valuable list of passages where, as here, a word is repeated in close context but bears an altered meaning. ✶

18. **summam hodieque:** so Cl., with *Σ*; Kl. reads, with *P²*, *summamque hodie*, but the adjective is essential in the first clause

47

if it is to have proper weight; yet there is a certain lameness of rhythm in the reading of *Σ*, and possibly one should read *habitam esse summam summamque hodie haberi*.

**§ 4. 20. equitis . . . poni**: see note on 3. 11; for a somewhat similar distortion cf. *Lig.* 9 'sed hoc quaero, quis putat esse crimen, fuisse in Africa ?'

**22. his: deíctic.** Quintil. thus comments (xi. 1. 28): 'quod fuisset tumidius, si accipiendum criminis loco negasset Cicero equitis Romani esse filium, se defendente, at ille fecit hoc etiam favorabile coniungendo cum iudicibus dignitatem suam'; cf. id. v. '13. 21 'quod est aut omnibus periculosum . . . aut ipsis iudicibus, ut pro Oppio monet pluribus, ne illud actionis genus in equestrem ordinem admittant'.

**nobis:** Cicero himself was the son of an *eques*.

**23. nam quod:** a formula of transition, which recurs in §§ 5, 6, 10, 17; in all these passages *nam* has no thought-connexion with the sentence immediately preceding, but is used to introduce a series of points that act as particular illustrations of the main theme expressed in the opening sentence of § 3; *nam*, in fact, acts here simply as a continuative particle (cf. Reid on *de fin.* i. 19), and needs no translation in English (*nam . . . dixistis* = 'to turn to your point about his feeling for his father'); cf. *de div.* ii. 68, *de nat. deor.* iii. 38, 41. Its recurrent use here suggests the closeness of the extant speech to that actually delivered. Cf. G. H. Poyser, *CR*, NS, ii, 1952, pp. 8 ff.

**est . . . parentis:** 'while on that subject we may form an opinion, the decision surely belongs to a parent'; *pietas*, being a matter of personal relationship (cf. *Planc.* 80 'quid est pietas, nisi voluntas grata in parentes ?'), can merely be surmised by an outsider, but his father's view is what matters, and this is evident to all.

*Ista* takes the place of an objective genitive, by a common Latin idiom; cf. *de am.* 3 'Scaevola cum in eam ipsam mentionem incidisset', Livy iii. 34. 7 'ea exspectatio . . . desiderium decemviros iterum creandi fecit' (see K. II. i, p. 65). Schöll expunged *ista*, quite unnecessarily (so too W.). *P* reads *est quidem ista* (so Müll.), but the force of *quidem* clearly belongs to *ista*, and Kl. supports Cl. in accepting the text of *Σ*. *Nostra existimatio* is taken up by *quid nos opinemur* below, and Halm's conjecture *vestra* for *nostra* is invalid.*

**24. opinemur:** see Laur., pp. 97 f., for a discussion of Cicero's use of the forms of this verb.

**25. audietis:** the interrogation of witnesses was done after the pleading (cf. §§ 19, 20, 66); where evidence of witnesses is treated as already given, as in the *pro Flacco*, they would have been heard after a first *actio* before an adjournment (see Webster, *pro Flacco*, Appendix A; Greenidge, *LP*, pp. 477 f.).

iuratis: in a criminal case the defence was confined to voluntary evidence, while the prosecution alone had the right to sub-poena (cf. Quintil. v. 7. 9).

lacrimae ... luctusque: 'his mother's sobs and unimaginable affliction, his father's dismal state, the melancholy and misery that you see before you in this court'. *Squalor* and *sordes* are regularly used of the mourning garb customary on such occasions, as part of the emotional appeal to the jury; cf. Quintil. vi. 1. 30 'non solum autem dicendo, sed etiam faciendo quaedam lacrimas movemus, unde et producere ipsos qui periclitentur squalidos atque deformes et liberos eorum ac parentes institutum', ibid. 33 'at sordes et squalorem et propinquorum quoque similem habitum scio profuisse, et magnum ad salutem momentum preces attulisse'. Many devices were used in the courts to harrow the emotions, and a weeping child was always good value (cf. the story of Ser. Galba in *de or*. i. 228); but sometimes unexpected contretemps would occur, as when an advocate asked a child the reason of his tears, and the boy replied that he had just been pinched (Quintil. vi. 1. 41). 'Serjeant Buzfuz rubbed his eyes very hard with a large white handkerchief, and gave an appealing look towards the jury, while the judge was visibly affected, and several of the beholders tried to cough down their emotions.'*

27. luctus: defined in *Tusc*. iv. 18 as *aegritudo ex eius qui carus fuerit interitu acerbo*, whereas *maeror* is *aegritudo flebilis* (an interesting passage, giving various Stoic definitions of the emotions).

§ 5. 27. nam quod: 'as to your objection . . .' (see note above). Probably no definite allegations had been made, only some insinuations on the same grounds as in § 3; the presence of *laudatores* (see below) could easily have been anticipated.

28. non probatum suis: cf. *Rosc. Am*. 152 'probatum suis filium', where Landgraf compares the expression *probis probatus* found in sepulchral inscriptions (e.g. *CIL* ii. 3476 'vixit probus probis probatus').

1. Praetuttiani: see Appendix II. If Baiter's *Tusculani* had been the true reading it would be amusing to compare Cicero's attitude in *Planc*. 19–20 'alteros [*sc*. Tusculanos] . . . nunquam intellexi vehementius suorum honore laetari . . . . num quando vides Tusculanum aliquem de M. Catone . . . num de Ti. Coruncanio municipe suo . . . gloriari ?'

3. in amplissimum ordinem: Caelius had been elected as a *decurio*, or member of the local senate. *Cooptarunt* is used loosely, as the enrolment was done by the *quinquennales* (Marquardt,

49

*Staatsverwaltung* i. p. 502, note 7). Wegehaupt inferred that Caelius must have been over 30 at the time of the trial, since according to the Lex Iulia Municipalis (45 B.C.) this was the minimum age prescribed for such membership; but the law itself made certain exceptions, and it looks as if in fact Caesar was making an innovation, since a date is given on which the ordinance was to begin, so that the argument is not valid.

**ea non petenti ... denegarunt:** cf. *ad Fam.* xiii. 55. 1 'quod ultro ei detulerim legationem cum multis petentibus denegassem'. W. infers from this passage that Caelius was *patronus* of his native town; but in that case Cicero would have made much of the point, and he is more probably still speaking of the honour of being made a *decurio*.

5. **lectissimos viros:** the members of such a deputation (*legatio*) would either bring accredited *mandata*, or would give personal evidence on oath; the usual number seems to have been at least ten, and it was better to have no *laudatores* at all than to appear unable to produce the customary minimum (*Verr.* v. 57). Pompey in 52 prohibited *laudationes*, but the enactment soon lapsed. See Greenidge, *LP*, pp. 489 f.

7. **ornatissima:** 'highly eloquent', of the style of the *laudatio* (cf. 8. 17 'ornate politeque dixisti'); cf. Nisbet on *de domo* 69. 7.

**videor ... iecisse:** 'I fancy that I have laid'; *videor mihi* is the normal Latin idiom for 'I think (I have done something)'. Cicero now ends the *locus de dignitate*; he feels that by removing misapprehensions of this kind he has put his case on a firm basis, and turns shortly to something much more serious.

8. **si ... suorum:** Schöll and W. delete the clause, leaving an intolerably lame sentence; that it is genuine is shown by *commendatione ac iudicio meorum* below. *Sui* often means 'one's own people' (family, friends, *municipes*, etc.), with no definite grammatical antecedent; cf. *Clu.* 11 'Melino ... inter suos et honesto et nobili' (where see Peterson), *Rhet. ad Herenn.* iv. 2 'cum possimus ab Ennio sumere ... exemplum, videtur esse arrogantia, illa relinquere, ad sua devenire'; see Lebr., p. 137, Schönb., p. 22. The reflexive pronoun is used similarly; cf. *de fin.* i. 67 'amicitiae ... effectrices sunt voluptatum tam amicis quam sibi', ii. 78, and Reid's notes ad loc.

10. **aetas:** = *adulescentia*; *huius aetas*, 'this young man'.

**§ 6. 12. ut ... revertar:** 'to come to my own case'; *reverti* means to pass to a fresh point connected with the main theme; here the way has been paved by the generality of *quae ... suorum*. This use of *reverti*, with no sense of 'return', is quite well defined; see Müll.'s examples ad loc., p. xxxii, and Schönb.'s interesting discussion (pp. 22 f.); *redeo* is used similarly in 37. 7. Schöll, not realizing this, unnecessarily removed the clause.

**ab his fontibus . . . meorum:** 'it is from a source of this kind that I have gone steadily forward to my reputation in the world; my work here at the bar and my professional career have found a rather wider course to public recognition, owing to the approval and the favour of my friends.'

The metaphor is a normal Latin one, though difficult to turn in English; cf. Q. Cic. *pet. cons.* 17 'fere omnis sermo ad forensem famam a domesticis emanat auctoribus', *Orat.* 96 'hoc totum e sophistarum fontibus defluxit in forum', *Epp. ad Brut.* i. 15. 6 'Caesarem hunc adulescentem, per quem adhuc sumus si verum fateri volumus, fluxisse ex fonte consiliorum meorum'. Kl. reads *dimanavit* (so *P*); this verb is not found elsewhere in classical Latin, but suits the picture better. The deletion of *ad hominum famam* (Kl.) is not necessary.

**§§ 6–9.** '*The criticisms made against Caelius' morals in his early days are mere baseless abuse, and I felt sorry that Atratinus should have been given the task of making them; why, his father put him in my own charge, and I need say no more than that.*'

Cicero now turns to a new point brought *deformandi Caeli causa*, first dealing with it in general terms and afterwards (§§ 10–14) with reference to Caelius' alleged connexion with Catiline. If Caelius' later life was to be successfully defended, it was essential that his early years should be shown to have been irreproachable.

**§ 6. 16. nam quod . . . pudicitia:** 'as regards the criticisms passed on his morals'.

**19. paeniteat:** the verb need not imply personal responsibility for what is regretted; cf. *de off.* i. 2 'tam diu autem velle debebis, quoad te quantum proficias non paenitebit' (where see Holden), *de sen.* 19 'num . . . senectutis eum suae paeniteret?', *ad Att.* i. 20. 3 'a senatu quanti fiam, minime me paenitet', Apul. *Apol.* 92 'iuvenem neque corpore neque animo neque fortuna paenitendum'. Yet this passage is quoted by Gellius (xvii. 1) to illustrate criticisms brought against Cicero's latinity by the authors of a 'Ciceromastix', *liber infando titulo*: Caelius, they said, could not 'repent' of what was not within his control. Gellius stoutly defends Cicero's language as *festivissimum adeo et facetissimum*, but it is doubtful if he himself realized that it is a normal usage.*

**non deformem:** 'not without good looks' (see § 36); cf. *Tusc.* iv. 70 'cur neque deformem adulescentem quisquam amat neque formosum senem?'

**sunt . . . liberalis:** 'scurrilous talk of that kind is commonly

directed against any young man of handsome figure and appearance'. *Liberalis* (lit. 'befitting a free man') is often used of well-
bred appearance: cf. Plaut. *Pers.* 521 'forma expetenda liberalem
virginem' ('an attractive, handsome girl'), Apul. *Apol.* 4 'licere
etiam philosophis esse voltu liberali' ('it is not wrong for a philosopher to look handsome'). For the argument cf. Quintil. v. 10. 26
'ducitur enim frequenter in argumentum species libidinis, robur
petulantiae'.

21. **sed . . . accusare:** 'defamation and accusation are entirely
different'. Note the idiom *aliud . . . aliud* to express differentiation
(cf. 67. 19), and cf. § 30 'omnia sunt alia non crimina sed maledicta',
Livy xlii. 41. 3 'ut accusare potius vere quam conviciari videantur',
Apul. *Apol.* 1 'Sicinium Aemilianum . . . accusationem . . . penuria
criminum solis conviciis impleturum'. See Quintil. xii. 9. 8 ff. for
an interesting and sensible attitude towards the employment of
abuse by advocates; Cicero's audience when he delivered the speech
*in Pisonem* a year later might justifiably have reminded him of his
present remarks. But lurid personalities were a feature of Roman
public life, and were often neither intended seriously nor taken so:
no one would go to Catullus for a valid picture of Caesar (cf. Warde
Fowler, *Social Life at Rome in the Age of Cicero*, p. 107, Munro,
*Criticisms and Elucidations of Catullus*, pp. 75 f.). For a parallel
contrast between κατηγορία and λοιδορία, see Demosth. *de cor.* 123.

22. **crimen:** 'a basis for a charge' (cf. 1. 10, note).

23. **hominem notet:** so Cl., with Σ; *hominem ut notet*, Kl., *P*,
which perhaps gives a better balance (see Kl. ad loc.). The object
of *probet* and *confirmet* is the 'case' which has been established
by marking the facts and stigmatizing the person responsible;
Manutius' emendation of *hominem* to *nomine* is unnecessary
(Fra., p. 205, supports it, but would remove *ut*, which Manutius
retains).

**maledictio . . . nominatur:** 'on the other hand, the sole
object of defamation is insult: if it is aimed with coarseness, it is
termed noisy rating, but if there is some wit behind it, it passes for
elegance'. Cf. Quintil. viii. 6. 74 'pervenit haec res [*sc.* hyperbole]
frequentissime ad risum; qui si captatus est, urbanitatis, sin aliter,
stultitiae nomen adsequitur.'

25. **petulantius:** see note on 50. 25, and my note on Quintil. xii.
9. 9.

**convicium:** the word always implies something noisy, and is
often coupled with *clamor* and similar terms (see *Thes. L. L.* s.v.,
and cf. Landgraf on *Rosc. Am.* 134); note Ulp. *Dig.* 47. 10. 15. 11
'non omne maledictum convicium esse, sed id solum quod cum
vociferatione dictum est'.

urbanitas: see some useful remarks on the various terms for 'wit' by Sandys, on *Orat.* 87, and the whole context there, especially § 90.*

An adequate translation of *urbanitas* is impossible. It is not only an abstract idea, but an attitude of mind; it represents all that seemed to a Roman gentleman to constitute 'good form' in manners, *ton*, the opposite of the boorish clumsiness of those *rustici* who had not the advantage of living in the *urbs*; it was something instinctively and naturally Roman (cf. *ad Att.* vii. 2. 3 'est, quam facile diligas, αὐτόχθων in homine urbanitas'). P. de Labriolle, *Les Satires de Juvénal*, p. 351, compares it to the conception of *politesse* in France during the seventeenth and eighteenth centuries, 'le produit exquis, la fleur de leur civilisation'. The essence of such 'good form' was sparkle, subtlety, wit, elegance: the unforgivable sin was to be clumsy, stupid, dull.

The best picture of what was meant by the *homo urbanus* as a type may be seen in the poems of Catullus. The poetaster Suffenus (22), *bellus ille et urbanus*, becomes *infaceto infacetior rure* the moment he starts to scribble—he is no longer then *venustus* or *dicax*, the significant terms that imply *urbanitas*. The napkin-stealer (12) plays a trick that is *res invenusta*; the minx who wittily catches Catullus out (10) is *non sane illepidum neque invenustum*; the death of Lesbia's sparrow affects all men who are *venustiores*; above all, Quintia, whom so many think *formosa* (86), has no real claims to beauty, 'nam nulla venustas, nulla in tam magno est corpore mica salis'—there is the indefinable ingredient of *urbanitas*—what lacks wit and sparkle is clumsy and rustic.

*Urbanitas* of style is similarly indefinable; in the *Brutus*, when certain non-Roman orators are being discussed (170), the essential difference between them and Roman speakers proper is said to be that their style is not *urbanitate quadam quasi colorata*, and when Brutus asks the meaning of *urbanitatis color*, the reply is given 'Nescio, inquam, tantum esse quendam scio'. Quintilian gives a definition of it (vi. 3. 17): 'urbanitas dicitur, qua quidem significari video sermonem praeferentem in verbis et sono et usu proprium quendam gustum urbis et sumptam ex conversatione doctorum tacitam eruditionem, denique cui contraria sit rusticitas'; his own definition is (vi. 3. 107) 'illa est urbanitas, in qua nihil absonum, nihil agreste, nihil inconditum, nihil peregrinum neque sensu neque verbis neque ore gestuve possit deprehendi; ut non tam sit in singulis dictis quam in toto colore dicendi, qualis apud Graecos ἀττικισμός ille reddens Athenarum proprium saporem'.

It is clear from this passage that abuse backed by wit was 'gentlemanly', otherwise it was vulgar and in bad taste; Cicero implies that Atratinus' remarks were far too uncouth for such an *optimus adulescens*. This definition of *maledictio* is an illuminating 'social document'.

**§ 7. 28. aetas illa:** Atratinus was only 17.

1. **pudor:** 'sense of fitness', feeling for τὸ πρέπον; practically = 'conscience', 'scruples'.

3. **robustioribus:** 'older', 'more mature', through the acquisition of *robur*; cf. Quintil. i. 8. 12 'priora illa ad pueros magis, haec sequentia ad robustiores pertinebunt.'

**male dicendi:** the words should not be deleted as Schöll thought (so too W.); their repetition in the same sentence is deliberate; Löfstedt (*Synt.* ii, p. 175, note) remarks that the apparent pleonasm is a stylistic method of stressing what is important.

4. **liberius:** 'more outspokenly'; *libertas* often = παρρησία.

6. **agam lenius:** cf. § 2. Cicero's treatment of the young Torquatus (*Sull.* 46) is comparable; see Laur., p. 252.

7. **beneficium tueri:** 'to keep the service unspoilt'; Manutius' conjecture that Cicero had defended Atratinus' father is now corroborated by the latter's identification with L. Calpurnius Bestia (see on I. 13); for this use of *beneficium* cf. *de off.* ii. 66 'multorum causas et non gravate et gratuito defendentis beneficia et patrocinia late patent', Quintil. xii. 7. 12 'non enim, quia venire hoc beneficium [*sc.* patrocinii] non oportet, perire oportet', Sen. *Suas.* vi. 11 'Deiotari regnum obligatum beneficiis, Aegyptum et habere beneficii memoriam'.

**§ 8. 8. esse admonitum:** see K. II. i, pp. 713 f. for the use of the participle with *volo* (*esse* is more usually omitted); the construction gives a stronger tone than would be suggested by the infinitive *admoneri*; the action expressed in the participle is regarded as finished and settled.

**primum . . . existiment:** so *Σ*; *P* has *primum qualis es talem te existiment* (*te* om. *P*¹), a corruption which led to many conjectures (see Müll., p. xxxiii). Lambinus knew the reading of *Σ* from the Cod. S. Victoris (though he read *primum ut qualis es talem hi te esse existiment*); Gruter's comment is amusing, 'Lambinus locum istunc foede collutulavit . . . in nullo autem nostrorum exstat illud Lambinianum *ut* post *primum*, nisi in S. Victoris, sed a manu secunda'. Kl. reads *homines* for *omnes* (see his note).

The construction is troublesome. As the text stands, *ut . . . existiment* can only be co-ordinate with *ut . . . seiungas*, the second clause explaining and particularizing the first, and both acting (in apposition to *illud*) as object to *esse admonitum*; *Verr.* iv. 100, previously adduced, is not in any way parallel. But it is difficult, as *ut . . . existiment* does not refer to the person who is being given the advice (hence various emendations); yet, harsh as it is, it is not an illogical construction—*ut . . . existiment* = 'to let people form an accurate impression of you'—and I think it can stand. A simple alternative, however, is to accept a proposal by Kl. (not in his edition; see *Rh. Mus.* lxvii, 1912, pp. 379 f.) to transpose *primum* to precede *ut quantum*, leaving *ut . . . existiment* as an independent final clause.*

For the thought cf. *de off.* ii. 44 'ut facillime quales simus tales esse videamur', *de am.* 56 'ut quanti quisque se ipse facit, tanti fiat ab amicis'. See Schönb., p. 24.

11. **ut . . . erubescas**: 'you should not say against another what you would blush to hear baselessly cast up at yourself'. For this 'stipulative' use of *ut ne*, with jussive subjunctive (cf. 30. 11), see L.-H., p. 761: an anticipatory *ita* or *sic*, or, as here, *illud*, generally precedes the clause. Cicero uses it less in his later works (see Parzinger, *Beiträge*, pp. 2 ff.); it occurs in Caesar, *B.C.* iii. 55. 1, occasionally in Livy, Quintil. vi. 3. 64, Tac. *H.* iv. 58. 6; see Reid on *de fin.* ii. 24, *Sull.* 27, Landgraf on *Rosc. Am.* 55.*

12. **erubescas**: the accusative after *erubescere* is rare in prose; *Thes. L. L.* quotes no other examples from Cicero; cf. Livy xxxviii. 59. 11 'non id Corneliae magis familiae quam urbi Romanae fore erubescendum'. Note St. Aug. *Enarr. in Ps.* lxviii. 20 (p. 856 M) 'verecundia est quae facit ingenuam frontem etiam de falsi criminis obiectione erubescere'.

13. **huic . . . dignitati**: so *Σ*. The passage is quoted by Agroecius (fifth century), in his treatise *de orthographia* (Keil, *GL* vii. 118. 28), to show the use of *dignitas* to mean 'beauty' in a man, reading *huic* before *dignitati*. P has *isti aetati* only (so W.), *ge* read *isti aetati atque etiam isti dignitati*, whence Kl. prints *isti aetati atque isti dignitati* (see *Rh. Mus.* lxvii, 1912, pp. 366 f.). With Cl.'s text, *huic aetati* is general, = *adulescentiae*, *isti dignitati* = 'a personal grace like yours'; Cicero both compliments Atratinus and implies that he too might be similarly attacked (Kl. takes *isti* of Caelius—cf. Reid on *Mil.* 68—but then the point of *quae cum tibi falso responsa sint* is lost).

For the meaning of *dignitas*, cf. *de off.* i. 130 'cum autem pulchritudinis duo genera sint quorum in altero venustas sit, in altero dignitas, venustatem muliebrem ducere debemus, dignitatem virilem'; but in *de inv.* ii. 2 it is used of girls and boys alike.

14. **suspicione . . . argumento**: 'ground for suspicion . . .', 'basis of accusation' (cf. 55. 11); W., following Schöll, deletes *at . . . argumento*, needlessly.

15. **partium**: 'role' (the plural is regular in this sense).

**§ 9. 19. quoad**: *quod* Kl., *ge*; but in his 1919 preface (p. lxviii),

Kl. shows this as a misprint for *quoad* which, of course, suits the context far better.

**22. togam virilem:** cf. Warde Fowler, *Roman Festivals*, p. 56; Marquardt, *Privatleben*, pp. 122 ff.

**nihil dicam . . . me:** the parenthesis causes an anacoluthon (less common in the speeches than in the philosophical and rhetorical works; see K. II. ii, pp. 584 ff.).*

**23. hunc . . . deductum:** see introd., p. v; Caelius was put in Cicero's charge, to learn the practice of the forum (cf. 11. 19), just as Cicero himself had been entrusted to Q. Mucius Scaevola (*de am.* 1). Cf. Tac. *Dial.* 34 'apud maiores nostros iuvenis ille qui foro et eloquentiae parabatur . . . deducebatur a patre vel a propinquis ad eum oratorem qui principem in civitate locum obtinebat. hunc sectari, hunc prosequi, huius omnibus dictionibus interesse sive in iudiciis sive in contionibus adsuescebat'; cf. Mayor on *Phil.* ii. 3; Warde Fowler, *Social Life*, p. 194.

For the evidence that this passage provides for the date of Cae'ius' birth, see Appendix I, p. 144.

**24. deductum:** the verb seems to have been a t.t. in this connexion (cf. Tac. *Dial.* l.c.). Quintilian alludes to the practice in his picture of the retired orator (xii. 11. 5 'frequentabunt vero eius domum optimi iuvenes, more veterum, et veram dicendi viam velut ex oraculo petent', cf. x. 5. 19).

**25. aetatis flore:** 'his early youth'; see *Thes. L. L.* s.v. *flos*, col. 934. 60 ff.

**26. M. Crassi:** for his domestic virtues cf. Plutarch, *Crass.* 3.

**§§ 10–14.** *'Caelius has been attacked for his connexion with Catiline. But his years of restraint were over by then; and Catiline had many remarkable attractions; why, he once almost deceived me myself.'*

**§ 10. 1. nam quod:** a new aspect of the theme that begins in § 6; Cicero now passes from the general to the particular.

**2. debet:** the subject is Caelius (but cf. H., p. 208, note 1). *Ista suspicione* = 'suspicion of the kind you mention'.

**enim:** the connexion is loose, for Cicero's explanation is contained not in this sentence only, but in the whole succeeding passage with its chronological argument, summed up by *qua re . . . haereat* in 14. 3.

**3. consulatum . . . petisse:** 64 B.C.

**si accessit:** *tum si* Lehmann (*Hermes* xiv, 1879, p. 216), unnecessarily.

**4. si a me discessit:** cf. *de am.* 1 'a patre ita eram deductus ad Scaevolam . . . ut . . . a senis latere nunquam discederem'.

5. **boni adulescentes:** for a far different picture of Catiline's following, see *in Cat.* ii. 10, Sall. *Cat.* 14.

**nequam atque improbo:** a frequent collocation; cf. Plaut. *Bacch.* 573, *Rosc. Am.* 130, *Verr.* iii. 84.

6. **tum existimetur:** *tum Σ*, Kl.; *tamen P*, Madvig (cf. Schönb., p. 25).

7. **at enim:** 'but, I am told' (*occupatio*, see K. II. ii, p. 85).

8. **etiam amicis:** *amici* here must mean more than *familiares*, or *etiam* would be meaningless; it = 'political adherents' (cf. *ad Fam.* v. 7. 1), referring to Caelius' support of Catiline in his second candidature, which Cicero does not deny (11. 16).

9. **sua sponte:** this is the usual order (cf. L.–H., p. 617; Krebs s.v. *sponte*).

10. **infestum:** cf. *Planc.* 1 'dolebam . . . si huius salus ob eam ipsam causam esset infestior'; this passive use ('endangered') is especially found with *iter*, *via* (see Landgraf on *Rosc. Am.* 30).

**id:** this takes up *illud tempus*; the redundant use is not infrequent after a parenthesis, to serve clarity or emphasis; cf. *Phil.* ii. 30 'ille, qui stillantem prae se pugionem tulit, is a te honoris causa nominatur', *de off.* iii. 13 'atque illud quidem honestum, quod proprie vereque dicitur, id in sapientibus est solis', *Tusc.* iii. 71 'Oileus ille apud Sophoclem . . . is cum audisset'. See K. II. i, p. 625; Havet, not understanding the idiom, proposed to delete *id* here (*Manuel de critique verbale*, p. 378).

11. **praetore me:** 66 B.C.; Cicero retraces the history of Caelius' impressionable years (cf. Appendix I, p. 144).

**Africam:** Catiline returned to Rome late in 66; there were two consular elections this year, owing to the unseating of Autronius and Sulla, and he wished to stand at the second, but was refused admission. Probably the refusal was made on political grounds; his trial for *repetundae* did not take place till the middle of 65, and it is unlikely that this had yet caused any technical disability. Cf. Sall. *Cat.* 18, Ascon., pp. 75, 80, Dio Cassius xxxvi. 44, and see Hardy, *The Catilinarian Conspiracy in its Context*, pp. 5 f.

12. **tum annus:** 65; Catiline was acquitted. *Annus = unus annus*; *unus* is generally omitted unless one year is contrasted with a number (cf. 11. 20); cf. *de am.* 11 'ut memini Catonem anno ante quam est mortuus', and S.–M. ad loc., *Quinct.* 15 'annum fere una sunt', Sen. *Suas.* iii. 1 'haec interdum anno lex est'; see Reid on *de sen.* 10, and cf. 56. 1, note. The reading of the text is quite compatible with the staccato style of the passage (which should be contrasted with Cicero's earlier manner in §§ 6–9); but W. adopts Garatoni's proposal *cum* before *causam*, and Kl. marks a lacuna.

14. **advocatus:** a supporter present in court to give help in legal

matters, the normal sense at this period; in Silver Latin it often =
*patronus* (see *Thes. L. L.* s.v., Peterson on Quintil. x. 1. 111, and
my note on Quintil. xii. 1. 13).

   **deinceps fuit annus:** 64, when Catiline could at last stand.
   **§ 11.** 18. **iterum petenti:** 63, when Caelius would be in his
twentieth year (see Appendix I, p. 145); cf. *Caec.* 54, with Jordan's
note, for evidence that at this age a youth was considered a responsible person.

   19. **nobis quidem . . . militaris:** 'in my young days, a single
year was the normal time for "keeping one's arms confined", and for
our athletic training on the *campus*, tunic-clad; and if we began our
army service at once, the same rule held for our training in camp
and on the field.' Cicero appears to contrast the normal practice
with what he pretends is a new fashion implicit in the argument of
the prosecution.

   **annus erat unus:** the *tirocinium* or probationary period (cf.
9. 23); see Gwynn, *Roman Education*, pp. 16 f.; Marrou, *Histoire
de l'Éducation dans l'Antiquité*, pp. 318 f., 387. Cicero means that
Caelius had already had an unusually long period of such apprenticeship by 63 (cf. Appendix I, p. 145).

   20. **ad . . . toga:** a picturesque way of putting 'for being on pro-
bation'. Literally taken, it means that at this stage extravagant
gesture was forbidden; cf. Sen. *Contr. Excerpt.* v. 6 'apud patres
nostros, qui forensia stipendia auspicabantur, nefas putabatur
bracchium extra togam exserere'; so Quintil. has the phrase *manum
intra pallium continentes* (xii. 10. 21) of the 'plain style' in oratory.
The early form of toga had the *sinus* very confined, so that elaborate
gesture was impossible (cf. Quintil. xi. 3. 137 f.); this may be seen
in some of the reliefs from the Ara Pacis; the early fashion in Greece
was similar (cf. Aeschin. *in Timarch.* 25, Demosth. *de fals. leg.* 251,
Plutarch, *Phoc.* 4).

   21. **campestri:** these athletics, which were performed without
the toga (*tunicati*), were not only useful training for military service
to follow, but would be of much importance for the practice of oratory,
which involved severe bodily strain (see Quintil. xi. 3. 22 ff., an
important passage for the comprehension of the physical side of
Roman oratory; cf. *de or.* iii. 220 'laterum inflexione hac forti ac
virili, non ab scaena et histrionibus, sed ab armis aut etiam a
palaestra').

   22. **si statim . . . coeperamus:** a probationary year was the rule
in the army also, for those who omitted the *tirocinium fori*.

   23. **qua . . . poterat:** even under this careful tutelage strength
of character was needed to escape ill report; but if this period was
passed without reproach, no scandal could later arise. Caelius had

had an unusually long *tirocinium*, and his reputation had remained
unblemished: therefore, Cicero argues, his ultimate support of
Catiline cannot carry any moral stigma.

**se ipse**: note *ipse*, not *ipsum* (cf. 77. 23); it is the young
man's own responsibility, not someone else's, to protect himself;
the accusative would shift the emphasis to the man as object of the
verb, not subject. See my note on Quintil. xii. 1. 10, and cf. K. II.
i, p. 617, Lebr., pp. 145 f.

**castimonia**: 'clean living'; not a common word in classical
Latin (see *Thes. L. L.* s.v.).

26. **esset**: the indicative would be normal; the subjunctive is due
to attraction (see K. II. ii, pp. 198 f.).

**infamiam veram**: a much-emended passage; to the list in
Müll., p. xxxiii, add now Sydow's *infamiae umbram* (*Rh. Mus.* xci,
1942, p. 356—but his parallel from *de off.* iii. 69 is inadmissible).
But no correction is needed; *vera* = 'backed by truth' (cf. *Clu.* 7
'falsae infamiae finis'), and the clause must be taken with *quoquo
modo . . . esset* ('however much his friends protected him, yet he
could not avoid giving ground for justifiable scandal, *if* it were not
for his own strength of character'—and this is where Caelius has
triumphed).

28. **cum . . . conroboravisset**: 'when he had at last grown up'
(cf. note on 7. 3).

29. **loquebatur**: for this use of *loqui de*, in the sense 'to speak
evil of', see Löfstedt, *Vermischte Studien*, pp. 69 ff.; he compares
Sen. *Epp.* 47. 4 'sic fit ut isti de domino loquantur, quibus coram
domino loqui non licet', Martial iii. 80. 1 'de nullo loqueris, nulli
maledicis, Apici'; the usage is probably colloquial in origin, but
this passage shows it to have reached literary Latin quite early.
Cf. 75. 24 'nequaquam enim tantum erat quantum homines loquebantur'; perhaps the usage supports the reading *uritur et loquitur*
in Catull. 83. 6 (cf. *mala plurima dicit*, ib. 1).

**§ 12. 29. at studuit**: Cl. is wrong in stating that Fra. proposed
*at* here; the suggestion made by Fra. (p. 207) was to insert *at* after
*infamia* in 11. 17. *At* is therefore Cl.'s own conjecture, based on
*ac* in Σ (om. *P*); Kl. accepts it. It resumes the statement made above,
*studuit Catilinae iterum petenti*, after the digression, i.e. it restates
Cicero's answer to the objection *at enim postea scimus*, etc. (10. 7),
which first took the form of a piece of personal history (*fuit adsiduus
. . . a me nunquam recessit*), was then summed up in *tot igitur annos
. . . petenti*, and is now given again after Cicero has stressed the
difficulty of Caelius' achievement. *At* here introduces the answer
to an objection, not the objection itself, by a clearly defined use
(K. II. ii, p. 86): 'yes, I grant that Caelius supported Catiline

politically, but it was after several years' apprenticeship to public life'. Schönb. seems not to have understood the argument, in his defence of *P* (p. 27).

**1. et multi . . . fecerunt:** Cicero now enlarges on the reasons which make him understand Caelius' attraction to Catiline. The brilliant portrait which follows is very different in tone from the familiar denunciations of the Catilinarian speeches; Caesar and Crassus certainly treated Catiline badly, by throwing him over after intending to use him as an instrument against Pompey, and at first he may have been no worse morally than many others; his ability is obvious. Of course, Cicero has an axe to grind here, yet the passage is significant; cf. Hardy, *The Catilinarian Conspiracy*, pp. 8 f.

**4. non expressa . . . virtutum:** 'marks of excellence not indeed firmly developed, but in outline'. *Expressus* is a metaphor from statuary (cf. *solidus*), *adumbratus* from drawing; the former is used of the finished work, the latter of an imperfect sketch (see Madvig on *de fin.* v. 62, and cf. *de nat. deor.* i. 75, *Tusc.* iii. 3); cf. *de off.* iii. 69 'veri iuris . . . solidam et expressam effigiem nullam tenemus, umbra et imaginibus utimur', *Planc.* 29, and Holden's useful notes, [Quintil.] *decl. mai.* 10. 11 'rictus oris expressos et adumbratos artificis manu vultus'. The passage is imitated in St. Jerome, *Epp.* 60. 7 'in parvo isto volumine cernas adumbrata non expressa signa virtutum', St. Ambr. *de fug. saec.* iii. 14 'genera non adumbrata sed expressa virtutum'. Fra. needlessly inserted *lineamenta* before *virtutum*.

**5. et quidem:** the adversative use of *quidem*, in a concessive statement ('yes, but . . .'); see Sandys on *Orat.* 168, Landgraf on *Rosc. Am.* 31, Reid on *de fin.* i. 35, K. II. i, p. 804.*

**6. erant . . . militaris:** 'men found much about him that attracted them to debauchery; but he also displayed definite qualities that were an incentive to unremitting toil. He was a fiery furnace of profligate passions; yet he had a strong and healthy interest in soldiering'.

**apud illum:** note that this is repeated below with a different shade of meaning and from a different angle; the *inlecebrae libidinum* were what others found 'in' Catiline, the *vitia libidinis* were 'in' him as forming part of his character.

**7. libidinum:** objective genitive (so too *industriae, laboris*); contrast *vitia libidinis* below.

**10. monstrum:** 'a portent'; the word implies something uncanny (the idea of size is only secondary), cf. *prodigium, portentum*. Note the echo of this passage in St. Jerome, *Epp.* 125. 18 'procedebat in publicum intus Nero, foris Cato, totus ambiguus, ut ex contrariis diversisque naturis unum monstrum novamque bestiam diceres esse compactum'.

**tam ... conflatum:** 'such an admixture of opposite, divergent, and incompatible natural passions and appetites'; *conflatum* (a metaphor from welding, cf. N., p. 585) implies something made into a unity; cf. *de nat. deor.* ii. 100 'ipsum autem mare sic terram appetens litoribus eludit, ut una ex duabus naturis conflata videatur', *de inv.* ii. 8 'ex his duabus diversis sicuti familiis ... unum quoddam est conflatum genus'.

**§ 13.** 12. **clarioribus viris:** possibly a covert reference to Caesar and Crassus; if so, *quodam tempore* must refer to 66-65. The passage (from *quis clarioribus ... effusior*) is quoted by Fronto, *ad Anton.* ii. 6 (p. 108 N), to illustrate the figure ἐπαναφορά (i.e. the repeated *quis*).

13. **meliorum partium:** cf. 77. 19; the phrase is parallel to *optimis viris* above, and implies political 'soundness' (see note on 14. 7), a curious claim to make for Catiline.*

14. **taetrior:** 'loathsome', suggesting disease; cf. *in Cat.* i. 11 'quod hanc tam taetram tam horribilem tamque infestam rei publicae pestem toties iam effugimus'.

16. **quis ... effusior:** 'who was ever more covetous in robbing others, who more open-handed in making gifts?' Cf. Sall. *Cat.* 5 'corpus patiens inediae, algoris ... alieni appetens, sui profusus'.

17. **admirabilia:** 'paradoxical' (so the Stoic παράδοξα are termed *admirabilia* in *de fin.* iv. 74; see Reid on *Acad.* ii. 136). The force of the compound is that there is an *object* of wonder (see S.-M. on *de am.* 2, p. 16), and *mirabilis* would not be used in a context where a person or thing is considered from that point of view; see Schönb., p. 28.

18. **obsequio:** 'devotion'; the modern sense of 'obsequious' has lost this aspect of the Latin root, which older English retained; the meaning of 'officious' has likewise changed. An epitaph in Gloucester Cathedral, where it is said of a girl 'obsequiosa viro fuit, officiosa parenti', would suggest a strangely unattractive picture if the adjectives were given their present-day sense.

**cum omnibus ... habebat:** Fronto comments, l.c., that this clause is incongruous in its surroundings, and is 'paulo volgatius et ieiunius'.

19. **temporibus:** 'times of need' (cf. καιρός); so *Sest.* 14 'huius potius tempori serviam quam dolori meo', *Arch.* 12 'ut a nullius unquam me tempore aut commodo aut otium meum abstraxerit aut voluptas avocarit'.

21. **versare ... flectere:** 'his ability to adapt and control his

ways to suit the occasion, twisting and manipulating his character this way and that'.*

22. **tristibus**: not 'sad', but 'stern', 'austere' (cf. σκυθρωπός). Catiline 'behaved with austerity among the puritanic, and with gaiety among the lax'. The antitheses in these three lines are notable, and Cicero obviously relished this mannerism, a famous example of which is *Rosc. Am.* 72, though he realized that it could be overdone (*Orat.* 107, cf. Quintil. xii. 6. 4). See Norden, *Die Antike Kunstprosa* i, pp. 226 ff., for a discussion of Ciceronian antithesis; the device used here is an ancestor of an antithetical method much affected by medieval Christian poets (cf. Raby, *Christian Latin Poetry*, p. 304).*

24. **cum facinerosis . . . vivere**: 'he could be a dare-devil among criminals and a roué among the vicious'. The form *facinerosus* is the earlier form (cf. *facineris, temperi*); the *-e-* forms were originally used in the oblique cases of these nouns, whose original nominative ending was *-os* (Greek *-os*); the genitive *-eris* (for *-esis*) corresponded to the Greek *-ε(σ)ος*, and the normal *-o-* forms are due to analogical transference from the original nominative (Lindsay, *Latin Language*, p. 192). For the form *audaciter*, see L.–H., p. 299, Neue–Wagener, *Formenlehre* ii, p. 685; it occurs also in *Rosc. Am.* 104, where it is vouched for by Priscian (Keil, *GL* iii, p. 76. 24), *de domo* 28, *de sen.* 72, *Font.* 11; cf. Reid on *de fin.* ii. 28. By Quintilian's time it was pedantic (i. 6. 17).

**§ 14. 25. multiplici**: 'complex'; see the interesting note of S.–M. on *de am.* 65. Catiline was a kind of Proteus among men.

27. **bonos**: see on 14. 7 below.

**specie . . . adsimulatae**: the pleonasm is deliberate, for emphasis (cf. note on 7. 3); Löfstedt (*Synt.* ii, p. 176) quotes *leg. agr.* ii. 10 'aliud quiddam obscure moliuntur, aliud spe ac specie simulationis ostentant', *de nat. deor.* i. 3 'in specie . . . fictae simulationis' (cf. Plasberg ad loc.).

2. **immanitas**: the word implies not only size but cruelty, frightfulness, 'enormity' in two senses.

**facilitatis**: so MSS.; *facultatis* Madvig (*Adv. Crit.* iii, p. 144), Kl. It is hard to see how the MSS. text would give the antithesis to *vitiorum tanta immanitas* that is needed; Abrami takes *facilitas* to be one of the *adumbrata signa virtutum* mentioned earlier, Manutius connects it with *clarioribus viris iucundior*; but the normal use of *facilitas* (so often joined as it is with *lenitas, comitas*, etc.) does not suggest that it could mean more here than 'affability', 'pleasantness' (cf. *de off.* i. 90 'Philippum . . . facilitate et humanitate video superiorem fuisse', where Holden translates *facilitate* by 'accommodation to circumstances'—a sense which

would suit the general picture here but not this particular antithesis).
Madvig's emendation (*facultas* = 'ability') gives far better sense;
cf. Schönb., p. 28, and for the meaning of *facilitas* see S.–M. on
*de am.* 19, p. 115.

3. **condicio**: 'consideration', 'possibility'; cf. *Planc.* 6 'si illam
accusationis condicionem sequar' (= 'that line of accusation');
*Rab. Perd.* 16 'harum enim omnium rerum non solum eventus
atque perpessio, sed etiam condiciô, exspectatio, mentio ipsa . . .
indigna cive Romano . . . est'; see N., p. 260, and Müll. ad loc.,
p. xxxiv. *Ista condicio = istius rei condicio*, i.e. the idea that
Caelius' intimacy with Catiline offers any *crimen*; with the connective *qua re*, Cicero has returned to the argument from which he has
digressed since 12. 2.

4. **nec . . . haereat**: 'do not let a ground for charge attach to him
in connexion with his association with Catiline'.

5. **bonis**: *etiam bonis P*, Kl.; I cannot see why Kl. regards *etiam*
as essential for the sense.

6. **me . . . decepit**: Cicero once thought of defending Catiline
for *repetundae* in 65, though he believed him guilty (*ad Att.* i. 2. 1);
Fenestella asserted that he really did so, but Asconius disbelieved
this (Ascon., p. 76).

→ 7. **civis . . . bonus**: a party term (cf. 10. 5 *boni adulescentes*,
14. 27 *fortis viros et bonos*), = a 'loyal citizen' in the Ciceronian
sense, a supporter of the Senate, no revolutionary or 'leftist' (cf.
note on 60. 24); see Kroll, *Die Kultur der Ciceronischen Zeit* i,
p. 15. *Optimi cuiusque* contains the same idea (for this use of
*cupidus* with a gen. of person, = *studiosus*, see *Thes. L. L.* s.v.,
col. 1427. 63 ff.). The idea of Catiline as a potential 'constitutional-
ist' must have made the jury smile.

11. **est ut**: 'it is reasonable that' (nearly the same as *est cur*; cf.
Clark on *Mil.* 35, Nisbet on *de domo* 65; see K. II. ii, p. 237).

**§§ 15–16.** *'From abuse of Caelius' morals you have passed to charg-
ing him with complicity in the Catilinarian Plot; this shows a
striking disregard for probabilities. With like brevity I can dismiss your charges of bribery and corrupt practices.'*

Cicero now leaves the *locus de pudicitia*. It is unlikely that
Caelius was connected with the conspiracy, in spite of his support
for Catiline's candidature in 63, and the insinuation was obviously
made half-heartedly. A man with Caelius' keen political flair would
quickly realize the significance of the withdrawal of Caesar and
Crassus from their support of Catiline's party.

**§ 15. 14. impudicitiae**: so *Σ*, confirming Garatoni's conjecture
(cf. Quintil. iv. 2. 27 'si defendendus sit M. Caelius, nonne optime

63

patronus occurrat prius conviciis luxuriae petulantiae impudicitiae quam veneficii?'); the genitive is objective. Kl. reads *pudicitiae* (so *P*); see his note for parallels (but at *Deiot*. 10 the text is doubtful). Cf. Sen. *de ben.* vi. 32. 1 'Augustus filiam ultra impudicitiae maledictum impudicam relegavit'.

**ad coniurationis invidiam:** 'to arousing prejudice in connexion with the conspiracy'. *Delapsa* implies that the matter is less important.

16. **titubanter et strictim:** 'in a hesitating and superficial manner'.

17. **in quo . . . oratio:** 'on this point, so far from any charge holding good, my brilliant young friend's argument scarcely held together'. *Haerebat* is absolute, as in 14. 4, 56. 26: a charge did not 'lie'; *in quo = qua in re* (see Schönb., pp. 29 f., a useful note).

18. **diserti:** the word is not always complimentary, but takes its tone from the context (cf. 67. 19, where it = 'glib'), and is often contrasted with *eloquens*; see Wilkins on *de or.* i. 94, and my note on Quintil. xii. 1. 23. Here it is pleasantly ironical.

19. **furor:** another party-term ('revolutionary madness'); see on 60. 24.

20. **volnus:** 'flaw', 'disability': 'was Caelius so far crippled?'

21. **nimium . . . loquor:** cf. *har. resp.* 20 'ne plura de re minime loquar dubia'; Cicero's crafty answer does not sound entirely convincing.

22. **non modo . . . voluisset:** 'he would never have sought to bring himself distinction as a young man in this particular way, by accusing another for complicity in the plot, if he had himself been privy to it, or rather if he had not been violently hostile to such a piece of criminality'. A negative must be understood with *non modo*, from *nunquam* below. The reference is to Caelius' accusation of Antonius in 59 B.C.; see introd., p. vi, and Appendix VII; the result much pleased the Catilinarians (*Flacc.* 95), which certainly suggests that Caelius was *persona grata* to them (see H., p. 211).

24. **coniurationis:** Antonius was, in fact, charged either with *maiestas* or with *repetundae*, more probably the former (see Appendix VII); the other prosecutors were Q. Fabius Maximus (*in Vat.* 28) and Caninius Gallus (Val. Max. iv. 2. 6).

§ 16. 25. **haud scio an . . . putem:** 'I am inclined to think'; *haud scio an* is one of the best ways of translating 'probably' (the force of *scio* is quite weak). *Quod* is adverbial ('in this connexion').

26. **de ambitu . . . sequestrium:** 'on the matter of corrupt electoral practices and on the charges of belonging to political bribery-clubs'. These were not formal charges, but were part of the series of points brought *deformandi Caeli causa.*

The passage has been used to prove that Caelius stood for the quaestorship about this time (Wegehaupt, p. 11, Wieschhölter, p. 27, Antoine, *Lettres de Caelius à Cicéron*, p. 22). But if Caelius had been quaestor, or was now quaestor-elect, Cicero could hardly have failed to mention it in his detailed biography in §§ 72 ff. (see Appendix I, p. 144). It is more probable that the charge **was** incurred in connexion with the candidature of some friend for office, perhaps at the pontifical elections mentioned in § 19 (see H., p. 212), perhaps even at Bestia's candidature for the praetorship in 57 (§ 26), for the fact that Caelius himself accused Bestia of *ambitus* need not exclude the possibility that he was himself suspected of it on that occasion, while Cicero's own language here suggests that this is what is meant. Drexler (see bibliography) thinks (p. 13) that the reference is to the elections of 63, when Caelius lent his support to Catiline (§ 11); this is possible, in view of the context here.

**sodalium ac sequestrium:** *sodales* were the members of a *sodalicium* (a private political club established for the purposes of bribery), *sequester* was the t.t. for the agent with whom the money was deposited; see Holden's *pro Plancio*, pp. xxx ff., Tyrrell and Purser, *Correspondence of Cicero* iii, Addendum i. In 55 B.C. the Lex Licinia de sodaliciis was passed to suppress these clubs; this had already been foreshadowed by a senatorial decree of February 56 (*Q.F.* ii. 3. 5), and the proposed penalty was to be the same as that for *vis*, which may have made it easier for the prosecution to include this point against Caelius (see H., p. 212).

27. **quoniam . . . incidi:** 'since I have reached this point'.

28. **tam . . . amens:** note the separation of *tam* from the adjective; cf. Reid on *Acad.* ii. 83 (p. 277), S.–M. on *de am.* 10 (p. 49); Löfstedt, *Synt.* ii, p. 397. The reference in *alterum* below is to Bestia.

2. **periculum:** here, as often, of a criminal trial; see Reid on *Arch.* 13, Landgraf on *Rosc. Am.* 85; this usage (so too *periclitari*) is common in Quintilian (see my note on xii. 1. 40).

4. **nec sapienter:** Cicero nowhere condones Caelius' persecution of Bestia (cf. § 76).

5. **cupiditas:** Cl.'s reasons for adopting this reading (that of *b²ψ²*)are obscure; I agree with Kl., who reads *cupiditatis* (so *Σ*); *P* has *cupidus*, deleted as a gloss by Lambinus and variously emended by others (see Müll. ad loc., p. xxxiv). The nominative can hardly stand here without a possessive genitive (*eius*, Koch; see Kl.). This absolute use of the word, which made early edd. uneasy, is not common but has some parallels (see *Thes. L. L.* s.v., col. 1416. 56); here it = *studium accusandi* (cf. Landgraf on *Rosc. Am.* 83).*

**§ 17.** '*You have accused Caelius of debt: there is no proof. You have grossly exaggerated the rent he pays for his house.*'

**§ 17. 7. nam quod:** see note on 4. 23: Cicero now returns to the series of points connected with the general theme of Caelius' behaviour; probably this was part of the issue which he chose to distort in 3. 11 (*parum splendidus*). For this type of *argumentum e victu* (*de inv.* i. 35 'in victu considerare oportet . . . quo modo rem familiarem administret, qua consuetudine domestica sit') cf. Landgraf on *Rosc. Am.* 39, p. 96.

**8. tabulae:** 'account-books'. Production of accounts was a common feature of documentary evidence; cf. the case of Aebutius in the *pro Caecina*.

**9. in patris potestate:** cf. Leage–Ziegler, *Roman Private Law*, pp. 90 ff. At this period a *filiusfamilias* owned no property that was legally his; and Cicero states here that he was not liable to keep accounts. Presumably the prosecution knew this, and it is probable that Cicero is again exaggerating the point raised against Caelius, to score against his adversary.

**conficit:** a t.t. in this connexion; cf. *Verr.* i. 60, *de or.* ii. 97, with Wilkins's note; see *Thes. L. L.* s.v., col. 198. 18 ff.

**versuram:** here = 'loan'; strictly it implies money borrowed to pay an existing loan, thus involving a change of creditor (*vertere*); cf. Ter. *Phorm.* 780 'in eodem luto haesitas, vorsuram solves', of a man who is becoming more deeply involved.

**11. habitationis:** this may mean 'house-rent'; cf. Suet. *Iul.* 38. 2 'annuam . . . habitationem Romae usque ad bina milia nummum . . . remisit'.

**triginta milibus:** abl. of price; so *habitare* is used with *tanti* (Vell. Pat. ii. 10, Pliny, *N.H.* xvii. 3), *gratis* (*de off.* ii. 83). The sum is about £250, by the conventional reckoning. Rents in the better quarters of Rome greatly increased during the last century of the Republic; in 125 B.C. a rent of HS. 6,000 caused an augur to be summoned by the censors, but by A.D. 30 this seemed contemptible (Vell. Pat. ii. 10 'at nunc si quis tanti habitet, vix ut senator agnoscitur'). Clodius' exorbitant charges (see below) were no doubt possible because the Palatine was so fashionable.

**nunc demum:** 'aha! *now* I understand'; Cicero pretends suddenly to see the reason for the exaggerated figure: Clodius wants to sell his property, and the lie will help him to get a better price.

**12. insulam:** a block of apartment-houses; see Jordan, *Topographie der Stadt Rom im Altertum* I. i, p. 538; Pauly–Wissowa, *RE* s.v. In the more luxurious type of *insula*, at least under the Empire, the ground floor would be let as a whole to one tenant, giving him virtually the advantage of a private house, while the poorer sort would have shops or booths occupying it: possibly Caelius' enemies had circulated the tale that he rented such a ground-floor flat, whereas in reality, according to Cicero, he occupied a much less grand apartment. See Carcopino, *Daily Life in Ancient Rome*, ch. ii.

T. Frank, *Catullus and Horace*, p. 281, has a conjectural plan of these houses on the Palatine (cf. Nisbet, *de domo*, p. 206); but his identification of Caelius' house as being 'the ninth from the temple of Castor' (Catull. 37. 2) is pure guesswork. Caelius moved later; in 50 B.C. he had a house near the *porta Flumentana* (*ad Att.* vii. 3. 9).

13. **aediculis:** one of the apartment-houses in the block; the plural seems usual in this sense (Ter. *Ph.* 663, Petron. 90. 7).

**ut opinor:** pretended ignorance; see Landgraf's interesting note on *Rosc. Am.* 46.

§ 18. *'Caelius certainly left his father's house, but it was with his father's sanction and on his advice: a pity he ever did so, for it was on the Palatine that he met his Medea.'*

This was presumably part of the charge of disrespect (3. 12) shown to the elder Caelius by his son. Two years later, in his defence of Plancius, Cicero took credit for his client that he lived at home (*Planc.* 29 'ut vivat cum suis, primum cum parente—nam meo iudicio pietas fundamentum est omnium virtutum—quem veretur ut deum', etc.).

§ 18. 17. **in hac aetate:** 'in a man of his age' (note this use of *in* = 'in the case of', 'where someone is concerned'); *hac* is either deictic or = 'this of which I am speaking'. Müll. needlessly distinguishes between *haec aetas* and Cicero's previous use of *illa aetas* or the like in speaking of Caelius' earlier days. Kl. reads *iam in hac aetate* (so *P*), with some doubt (see his note); *iam* would then = 'precisely' (cf. Schönb., p. 31).

**qui:** the connexion is loose, but possible, and it is quite unnecessary to regard the previous sentence as interpolated (so Schöll, W.).

18. **publica causa:** so *Σ*, confirming Fra.'s conjecture; Schönb., p. 32, offers a defence of *P*'s *rei publicae causa*, but the expression is in no way appropriate here (see Kl.). The reference is to Caelius' prosecution of Antonius.*

19. **magistratus petere:** probably this means simply that Caelius was now of an age to look forward to office; if any definite office is meant, it may be the military tribunate (so Fra., p. 209) or one of the minor magistracies (cf. H., p. 194, note 3). Wegehaupt (p. 6) argued that the quaestorship is meant, and adduced the

passage to support his view that Caelius was born in 88 (see Appendix I); but Cicero's words are far too vague for this.

**22. nostras domus:** Cicero may refer to Crassus as well as himself. Caelius' father possibly lived on one of the more distant hills, where his economical tastes would be satisfied by a lower rent (perhaps, like Atticus, on the Quirinal). The move was sensible enough in view of Caelius' obvious ambitions. See the maps in Hülsen–Jordan, *Topographie* I (iii), and cf. T. Frank's plan.

**23. suis:** quite general, as in *iudicio suorum*, 5. 9.

**conduxit ... domum:** 'leased a house on the Palatine at a low rent'.

→ **24. M. Crassus ... Ptolemaei:** see on § 23, and Appendix V, p. 152.

**27.** Cicero quotes the beginning of Ennius' *Medea exsul*, adapted from the opening of Euripides' play:

> utinam ne in nemore Pelio securibus
> caesa accidisset abiegna ad terram trabes,
> neve inde navis incohandae exordium
> coepisset, quae nunc nominatur nomine
> Argo, quia Argivi in ea delecti viri
> vecti petebant pellem inauratam arietis
> Colchis, imperio regis Peliae, per dolum.
> nam nunquam era errans mea domo ecferret pedem
> Medea, animo aegra, amore saevo saucia.

Crassus probably quoted the lines to show how disastrous it was that the embassy led by Dio (§ 23)—*delecti viri*—had come to Rome. Cicero adapts the passage differently, to entertain his audience; cf. Quintil. i. 8. 11 'apud Ciceronem ... videmus inseri versus summa non eruditionis modo gratia, sed etiam iucunditatis, cum poeticis voluptatibus aures a forensi asperitate respirant'. An anecdote in *de or.* i. 154 shows how Ennius was used in declamation-exercises; Cicero's fondness for him made Seneca once remark (Gell. xii. 2. 6) 'apud ipsum quoque Ciceronem invenies etiam in prosa oratione quaedam ex quibus intellegas, illum non perdidisse operam quod Ennium legit'.

Another possibility is that Crassus used the quotation to show the remote bearing of the charges *de legatis* on the case, for it is clear from Quintilian (v. 10. 84; cf. *de inv.* i. 91) that it was a stock instance of the *argumentum longius repetitum*, 'quo modo pervenire quolibet retro causas legentibus licet'. A strange example of its adaptation occurs in St. Jerome, *Epp.* 127. 5 'nec erubuit (Marcella) profiteri quod Christo placere cognoverat. hanc multos post annos imitata est Sophronia et aliae, quibus rectissime illud Ennianum aptari potest, Utinam ne in nemore Pelio.'*

→  1. **longius ... contexere**: 'to continue the context farther'; cf. *de leg.* i. 9 'neque tam facile interrupta contexo quam absolvo instituta'.

5. **sic**: anticipatory of *hanc ... fuisse.*

6. **Palatinam Medeam**: Fortunatianus quotes this gibe (Halm, *RLM*, p. 124), and adds that Atratinus had called Caelius *pulchel-lum Iasonem.* Caelius' own phrase *Pelia cincinnatus* (cf. introd., p. vii) may well have been a retort to this, as Münzer suggests, for if Caelius is a Jason, his accuser is a Pelias, who tried to destroy Jason. Possibly Atratinus had said that Caelius had won his golden fleece and kept it (cf. 30. 17 *aurum sumptum a Clodia*), deserting his Medea, though certainly this afforded an obvious means of retort. *Pulchellus* and *cincinnatus* both imply effeminacy (cf. *Sest.* 26, *post red.* 12, *de or.* ii. 262, etc.). See *ad Att.* i. 18. 3 for similar allusiveness, and Apul. *Apol.* 56 'igitur adgnomenta ei [*sc.* Aemiliano] duo indita, Charon ... ob oris et animi diritatem, sed alterum, quod libentius audit, ob deorum contemptum, Mezentius'.

**migrationemque hanc**: so Cl., for *migrationemque huic Pπδ.* A demonstrative is plainly needed with *migrationem*: *hanc migra-tionem Palatinamque Medeam huic* Kl. (see his note); *hanc ad Palatinam Medeam migrationem huic* Sydow, *Rh. Mus.* xci, 1942, p. 357; W. follows Schöll in expunging *migrationemque*, but this is plainly needed; Schönb. defends *P*'s text (p. 33). Cl.'s reading seems the best of these proposals, for it gives a better balance of stress and rhythm: further, *hic* alone, or *adulescens* alone would be expected in reference to Caelius, but *hic adulescens* is unnatural.

**§§ 19–22.** '*I am not afraid of the mysterious senator who is allegea to have been beaten up by Caelius at the pontifical elections, nor of those shadowy witnesses who are to state that Caelius assaulted their wives after a dinner-party. But really, the truth cannot be discovered in that way: let us come to facts.*'

Cicero now deals with two further points of the *Caeli diffamatio*, intended to show him up as a young Mohock; these differ from the preceding ones in that witnesses are to be produced—but, says Cicero, they will be tainted witnesses.

**§ 19. 9. quam ob rem**: again the connexion is loose; Cicero is going to show that these persons' evidence clearly goes back to the same *causa malorum* that he has just mentioned.

**praemuniri ... fingi**: 'invented and contrived to bolster up their case'; for *praemuniri*, see on § 3 (p. 45).

10. **prudentia**: 'common sense' (which is never *communis sensus* —this means 'feelings common to humanity', either in general or

in a particular form, such as 'tact'; see H. J. Thomson, *CR* xxxiv, 1920, pp. 18 ff.).*

11. **aiebant**: Sydow (*Hermes* lxv, 1930, p. 319) defends *iaciebant* (*Σ*), comparing *Scaur*. 5 'iecit quodam loco vita illam mulierem spoliari quam pudicitia maluisse' (his parallel from *Flacc.* 35 is hardly valid).

12. **pontificiis comitiis**: in 63 the Lex Domitia of 104, abolished by Sulla, was restored; it gave the elections in connexion with the pontifical and augural colleges to a special assembly of the people (Greenidge, *Roman Public Life*, p. 124). Thus the malpractices common to popular elections could be expected (cf. note on 16. 26). Fra. (pp. 209 f.) suggests that the reference is to the pontifical elections of 57, when C. Scribonius Curio the elder was elected.

**pulsatum**: this would constitute *iniuria*, not *vis*.

13. **quaeram**: cf. 67. 11, where Cicero similarly indicates his intentions; in so doing he merely implies that his opponents have no case, and he is not giving away anything of importance. It cannot be argued from these passages that they were added afterwards when Cicero edited the speech (cf. Laur., p. 7)

**egerit**: 'took no legal action'.

16. **acute arguteque**: 'shrewdly and to the point'.

18. **si ... sese**: 'if he turns out to be himself the main source and supply'; cf. Reid's notes on *de fin.* ii. 78 and *Acad.* ii. 23.

19. **rivolus . . . vestrae**: 'a tributary, drawn and laid on from the very fountain-head of the prosecution'. For this contrast of *rivolus* with *fons* cf. *de or.* ii. 117 'tardi ingeni est rivolos consectari, fontis rerum non videre, et iam aetatis est ususque nostri a capite quod velimus arcessere et unde omnia manent videre', and see Reid on *Acad.* i. 8; there is an echo of such passages in St. Jerome, *Epp.* 20. 2. 1 'omissis rivolis . . . ad ipsum fontem . . . recurramus'.

20. **cum**: concessive, not causal.

23. **DE TESTE FVFIO**: this is found in *Σ* alone. The reference may be to Q. Fufius Calenus, tribune in 61 and a friend of Clodius; he is presumably the *unus senator* just mentioned (see H., p. 219, note 1, for a refutation of Klotz's view that the pontiff Curio is meant).

See *Mur.* 57 and *Font.* 20 for similar *tituli*, marking an abridgement made by Cicero himself (cf. Pliny, *Epp.* i. 20. 7): in those passages the context shows that there is an omission in the speech as published, but here the only indication (if it is one) of an omission is the difficult connective *tamen* below. This *titulus*, therefore, may not be genuine, as its presence is not necessary (contrast *Mur.* and *Font.*, l.c.); H. (pp. 217 f.) regards it as a marginal note that has been taken into the text of *Σ*, and this finds support in the fact that

COMMENTARY       §§ 19–20

Cicero's attack depends for much of its point on the assumption of
anonymity, both here and in § 20. Kl. and Norden (see bibliography) do not doubt the authenticity of the *titulus* in *Σ* (cf. Kl. in
*Rh. Mus.* lxvii, 1912, p. 363). The matter really turns on whether
the connexion in § 20 is intelligible without assuming a lacuna;
on the whole, I am inclined to think that it is, and that the *titulus*
is not a genuine mark of an abridgement made by Cicero himself.

For an interesting discussion of the desirability of 'editing' a
speech, and the difference between the spoken and the written versions, see Quintil. xii. 10. 49 ff.; cf. Laur., pp. 5 ff.*

§ 20. 24. nec tamen: can this connective not be taken simply
with reference to the concessions made in 19. 19 ? Cicero has said
there that if the senator proves to be independent of Clodia, he may
listen to him, though the possibility is unlikely; these other vague
witnesses, however, cause him no concern at all. But there are
passages where *tamen* (with *et* or *nec*) does not bear the usual adversative sense, but means 'in any case', 'in spite of what someone may
have said'; cf. *ad Fam.* ix. 2. 3 'haec ego suspicans adhuc Romae
maneo, et tamen λεληθότως consuetudo diurna callum iam obduxit
stomacho meo' (see Tyrrell and Purser ad loc.), ibid. iv. 12. 3 'ab
Atheniensibus locum sepulturae intra urbem ut darent impetrare
non potui, quod religione se impediri dicerent, neque tamen id
antea cuiquam concesserant'; see Friedrich's examination of these
and other passages in his note on Catull. 68. 143, and the important
discussion of *Q.F.* i. 2. 3, *ad Att.* vii. 3. 10, Lucr. v. 1120 ff., in
Löfstedt, *Kommentar zur Peregrinatio Aetheriae*, pp. 31 ff. This
is a possible alternative sense here; with either explanation, it is not
necessary to assume that Cicero has omitted a passage in editing
the speech for publication.

nocturnorum testium: 'night-bird witnesses'; cf. *Mil.* 9
'nocturnum furem'. The witnesses are not honest men, but skulk
away from daylight.

26. attrectatas: 'criminally assaulted' (cf. *contrectare*); *mala
tractatio* is a t.t. for 'maltreatment' (Quintil. iv. 2. 30, etc.).

1. se . . . experiri: 'that they never attempted to get legal
satisfaction for these horrid insults even by a private meeting and
settlement out of court'. Cf. *Caec.* 33 'homines inermos qui ad
constitutum experiendi iuris gratia venissent', *Quinct.* 38 'aut intra
parietes aut summo iure experiretur' (see *Thes. L. L.* s.v. *experiri*,
col. 1670. 28 ff.).

2. sed . . . debebitis: Cicero ends his comments on the miscel-
laneous points of the *diffamatio* by restating his view of the case as
he had given it in § 1, and by a 'locus communis de testibus' carefully directed to showing their complete dependence upon the

powerful clique behind the scenes. For such *loci* see *part. or.* 48 ff., Quintil. ii. 1. 11, 4. 27; for the general topic of dealing with witnesses see Quintil. v. 7, a very interesting chapter. Cf. H., pp. 216 f.

**§ 21. 7. in eos:** H. (p. 215) takes this to refer to the *gens Claudia* (cf. 68. 2), and Cicero's use of *oppugnandi* below, not *accusandi*, supports this: there is nothing wrong about family pride, he says, but it must not be made an excuse for injustice.

**etiam:** with *gloriosum*, in a position of emphasis.

**12. vobis quoque:** so *Σ*, confirming Garatoni's conjecture: *P* has *vobis quoque vos* which Schönb. defends (p. 34), adducing Madvig's note on *de fin.* iii. 10, but the close proximity of *vos* to *vobis* here is surely against the reading.

**alieno dolori . . . vestrae fidei:** 'someone else's spite . . . your own honour as a jury'.

**13. iam:** so Cl.; *nam* Kl. (see app. crit.). *Iam* = 'further', adducing a new point; Kl.'s reading offers a slightly better connexion.

**16. disertis:** cf. note on 15. 18; here it is uncomplimentary ('with plenty of talk').

**17. operam navare:** 'work energetically', cf. 67. 24 'navent aliam operam'; *opera* is the abstract counterpart of the concrete *opus*; *navare* (connected with *navus* or *gnavus*, 'energetic', 'industrious') is generally found with *opera* or *studium* as object, = 'to take busy pains' about something (*bellum navare*, Tac. *H.* v. 25; *flagitium navare* id. ib. iv. 59).

**§ 22. 18. se . . . proiecerint:** 'have intruded themselves'.

**19. excluditote:** when the imperative is accompanied by a subordinate clause referring to the future, this form is usual; see Lebr., pp. 194 ff.

**21. religioni:** 'sense of responsibility', like *fides* above; cf. *Rosc. Com.* 45 'propter fidem et religionem iudicis'. *Religio* always has some idea of a restraining force: see the analysis of its uses in Nettleship, *Contributions to Latin Lexicography* s.v., pp. 570 ff.

**potentias:** abstract for concrete ('dangerous, powerful personages'); see Lebr., pp. 47 f. The plural is probably due to the plural in *hominum. Potestas* is used similarly; cf. Quintil. vii. 1. 32 'interveniente aliqua potestate', 'if some Personage intervenes' (i.e. the Emperor), Juv. 10. 100 'Fidenarum Gabiorumque esse potestas'.

**25. fingi:** 'manipulated', parallel with *flecti ac detorqueri*; cf. *Scaur.* 15 'testis . . . quivis . . . impelli deterreri fingi flecti potest', *Brut.* 142 'eosque fingit, format, flectit, talisque oratores videri facit qualis ipsi se videri volunt'; cf. H., p. 219, note 2.

**26. argumentis . . . signis:** cf. 66. 4 'haec causa ab argumentis,

a coniectura, ab eis signis quibus veritas inlustrari solet ad testis
tota traducta est'; Cicero means 'artificial proofs', ἔντεχνοι πίστεις
(see note on 54. 12).

27. **causa cum causa**: cf. *Quinct.* 92 'si causa cum causa con-
tenderet, nos nostram perfacile cuivis probaturos statuebamus;
quod vitae ratio cum ratione vitae decerneret, idcirco nobis etiam
magis te iudice opus esse arbitrati sumus', Quintil. ii. 17. 33
'rhetorice non est contraria sibi; causa enim cum causa, non illa
secum ipsa componitur'.

The passage seems to have attracted Christian writers; cf. St.
Aug. *de util. cred.* 3 'ut quemadmodum ille [*sc.* Cicero] ait, separatis
nugis locorum communium, res cum re, causa cum causa, ratio
cum ratione confligat', Ennodius, *pro Synodo*, p. 187A (Migne) 'ut
vere dicam, res cum re, causa cum causa, ratio cum ea quam putant
ratione pugnabit', Victricius of Rouen, p. 452B (Migne) 'unde
amotis sermonum insidiis res cum re, ratio cum ratione confligat'
(see Weyman, *Wiener Studien* xvii, 1895, pp. 317 f.). See also on
8. 12, 12. 4, 12. 10, 62. 4; St. Augustine may have popularized the
speech, perhaps because of the importance given to it by Quintilian;
cf. Landgraf on *Rosc. Am.* 37 (p. 92), *Archiv für lat. Lex.* xii,
p. 468, for echoes of Cicero in St. Ambrose.*

**§§ 23–24.** *'Crassus has dealt competently with the charges which
he was left to answer; a pity that he did not also reply to the point
in connexion with Dio. But I may say that the murder of Dio
is completely irrelevant to the present proceedings, and I can prove
this. Let us come to the real point.'*

Cicero has yet another matter to dispose of, the allegation that
Caelius was involved in the murder of the philosopher Dio, the
leader of an embassy from Alexandria to Rome, by P. Asicius (see
Appendix V).

This allegation is evidently regarded by Cicero as a pendant to
the other *maledicta* already cleared away; it is plainly not connected
with the specific charge which he handles in §§ 51 ff., but was presumably dragged in by the prosecution in much the same way as the
allegation that Caelius had been one of the Catilinarian conspirators.
See H., pp. 220 ff.; Reitzenstein, *NGG* 1925, p. 27, note 5; Norden,
p. 19.

**§ 23.** 29. **itaque**: another difficult connective; presumably Cicero
means 'I am concerned with facts alone, not hearsay; *therefore* I
need not add to what Crassus has so well covered, because those
allegations were likewise based on irresponsible evidence'.

   **facile patior**: 'I am very pleased', a common idiom (see Landgraf on *Rosc. Am.* 56, Holden on *Planc.* 62).

**graviter ... peroratam:** 'that Crassus has dealt in full with it, in a dignified and eloquent manner'; for this sense of *perorare* cf. *Sest.* 3.

1. **de seditionibus:** probably some local dispute (see Appendix V).

**de ... pulsatione:** this must have had some connexion with the alleged attack by Caelius upon Dio; possibly the embassy was involved in a scuffle at Puteoli, in which Caelius was said to have been implicated.

2. **Pallae:** otherwise unknown. But Dio Cassius (xlvii. 24) mentions a Palla (so MSS.; Boissevain reads Πώλλα) who was the mother or stepmother of L. Gellius Poplicola; now there is evidence that Poplicola married Sempronia Atratina, the adoptive sister of Atratinus (Appendix VI, p. 155), so that if the Palla of this passage is the Palla named by Dio Cassius, the accusation appears as a family affair. Further, Poplicola is very probably the Gellius whom Catullus attacks (cf. Kroll on Catull. 74; Ellis, p. 443), and therefore a possible rival of Caelius for Clodia's favours: an entertaining situation.*

For the possible nature of the charge see Appendix V; it may have been more substantially based than the other counts mentioned, or at least have had greater technical importance, as it alone is named by Quintilian (iv. 2. 27; see H., p. 201, and Ciaceri, *Atti della R. Acc. di Archeologia, Lettere e Belle Arti di Napoli* NS, xi, 1929–30, p. 11).

3. **de Dione:** Crassus may have left this charge to Cicero, because of the latter's defence of Asicius (24. 14); Cicero means that it was as groundless as the rest, so that Crassus might as well have dealt with it. The murder took place in 57 (H., p. 198, note 1); Strabo implies (xvii. 1. 11) that Pompey was at the back of it. H. points out that Pompey was out of favour with the Senate, and that Clodius also was opposed to his ambitious scheme for commanding an army in the East (see Appendix V); the acquittal of Sex. Clodius, shortly before Caelius' trial (cf. 78. 4), was also a blow at Pompey; possibly, therefore, the proceedings against Asicius, Ptolemy's agent, were aimed indirectly at him, and the attempt to implicate Caelius in the affair may also have been meant to discredit him.

**de quo ... rex:** 'however, what statement can you possibly look for even in connexion with Dio ? Why, one which the person responsible either is not afraid to hear or else actually admits; for he is a king'.*

Ptolemy himself had openly taken responsibility for Dio's murder; his agent and abettor, Asicius, had been formally acquitted:

therefore, says Cicero, how can the prosecution expect any serious treatment of the attempt to implicate Caelius?

6. **P. Asicius:** he was defended by Cicero and prosecuted by Calvus, whose speech was apparently extant in Tacitus' time, though little read (*Dial.* 21). There is probably an allusion to him, and to his connexion with Ptolemy, in *Q.F.* ii. 8. 2; see Bücheler in *Rh. Mus.* xxv, 1870, p. 170.

7. **quod igitur . . . afuit:** 'Very well; here is a charge which is not denied by the responsible party; the person who disclaimed responsibility has been acquitted: is my client here to be scared by it, when he had absolutely no connexion with the crime and was never even near being suspected of complicity?' Note the use of *igitur* with the relative *quod* (which is anticipatory of *id*); see note on 3. 14.

10. **si . . . invidia:** 'if Asicius gained more advantage from his trial than damage from the odium attaching to it'. *Invidia* is surely nominative, not ablative as I formerly thought: *profuit*)(*nocuit invidiâ* is a most improbable antithesis. The advantage gained by Asicius was presumably the publicity given to Ptolemy's responsibility, which more than counterbalanced the slur sustained by his being brought to trial. W., following Schöll, deletes *causa*; Müll. emends to *in causa* (supported by Schönb., p. 34); Clark suggests *ea* for *causa* in his apparatus—confusion of *ea* and *câ* is common; but how could any form of *invidia* 'bring advantage'?

**§ 24.** 12. **at . . . liberatus:** 'but, it is argued, it was collusion that gained Asicius his acquittal'; *praevaricatio* is the t.t. for collusion between prosecutor and the defence (Greenidge, *LP*, p. 470); cf. *part. or.* 124 ff. Caelius' accusers had claimed that Asicius was not justifiably acquitted, and that therefore Caelius, his alleged accomplice, was not cleared either; Cicero denies both the collusion and the implied connexion between the two men.*

13. **loco:** 'point' (τόπος).

15. **cuicuimodi:** used for the non-existent form *cuiuscuiusmodi* (Neue–Wagener, *Formenlehre* ii, p. 513); it is found only with *est*, *sunt*, etc. (see Landgraf on *Rosc. Am.* 95, Kühner on *Tusc.* iii. 83, Wilkins on *de or.* iii. 94).

16. **seiunctam:** 'unconnected', as opposed to *coniuncta causa*, where the verdict in one case has a bearing on another; cf. *Clu.* 96, *Sest.* 31 (H., p. 221), *Verr.* iii. 153 'si condemnato Apronio coniunctam cum eo Verris causam omnes erant existimaturi, Metellus quidem certe iam hoc iudicabat, eorum rem causamque esse coniunctam, qui statueret Apronio condemnato de isto praeiudicium futurum'.

17. **humanissimi . . . praediti:** 'men of the highest possible

§ 24                           COMMENTARY

sensibility and scholarship, with the advantage of the finest kind
of literary training and the most virtuous principles'; *humanissimi*
implies their feelings as human beings (cf. Landgraf on *Rosc. Am.*
46), *doctissimi* shows the way in which they had developed this
quality; by a chiasmus, the latter is taken up in *rectissimis studiis*,
the former in *optimis artibus* (*ars* here, as so often, is used of moral
quality, almost = *virtus*): cf. 54. 21, *ad Fam.* xiii. 30. 1 'virum
optimum . . . iis studiis litterarum doctrinaeque praeditum quibus
ego maxime delector'. For a different interpretation see on 20
below.

19. **Coponii:** possibly the persons mentioned in *Balb.* 53 as
grandsons of T. Coponius, 'civis item summa virtute et dignitate';
there was a C. Coponius who was praetor in 49 (*ad Att.* viii. 12a. 4,
Caes. *B.C.* iii. 5). With this text *seiunctam esse causam putant*
must be supplied: the Coponii, close friends of Dio, feel the same as
Caelius does, and their high opinion of him will show the baseless-
ness of the insinuation made against him.
    This passage has an interesting textual history. The reading
given is that of *Σ*. The first hand in *P* omitted *Coponii . . . erat ei*
(cf. Vollgraff's text); the second hand (nearly contemporary, see
Kl., praef. 1919, pp. vi, xxi) partly filled the lacuna with a corrupt
version of what *Σ* presents (see Kl.'s app. crit.). But the reading
preserved in *Σ* was known, with two important discrepancies,
from cod. Mon. 15734 (*S*, late fifteenth century, cf. p. xix),
though its authority was not realized (Müll. prints this text, with
the warning 'admodum incerta auctoritate'). These discrepancies
are *is apud Luceium* and *fuerat* (so *P²*, with the addition of *L.*
before *Luceium*), where *Σ* has *apud Titum* and *Dio erat*. It was
left to Clark to show that the reading of *S* was not an interpolation
by some fifteenth-century scholar ('homo audacissimus' Madvig,
*Op. Ac.*, p. 319), but reflected the text of *Σ* and was consequently
based on eighth-century authority. Clark further restored from *Σ* the
true reading *Titum* for *Lucceium*, which is out of place here and
was clearly introduced from § 51 (see *An. Ox.*, pp. xxxiii f.; *Descent
of MSS.*, pp. 266 f.), and *Dio erat* for *fuerat*.
    Klotz has an important discussion in *Rh. Mus.* lxvii, 1912,
pp. 359–64. He omits *qui* before *cum doctrinae studio*, making
*tenebantur* the main verb. This is an improvement, as far as it
refers to the Coponii, but in its reference to Caelius it is abrupt and
improbable, as there has been no previous mention of any friendship between Caelius and Dio, nor is such an important fact spoken
of later in § 51; I therefore prefer Cl.'s reading here. Below, Kl.
accepts *fuerat* (*P²*), and reads *habitabat is apud Titum, ut audistis,
fuerat ei cognitus*, etc.; he takes the name *Dio* in *Σ* as a gloss, and

considers that the tense of *fuerat* is essential, since Dio's connexion with Titus at Alexandria had ended before the period which Cicero is discussing. But this involves an awkward construction, by which *is* refers to Dio and *ei* to Titus; and the form *fuerat* for the pluperfect is not needed (cf. 64. 8, and see H., p. 223, note 1). I would therefore follow Cl. in accepting the full text of *Σ*.

The passage is one of a number adduced by Kl. to prove the independent value of the readings of *P²ge*, which he has shown to be derived not from *P* but from a common archetype; see *Rh. Mus.*, l.c., and Kl.'s preface (1919), p. xi.

There is an interesting examination of repeated relative clauses in S.–M. on *de am.* 27 (p. 198). In such repetitions, the second clause often has a different shade of meaning from the first: here, although the passage is not quite parallel to the type considered by S.–M., the clause *qui . . . tenebantur* is really the explanation of the previous statement *qui . . . doluerunt*. The discomfort felt by Kl. at the double relative is largely due to the difference between modern idiom and that of Latin.

Schönb. (*Woch. für kl. Phil.* 1913, col. 54) proposed *qui cum communi doctrinae studio*; see further his note in *PhW* 1933, col. 1104.

20. doctrinae . . . humanitatis: 'by his devotion to scholarship and to the principles of human conduct'; *doctrinae* corresponds to *doctissimi* above, *humanitatis* to *humanissimi*; cf. *Rosc. Am.* 46 'natura certe dedit ut humanitatis non parum haberes; eo accessit studium doctrinae ut ne a litteris quidem alienus esses'. But it would be equally possible to take *doctrinae* and *humanitatis* as a single concept ('literary and cultural interests'); cf. *Tusc.* v. 66 'quis est omnium, qui modo cum Musis, id est cum humanitate et cum doctrina, habeat aliquod commercium, qui se non hunc mathematicum malit quam illum tyrannum?' In that case, the meaning of *humanissimi . . . praediti* (above, 17–18) will be 'men of the highest possible culture and learning, with the advantage of the finest kind of literary training and liberal studies' (*ars* being taken as 'accomplishments').

21. apud Titum: apparently Dio moved here from Lucceius' house, where he was living at the time of Caelius' alleged attempt to kill him (§ 51); see H., pp. 222 f. W. misunderstands the later passage, referring it to the actual murder.

25. ut . . . veniamus: 'that at last we may reach the real facts behind the case'. Cicero again distinguishes between the formal prosecutors and the real enemy (cf. Drexler, *NGG* 1944, p. 20). H. (p. 223, note 2) suggests *continetur* for *nititur* (*conititur g*, *conicitur e*), adducing *Mur.* 31 'neque enim causa in hoc continetur'. The suggestion is attractive: cf. *Verr.* ii. 118 'cum vero in communibus

iniuriis totius provinciae Stheni quoque causa contineatur', *Rosc. Am.* 34 'ita facillime, quae res totum iudicium contineat . . . intellegetis', *Rhet. ad Herenn.* iv. 58 'commoratio est, cum in loco firmissimo, a quo tota causa continetur, manetur diutius' (*contineri* = 'centres on'). However, the correction is not essential: even though *in quibus accusatio nititur* might have been expected, the whole *causa* for both sides depends upon the animosity of Clodia.

**§§ 25–26.** '*Herennius' speech impressed you deeply, as I could see; it made an impression on me too: why, he scolded Caelius so angrily, and read him such a long lecture on Sin! However, his initial points were quite negligible and absurd.*'

In this speech, as in *Planc.* and *Mur.*, Cicero deals separately with the different speakers for the prosecution; he passes now from Atratinus to Herennius (see Appendix VI). The obscurity of these sections could be removed only if Herennius' own speech were extant; Norden infers that it made Cicero change his whole plan of defence on the spot, not a very likely supposition, for he could certainly have foreseen the general line of attack. Herennius seems to have combined generalities with personalities in a very telling way (my former view that his speech fell into two distinct parts seems to me now most unlikely).

**§ 25. 1. animadverti enim**: the connexion is 'I want to come to the real issue; for Herennius put one side of it clearly before you'— the issue being that *either* Caelius is a vicious man *or* he has been represented as such by a vicious woman.

**familiarem**: Cicero's personal relationship with both Atratinus and Herennius was friendly. W.'s view that this was the Herennius who accused Milo is untenable if Clark's punctuation of Asconius p. 30 KS (adduced by W.) is accepted (contrast, however, Clark's earlier note on p. 99 of his *pro Milone*). Possibly he was related to the C. Herennius who furthered Clodius' transference to the plebs in 60 (*ad Att.* i. 19. 5); Schöll (*Rh. Mus.* li, 1896, p. 381) identifies him with one of the prosecutors of Flaccus in 59 (see Webster's edition, p. 56).

**2. perattente:** Cicero is fond of *per-* compounds in this speech, some of them not found elsewhere; cf. §§ 50, 58, 69. They are a feature of colloquial Latin: Laur. notes that there are more of them in the *pro Caelio* than in any other speech delivered after the Verrines (see his analysis, pp. 271 ff., and cf. Parzinger, op. cit., pp. 44 f., Madvig on *de fin.* iii. 36). See J. André, *RÉL* xxix, 1951, pp. 121–54.

**in quo:** 'where he was concerned' (to be taken with *verebar*, not with the concessive clause). Cicero means here that although

Herennius held his audience primarily by his brilliant style, yet (*tamen*) a more serious danger to Caelius lay in the imperceptible effect of his matter.*

3. **dicendi genere quodam:** 'a particular quality of style'; *quodam* is not contemptuous, as W. thinks, but complimentary; Cicero knew the value of such compliments (cf. § 8, and see Quintil. iv. 1. 11). *Dicendi genus* is one of the normal ways of expressing 'style' in oratory (*oratio* and *sermo* are also used for style in speech, but *stilus* refers always to written work).

4. **subtiliter ... inducta:** 'tellingly planned for an incriminating effect'; *subtilis* (originally 'finely woven', of textiles, as in Catull. 64. 63 'subtilem mitram') has various metaphorical uses in connexion with style, with the basic sense of 'precision' always present (see Sandys on *Orat.* 20, Wilkins on *de or.* i. 17), and is particularly associated with the 'plain style' in oratory, which was essentially dialectical in character (cf. my note on Quintil. xii. 10. 58). Cicero means that Herennius' speech was full of shrewd argument, a 'finely woven fabric' to incriminate Caelius, and he fears that its logic may affect the jury. *Inducta* suggests the idea of being 'laid on' to lead up to the desired effect.

5. **sensim ... accederet:** 'imperceptibly and gently insinuate itself'. The text is uncertain (*leniter g, leviter P; accederet Pge, accideret codd. recentiores*). Müll. and W. read *leniter accideret*, which may be ruled out as involving too dactylic a clausula; Kl. reads *leviter accideret*, which also provides a doubtful clausula.

As between the two verbs, *accedere* is the only possible choice. It is true that (as Schönb. points out, p. 35) *accidere* is commonly used of a sound or a voice impinging on the hearing (*Thes. L. L.* s.v., col. 290. 84 ff.), whereas for *accedere* in that sense there are no prose examples (*Thes. L. L.* s.v., col. 263. 1 ff.); but this is not the meaning required. It was not the sound of Herennius' voice falling upon the jury's ears that Cicero feared, but the 'approach' of his words to their minds, a meaning to which *accedere* is perfectly suited.

As between the adverbs, either *leniter* or *leviter* is possible as far as the clausula is concerned, with the balance slightly in favour of the former, judging from Zielinski's statistics. Löfstedt shows that *levis* and *leviter* often approach so nearly to the sense of *lenis* and *leniter* that they are almost interchangeable (*Coniectanea* i, p. 75); he notes Sen. *de tranq. an.* 13. 3 'necesse est autem levius ad animum pervenire destitutae cupiditatis dolorem, cui successum non utique promiseris', *Epp.* 78. 29 'quicquid exspectatum est diu, levius accedit'. But *leniter* seems to me to suit *sensim* better, and I see no good ground for departing from Cl.'s text.

7. **qui ... disseruit:** 'although he is a kindly man as a rule, and

79

generally is quite charming in his employment of those pleasantly well-bred manners which most people nowadays like, yet in this case he behaved like the sourest sort of uncle, critic, dominie: he hectored Caelius, as no father ever did his own son; he gave a long lecture on wild and riotous living.'

8. **esset . . . soleret:** concessive (English idiom needs a present tense); Cicero sometimes uses an indicative in this type of sentence, e.g. *Phil.* viii. 19 'Caesar ipse, qui illis fuerat iratissimus, tamen . . . cotidie aliquid iracundiae remittebat', *leg. Man.* 55 'nos, quorum maiores Antiochum . . . superarunt . . ., ii nullo in loco iam praedonibus pares esse poteramus'; see K. II. ii, pp. 294 f.*

**hac:** as often, 'this that we see round us', 'familiar', 'usual'. *Humanitas* implies civilized, gentlemanly behaviour.

9. **versari:** when used of moral or mental qualities, *versari in* nearly means 'to display' (N., p. 467); cf. *in Cat.* iv. 7 'uterque . . . in summa severitate versatur'.

10. **pertristis:** cf. note on 13. 22.

**patruus:** for the proverbially stern uncle, cf. Hor. *C.* iii. 12. 3, *Sat.* ii. 2. 97, 3. 88, Manil. v. 454, Persius i. 11; see Otto s.vv. *patruus, tutor.*

12. **quid quaeritis?:** 'in short'; a regular formula in summing up.

13. **ignoscebam . . . horrebam:** 'I began to excuse you for your close attention, because I myself was shivering before his extremely glum and grim manner of speaking'. *Horrebam* is probably ironical.

**audientibus:** this use of the participle is frequent after concessive verbs, although Lebr. (p. 405) claims that it is rare in Cicero; cf. *de off.* i. 71 'iis forsitan concedendum sit rem publicam non capessentibus' (where see Holden), *Tusc.* ii. 19, *de fin.* ii. 57, *de or.* ii. 203, Quintil. iii. 4. 4 'ut mihi in illa vetere persuasione permanenti velut petenda sit venia'.

**§ 26. 15. prima pars:** Herennius seems to have begun with some desultory remarks of a personal kind, to show that Caelius was habitually disloyal to his friends; Cicero no doubt distorts them to suit his purpose.

16. **Bestiae:** see Appendix VI, p. 154; the allusion would be obscure if Münzer had not shown that Bestia was Atratinus' father, towards whom Caelius was now so implacable.

18. **etenim . . . dicere:** the alleged witnesses to Caelius' presence at Bestia's dinner-table are either nowhere to be seen or so much under Herennius' influence that they say what he says.

20. **neque vero . . . dixit:** Cicero's point is not comprehensible without knowledge of what Herennius had said. Presumably at this period membership of the college of Luperci had fallen into

disrepute (cf. Wissowa, *Religion und Kultus der Römer*, pp. 484, note 7, 560); cf. the scandal resulting from Antony's behaviour at the festival: whatever had been the nature of Herennius' gibe (based upon his and Caelius' common membership of the college), Cicero evidently twists it to recoil upon him. See H., p. 226.

21. **fera ... videantur:** 'a quite savage brotherhood this, downright rustic and uncouth, consisting of those genuine wolf-men whose famous woodland pack was founded long before civilization and law! Why, its brethren not only lay information against one another, but even flaunt their membership of the brotherhood in so doing, afraid, I suppose, lest anyone should be ignorant of it.' Cicero malevolently pretends that the modern Luperci are just as primitive in their manners as the original priests of Faunus must have been.

**quaedam:** intensifying, as often with an adjective; cf. *Tusc.* ii. 11 'te natura excelsum quendam ... et altum ... genuit', *de domo* 60 'hostificum quoddam et nefarium ... bellum', where see Nisbet; see K. II. i, pp. 643 f.

22. **agrestis:** there is no *urbanitas* about them (cf. note on 6. 25).

23. **Lupercorum:** Cicero probably intended this in the popular sense, 'wolf-priests', nearly equivalent to *luporum* (cf. W. F. Otto, *Philologus* lxxii, pp. 165 ff.); if he meant 'wolf-averters' (the theory of Servius, see Pauly–Wissowa, *RE* s.v., Wissowa, *Religion und Kultus*, p. 209, Deubner, *Archiv für Religionswissenschaft* xiii, pp. 481 ff.), the sense would be 'genuine wolf-averters indeed, fighting as they do with their own pack'.

For the Luperci and the Lupercalia see Frazer, *The Fasti of Ovid* ii, pp. 327 ff., where there is a summary of theories, Warde Fowler, *Roman Festivals*, pp. 310 ff.; F. Altheim, *A History of Roman Religion*, pp. 206 ff., discusses the meaning of *luperci* in the light of the possibility that the name of Faunus himself (whom they served as priests) means 'wolf'; cf. also K. Kerényi in *Mélanges Marouzeau*, pp. 308 ff.

**silvestris:** here the passage contained in *Ox. Pap.* x. 1251 (*Π*) begins.

24. **si quidem:** causal, as often in Cicero; see K. II. ii, p. 427.

**§ 27. 27. omitto:** Schönb., p. 36, remarks that Cicero always uses the indicative in the singular formula, but the subjunctive *omittamus* is invariable in the plural.

**§§ 27–30.** '*Herennius spoke much about the dissipated manners of modern youth; but you must not allow yourselves to be prejudiced against Caelius' case by generalities.*'

Cicero now comes to the more serious aspect of Herennius'

speech, which might spell real danger to Caelius; for a discussion of the argument of these sections see Drexler, op. cit., pp. 22 ff.; H., pp. 226 f.

**§ 27. 1. deliciarum obiurgatio:** 'his scolding of dissipation'. *Deliciae* here corresponds to the *luxuries, libido, vitia iuventutis* of § 25. The word always implies the lighter forms of pleasure, and more often suggests moral decadence than innocent enjoyment (note Stat. *S.* i. 3. 92 'luxuque carentes deliciae'): so *deliciis diffluere* is used of complete sensual abandonment (cf. S.–M. on *de am.* 52, p. 354). Sometimes it means something like 'affectation', 'posing' (so Quintil. i. 11. 6 uses it of an affected manner in speech, Cic. *ad Att.* i. 17. 9 of irresponsible behaviour). *In deliciis esse* = 'to be a favourite', and *deliciae* is thence transferred to the person or creature that is a 'pet' (so Lesbia's *passer*, Catull. 3. 1; Suet. *Tit.* 1 'amor ac deliciae generis humani', of the Emperor Titus; cf. Plaut. *Poen.* 365 'mea voluptas, mea delicia'.) *Delicatus* likewise has generally a bad sense, 'spoilt', 'pampered', or worse (so Martial iv. 30. 16 speaks of some tame fish as *delicati*).*

   **etiam lenior:** so Cl., for *et ea lenior* of MSS., including Π (which Kl. retains); *et eo* Kayser; *et eo lenior quo plus disputationis* W.; *et verbis quam sententia lenior* H. (p. 225, note 1); Cl., noting that Σ reads *alienior* for *lenior*, suggested *et a causa alienior* (cf. 23. 10, note).*

   The textual problem is bound up with that of the meaning of *lenior*. Attempts to explain it have assumed that it must mean 'less severe', as compared with the passage about the Luperci (so W.) or with the *asperum genus orationis* of § 25 (so Norden, but those words clearly apply to the whole speech, including the *deliciarum obiurgatio*—cf. H., p. 225, note 1). Neither suggestion is acceptable; I regard *lenior* as being much more probably an 'absolute' comparative = 'on the quiet side': it must be connected with the following 'plusque disputationis habuit quam atrocitatis', and with Cicero's fears 'ne illa subtiliter ad criminandum inducta oratio ad animos vestros sensim ac leniter accederet', which show clearly the character of Herennius' speech. It was precisely this deadly quietness that won him his hearing, as contrasted with the ranting of P. Clodius, whom Cicero so contemptuously dismisses. An *obiurgatio* does not necessarily imply violent anger; cf. *de or.* ii. 339 'admonitio, quasi lenior obiurgatio', *de am.* 88 'et monendi amici saepe sunt et obiurgandi, et haec accipienda amice, cum benevole fiunt', *de nat. deor.* i. 5 'benevolos obiurgatores placare et invidos vituperatores confutare'.

   With this interpretation, there is no difficulty about the MSS. *et ea*, which I should prefer to retain. Cl.'s *etiam* is hard to understand, if indeed it has any meaning here; his other suggestion, *a causa alienior*, though very tempting palaeographically, is ruled out by two considerations—Herennius' main argument was only too relevant to the case, as Cicero well knew, and if it *had* been *a causa alienior* Cicero could not have said that it 'impressed him more' than the casual personalities that preceded it. Kayser's *eo lenior* seems unintelligible, and the emendations of both W. and H. give no improvement on the MSS. reading. Müll. obelizes the text. Drexler treats the passage sensibly (op. cit., p. 22, note 31).

2. **disputationis . . . atrocitatis:** 'subtlety' . . . 'savagery'; *disputatio* implies dialectical argument, *subtiliter ad criminandum inducta*.

3. **nam P. Clodius . . . pertimescebam:** 'I need hardly mention my friend P. Clodius: he certainly flung himself about with much vigour and energy, and was white-hot throughout in conducting his speech, employing the most acid language and shouting at the pitch of his voice; I gave him a good mark for his eloquence, but all the same he had no terrors for me'. Cicero dismisses Clodius (probably not the famous tribune, see Appendix VI, p. 155) as a mere *latrator* or *rabula*.

**nam:** this elliptical use, 'praetereuntis', has the effect of putting the statement into a position of minor importance; see S.–M. on *de am.* 45 (p. 312), K. II. ii, pp. 117 ff.

**amicus meus:** ironical; cf. *Mil.* 46 'ut Q. Arrius, amicus meus, dixit', and Clark ad loc.

4. **inflammatus:** the absolute use is abnormal; Cl. suggests *inflatius*.*

7. **Balbe:** i.e. Herennius.

8. **precario:** 'begging your leave', ironical (sometimes it means 'on sufferance', e.g. Tac. *G.* 44. 3, Sen. *Epp.* 53. 8, where see Summers).

**si licet:** W. and Kl. read *scilicet*, with later MSS.; but *si licet* (now supported by *Π*) balances admirably with *si fas est*; Sydow (*Rh. Mus.* xci, 1942, p. 357) notes *leg. agr.* ii. 19 'quoad fas esset, quoad liceret'.*

9. **qui in hortis fuerit:** these words are not in the MSS., but occur in the passage as quoted by Donatus, on Ter. *Hec.* 551. W. and Kl. delete them, following Oetling (p. 13). But in §§ 38 and 49 *horti* and *Baiae* are mentioned together, and Cicero is obviously picking up Herennius' remarks at random; his audience would know that the *horti* belonged to Clodia, but the irony is heightened by the omission of any name ('a man who has never refused an invitation to dinner, who has actually been in a park, who has used unguents, who has taken a trip to Baiae'), and the interruption of

thought between *convivium* and *unguenta* is not really important. For the meaning of *horti*, see on 36. 27; the plural is invariable in this sense.*

**10. Baias:** see note on 35. **10.** *Viderit* is taken by Leo (*Hermes* xxxvii, 1902, p. 315) as the perfect of *visere*; cf. *Verr*. iv. 7, where Baiter emends *viderit* (so MSS.) to *viserit*, as also here; *ad Att*. i. 4. 1 is said to be the only passage where the form *visi* finds support. But *videre* can bear the meaning 'go to see': cf. Pliny, *N.H.* ix. 172 'cuius (*sc*. murenae) propter famam nonnulli Baulos videre concupiverunt'.

**§ 28. 10. equidem . . . fuisse:** see the parallel passage in § 43 (cf. Appendix VIII); there may perhaps be a covert allusion to Caesar in both.

**11. primoribus labris . . . extremis . . . digitis:** quasi-proverbial expressions for superficiality; cf. *de nat. deor*. i. 20, *de or*. i. 87, Quintil. xii. 2. 4, Plaut. *Bacch*. 675 (*digitulis primoribus*), Lucian, *Demonax* 4 (κατὰ τὴν παροιμίαν ἄκρῳ τῷ δακτύλῳ ἁψάμενος); see Otto s.vv. *labrum*, *digitus*.

**14. se . . . recepisse:** 'turned over a new leaf'. *Π* reads *ad bonam frugem*, which Kl. adopts as being the more usual order (*bonae frugi* is especially common in Plautus); see *BPhW* 1914, col. 956. Cf. Lamprid. *Heliog*. 15. 1 'si . . . impuros homines . . . a se dimoveret atque ad bonam frugem rediret' Plaut. *Bacch*. 1085, *Trin*. 118, 270; *frugem* implies maturity, and hence excellence of mind (Quintil. i. 3. 3 'illud ingeniorum velut praecox genus non temere unquam pervenit ad frugem'). It is odd that these three proverbial expressions should occur in one sentence; but they give a pleasant touch of lightness to Cicero's irony.

**16. datur . . . aetati:** 'for everyone agrees in allowing a young man a few love-affairs'; for *ludus, ludere* in such a context cf. Livy xxvi. 50 'si frui liceret ludo aetatis, praesertim recto et legitimo amore', Plaut. *Bacch*. 129 'non omnis aetas, Lyde, ludo convenit', Varro, *Sat. Men*. 87 'properate vivere puerae, quas sinit aetatula ludere, esse, amare et Veneris tenere bigas'. See the parallel in § 42, 'detur aliqui ludus aetati'.

**17. profundit:** cf. 75. 22; the sense is made clear from the parallel in 41. 21 ff. For this use of *fundere* and its compounds to mean 'develop', cf. *de or*. ii. 88 'facilius sicut in vitibus revocantur ea quae se nimium profuderunt', Quintil. i. 3. 5 (*se effundere*), xii. 2. 23 (*se fundere*), Lucr. i. 175 (*fundi*); see N., pp. 446, 483.

**18. ita . . . ut:** limitative; 'if they have their outbursts without shattering anyone's life'. Cf. 42. 10.

**§ 29. 21. conflare:** 'to engineer' prejudice; cf. *in Cat*. i. 23 'mihi inimico . . . tuo conflare vis invidiam', *Clu*. 79 'summam illi iudicio invidiam infamiamque esse conflatam'.

COMMENTARY   §§ 29-30

24. **luxuriem:** 'profligacy', as often; so too *luxuriosus* (cf. the eurious passage in Quintil. *decl. min.* 298, Ritter, p. 179).

**dies ... deficiat:** 'daylight would soon fail me'; a rhetorical commonplace, cf. *de nat. deor.* iii. 81, *Tusc.* v. 102, *Verr.* ii. 52, *Rosc. Am.* 89 (*deficeret*, where see Landgraf), *Verr.* iv. 59 (*defecerit*), *de fin.* ii. 62, Macrob. *Sat.* vi. 6. 20, Apul. *Apol.* 54 (*deficiet*); so Demosth. *de cor.* 296 ἐπιλείψει με λέγονθ' ἡ ἡμέρα, Isocr. *Archid.* 81 ἐπιλίποι δ' ἂν τὸ λοιπὸν μέρος τῆς ἡμέρας.*

25. **expromere:** 'to bring to light', as if from a store.

26. **protervitate:** 'lascivious conduct'; the word implies misdirected animal spirits.

27. **ut ... potest:** 'even though one has no specific person to accuse, but only the general topic of such vices before one, the subject in itself offers scope for a lengthy and severe attack'. *Ista* is Cl.'s emendation of *ipsa* (Σ), which is omitted in *P*; it would not be a necessary change if *res tamen ipsa* did not follow. Kl. accepts *P*'s text, but this somewhat lames the rhythm. W., following Bake, deletes *sed vitia*, on no good ground.

28. **sed vestrae ... vocatus:** 'but sensible men like you must not be side-tracked from the accused; you are strict and responsible persons, and as such you have a sting to use; now the prosecutor has directed it against generalities, the dissolute behaviour and immorality of the age, and you must not employ it against a single individual in the dock, when it is not through his personal fault but through the laxity of the many that he has to face a form of prejudicial attack which he does not deserve.'

2. **aculeos:** cf. *Clu.* 152 'evellere se aculeum severitatis vestrae posse confidunt', *Sull.* 47 'noli aculeos orationis meae, qui reconditi sunt, excussos arbitrari', *Flacc.* 86 'eodem etiam M. Lurco ... convertit aculeum testimoni sui'. Here the 'sting' is in the jury's prospective verdict, not in a speaker's oratory or a witness's evidence; so Aristophanes says of the dicasts in the *Wasps* (225) ἔχουσι γὰρ καὶ κέντρον ἐκ τῆς ὀσφύος ὀξύτατον, ᾧ κεντοῦσι (contrast Eupolis' phrase of Pericles, quoted by Pliny, *Epp.* i. 20. 17, τὸ κέντρον ἐγκατέλειπε τοῖς ἀκροωμένοις).

**habeat:** so Π²P; *habet* Kl., Π¹Σ: see p. xx.

§ 30. 5. **itaque ego:** so Cl., Kl., with Σ; *ego* om. *P* (so Müll.); Schönb. notes (p. 37) that *ego* is rarely found immediately following *itaque*.

6. **tuae:** Cicero turns from the jury to Herennius.

**erat ... petere:** 'for I might have pleaded for the concessions that a young man should have, and have begged forgiveness for him'. *Deprecari* is used of interceding for something in danger; cf. *Planc.* 102 'non ego meis ornatum beneficiis a vobis deprecor',

85

and Holden's note. *Vacatio* = freedom from blame, trouble, etc., practically 'excuse'; cf. *de leg*. i. 10 'aetatis . . . vacationi confidebam'; Nep. *Att*. 7 'usus est aetatis vacatione' (both with reference to an old man).*

8. **perfugiis . . . aetatis:** 'I am not taking refuge in the plea of his youth.' Cicero has remarked in § 28 that 'boys will be boys'; here he pretends, magnanimously, that he will not use this argument on Caelius' behalf—all he asks is that Caelius shall not suffer as a scapegoat for others.

9. **ut . . . ne . . . noceant:** a good example of the 'stipulative' use of *ut ne* (see note on 8. 11).

**si qua est . . . iuventutis:** 'whatever general prejudice there is in our generation against the debts, profligacy, and debauched ways of young men'. See H., pp. 227 ff., for a discussion of the tactics of both sides here; he assumes that Herennius had been forced into generalities because he dared not mention Caelius' real relations with Clodia, which seems to me unlikely, for if Herennius had not spoken of it, Cicero need never have referred to the subject either. Herennius must have mentioned it, but only to throw all guilt on Caelius, not thinking that Cicero would dare to make a public attack upon Clodia: but Cicero did dare (§§ 49 ff.), and although he could not deny Caelius' conduct, he turned the tables on Herennius by a damning indictment of Clodia's whole life. See further Reitzenstein's remarks (op. cit., p. 32) on H.'s view, and Drexler's comments (op. cit., p. 25).

14. **proprie:** 'in person', as opposed to generalities. Sydow (*Hermes* lxv, 1930, p. 319), noting that the reading of *g* and *e* is *in hunc mundum*, proposed *in hunc eundem*, comparing (for the repeated use of *idem*) *Sull*. 20, *prov. cons*. 17.

15. **recuso:** this can seldom be translated 'refuse', which is normally *nego* or *nolo*; it implies 'kicking against something', to object or demur.

**§§ 30–32.** '*The real charges are two: one concerning some gold, one concerning some poison. Both are connected with Clodia. She is the real foe, but I will treat her mercifully.*'

Cicero pretends that he is at last to deal with the actual charges. But it is only a feint, and he uses Clodia's name (mentioned here explicitly for the first time) merely to play with it, cat-and-mouse fashion, to amuse the jury until he is ready for the kill. The passage from § 30 to § 50 forms a special part of the *praemunitio*, devoted to clearing away the awkward side of Herennius' revelations in so far as they were damaging to Caelius. Cf. H., pp. 230 ff.; Reitzenstein, op. cit., pp. 28 ff.

§ 30. 16. auri: apparently gold ornaments (see § 52).

→ 17. aurum ... dicitur: these words are nearly repeated in § 51, by obvious design. Schöll deletes the sentence as an interpolation, on the ground that the mention of Clodia's name is premature here; but it is excellent drama, and the name is tellingly placed. Kl. (*Rh. Mus.* lxvii, 1912, pp. 373 f.) accepted Schöll's argument, but retained *ut dicitur*; but in his text he rightly retracted this view. See Norden, pp. 26 f. (but his treatment of the sentence as an improvisation is fanciful), Reitzenstein, op. cit., p. 25, Opperskalski (see bibliography), p. 81.

19. alia: = *cetera*, a frequent use when *alius* and *omnis* are joined; see *Thes. L. L.* s.v., col. 1648. 16 ff.; Lebr., pp. 109 f.; Krebs s.v., p. 144.

iurgi ... quaestionis: 'more suited to some loutish brawl than to a court of justice'.

20. sequester: see on 16. 26; it seems at first sight strange after *adulter*, *impudicus*, but it implies the use of corrupt practices, and so is in place; perhaps 'briber's tout' might suit. For *convicium* below, see on 6. 25.

22. nullae sedes: Kl. may be justified in reading (with *P*) *nullo*, in spite of the authority of both *Σ* and *Π* for the plural; as he points out, the plural does not suit *fundamentum*; and in *part. or.* 31, Sen. *N.Q.* i. 1. 10, where *sedes* and *fundamentum* are also connected, the singular form is used.*

voces ... emissae: 'they are abusive taunts, hurled wildly by a man who has lost his temper and speaks with no one to back his words'.

§ 31. 24. horum ... caput: 'but as for the two charges that I have mentioned, I can see that someone is at the back of *them*, I can see a source, I can see a very definite personage as their fountain-head'. *Auctorem* is contrasted with *nullo auctore* above; this reading (*Σ*) gives a more forceful order than that of *P* and *Π*, which reverses *auctorem* and *fontem* (see Kl. ad loc.): Lindholm (*Stilistische Studien*, p. 170, note 2) has not realized the force of the juxtaposition. The point of this sentence is not the identity of the *auctor*, but the fact that there is an *auctor*, which enables Cicero to regard the two *crimina* as in a different category from the 'voces nullo auctore emissae': thus the mention of Clodia's name above does not weaken its effect.

25. caput: cf. *de or.* i. 42 'philosophorum greges iam ab illo fonte et capite Socrate', *Planc.* 18 'ad caput et ad fontem utriusque generis veniamus', *ad Fam.* xii. 10. 1 'cotidie quae volumus audimus, sed adhuc sine capite, sine auctore, rumore nuntio'; see *Thes. L. L.* s.v., col. 424. 53 ff., Landgraf on *Rosc. Am.* 74, and cf.

Warde Fowler, *Aeneas at the Site of Rome*, pp. 41 f., an interesting note.

**26. maximum . . . familiaritatis:** 'ah, I can detect valuable evidence of a quite unusual intimacy' (*egregius* is ironical, as often; for *quidam* intensifying an adjective see on 26. 21).

**27. necare . . . voluit:** note the disarmingly simple manner, as if such a proceeding was quite natural.

**1. sollicitavit:** 'bribed'; the verb is very common in the sense of 'tampering' with a person's honesty.

**servos, potionem:** so Cl., Kl., with Baehrens (*Revue de Philologie* viii, 1884, p. 47); *quos potuit Pπδ*. W. retains the MS. reading, but his defence is weak, and I cannot see how *paravit* can stand, without an object, following *sollicitavit quos potuit*. Kl. considered the passage afresh in his 1919 preface (p. lx), doubting the order of the different actions as Baehrens's conjecture shows them, and holding now that *quos potuit* is sound: he would eject *paravit*, however, and suggests that a satisfactory order is obtained by reading *quaesivit venenum, sollicitavit quos potuit, locum constituit, attulit*. But if *quos potuit* can be kept, *paravit* need not be deleted, but transferred to follow *venenum*, as Kl. appears himself to suggest as an alternative; cf. 58. 2 'ubi quaesitum est [*sc.* venenum], quem ad modum paratum?' (see also Sydow, *Rh. Mus.* xci, 1942, p. 357). In support of *quos potuit*, it should be stated that this is not only the reading of *P* but of *Σ* and also of *Π* (corrected here from *voluit* by a second hand); and it seems just possible that it is sound, weak though it appears, and that Cicero meant to be vague, since part of his subsequent defence lay in showing the improbability of the allegation that Caelius had had dealings with Clodia's slaves (57. 6 'cui denique commisit?' etc.). On the whole, I should prefer to accept it, and to read *quaesivit venenum, paravit, sollicitavit quos potuit*; Baehrens's conjecture is specious, but not essential to the sense, nor entirely satisfactory when the evidence for *quos potuit* is considered.

**2. clam attulit:** so Cl., noting that *Σ* reads *quam* before *locum*; but *attulit* alone is more dramatic (cf. Kl. ad loc.), and there is no real point in *clam* here. Housman proposed *horam locum constituit, attulit*, which gives admirable sense (*JPh* xxxii, 1913, pp. 267–8): he points out that *quam* must be seriously regarded as a remnant of an actual word, and compares Hor. *Sat.* i. 4. 15 'detur nobis locus, hora', Martial xi. 73. 2 'constituisque horam constituisque locum', with other evidence. The conjecture seems certain.

**3. rursus:** 'after all'; the *odium* is contrasted with the *familiaritas*.

**discidio:** 'rupture'; it applies both to a separation of lovers and to a divorce; for the form of the word, see Madvig's second excursus to his *de finibus*.

**exstitisse**: 'had taken shape' (*exsistere* = 'to come into existence').

Quintil. comments (v. 13. 30) 'artificis autem est invenire in actione adversarii quae inter semet ipsa pugnent aut pugnare videantur, quae aliquando ex rebus ipsis manifesta sunt, ut in causa Caeliana Clodia aurum se Caelio commodasse dicit, quod signum magnae familiaritatis est, venenum sibi paratum, quod summi odii argumentum est'.

→ **5. muliere**: Axelson (*Unpoetische Wörter*, pp. 53 ff.), after examining the use of *mulier* and *femina*, finds that the latter is rare in Republican Latin; *mulier* is the normal word in Cicero, *femina* (when not used in antithesis with *vir*) being used, generally with an adjective, to mark distinction in character or status; *femina* predominates in the poets, and Tacitus prefers it to *mulier*. Cf. note on 34. 23, 63. 9.

**nobili . . . nota**: 'of noble birth . . . of notoriety' (cf. *Verr. Act. Prim.* 15, *Flacc.* 52); but Cicero's audience would find another sense present in *nobilis* (cf. Donatus on Ter. *Hec.* 797 'et meretrix et gladiator nobiles dici solent', Ter. *Heaut.* 227 'procax, magnifica, sumptuosa, nobilis', also of a *meretrix*). Quintil. (ix. 4. 98) quotes the words to illustrate a type of clausula.

**§ 32. 7. Cn. Domiti**: the president of the court, Cn. Domitius Calvinus, tribune in 59 (when he supported Bibulus against Caesar), consul in 53; he was a Caesarian in the Civil War, was consul again in 40, and then went to Spain as governor (see Drumann–Gröbe ii, p. 9; *CIL* ii. 6186). He had presided at Bestia's trial for *ambitus* (*Q.F.* ii. 3. 6), yet the case of Sestius *de vi* in March of this year was heard before M. Aemilius Scaurus (*Sest.* 101, 116). Probably the arrangements concerning presidents were adjustable (see Greenidge, *LP*, p. 430).

**10. petulanter . . . nominamus**: 'our conduct is grossly offensive, in that we are using the name of a Roman lady in a manner which is far from the due of a married lady's virtue'. Cicero maliciously stresses Clodia's position as a *matrona* (cf. § 57), to which her behaviour was so unsuited; cf. Hor. *Epp.* i. 18. 3 'ut matrona meretrici dispar erit', and Plautus *passim*.

**13. quid est aliud . . . repellamus**: 'the refutation of those who attack him is the only course open to us who are his counsel'; the emphasis lies on the *nisi*-clause (cf. Reid on *de sen.* 5, p. 74, Landgraf on *Rosc. Am.* 54, p. 121).

**16. inimicitiae**: the plural is always used, except where the abstract conception of enmity is meant, as in *Tusc.* iv. 16 and 21.

Cicero pretends that he does not want to seem spiteful because of his quarrel with Clodia's brother.

**viro:** Cicero's wit is not always in good taste. For the figure *reprehensio* or 'self-correction' (ἐπανόρθωσις), see Sandys on *Orat.* 135.

**fratrem:** so *Σ*, Cl.; *fratre P*, Kl. (cf. *Rh. Mus.* lxvii, 1912, p. 373); both readings have the support of an ancient *testimonium* (see app. crit.), but Ciceronian usage is in favour of the ablative, for normally a word repeated from an oblique case remains unaltered; contrast *Flacc.* 13 'qui comitatus in inquirendo—comitatum dico ?' with *Phil.* v. 49 'utinam C. Caesari, patri dico, contigisset'. See the careful discussion in Schönb., pp. 37 f., Mayor on Pliny, *Epp.* iii. 2. 2; K. II. i, p. 245.

→ **20. amicam omnium:** another jest (cf. Quintil. ix. 2. 99); Cicero's ironical gallantry makes it pleasant to think of Plutarch's wild story (*Cic.* 29) that Clodia wished to marry him.

**§§ 33–34.** '*Well, how would she like me to treat her? Suppose, to begin with, I conjure up one of those grand old Claudii to talk to her, say, Appius Claudius Caecus: he will know how to sum her up.*'

The following passage is a particular form of what was called in rhetoric προσωποποιία, a 'speech in character', by which someone long dead was made to speak, or some other impersonation given. It excited the admiration of ancient critics, and is a first-rate piece of acting; see Quintil. iii. 8. 54, xii. 10. 61; Priscian, *GL* iii. 437. 34; Halm, *RLM* i, pp. 23, 72. Two other famous Ciceronian examples are *in Cat.* i. 18 ('tecum, Catilina, sic agit [patria] et quodam modo tacita loquitur') and 27 ('si mecum patria . . . si cuncta Italia, si omnis respublica loquatur: M. Tulli, quid agis ?'); cf. *Planc.* 12, *de fin.* iv. 61, *Tusc.* ii. 46, and note Demetrius π. ἑρμ. 265 παραλαμβάνοιτο δ' ἂν σχῆμα διανοίας πρὸς δεινότητα ἡ προσωποποιία καλουμένη, οἷον· Δόξατε ὑμῖν τοὺς προγόνους ὀνειδίζειν καὶ λέγειν τάδε τινὰ ἢ τὴν Ἑλλάδα ἢ τὴν πατρίδα, λαβοῦσαν γυναικὸς σχῆμα.

It was essentially a feature of the 'grand style' in oratory; so Quintil. says of such a speaker (xii. 10. 61) 'hic orator et defunctos excitabit ut Appium Caecum, apud hunc et patria ipsa exclamabit'; Cicero remarks of a 'plain-style' speaker 'non faciet rem publicam loquentem nec ab inferis mortuos excitabit', and adds 'valentiorum haec laterum sunt', i.e. the figure needs 'stronger lungs' than such an orator will possess (*Orat.* 85; see Sandys's notes there, and his extract from Robert Hall's *Sermon* of 1803). Quintil. discusses its technique at some length in ix. 2. 29 ff.; in xi. 1. 39 he shows that the speaker changed his tone to suit the character ('dandique sunt iis, quibus vocem accommodamus, sui mores; aliter enim P.

Clodius, aliter Appius Caecus, aliter Caecilianus ille, aliter Terentianus pater fingitur'). See also *Brut.* 322, *de or.* i. 245, iii. 205, *part. orat.* 55, *Top.* 45.

In a wider sense, the term is used of any passage where the orator imagines another person as speaking, e.g. the prosecuting counsel, or the defendant (as in *Rosc. Am.* 32); see Oetling, *Librorum manuscriptorum qui Ciceronis orationem pro Caelio continent, qualis sit conditio, examinatur,* Göttingen, 1868, p. 48. It is also used of certain types of rhetorical exercise (Quintil. iii. 8. 49 ff.; cf. Colson on i. 8. 3). Cf. Sir P. Sidney on the Psalms, in his *Apologie for Poetrie.*

Cicero's tactics here are masterly; even by the end of § 38 he must have known that he had won his case, with Clodia laughed out of court.

**§ 33. 23. severe ... urbane:** 'in a stern, solemn, antique manner, or light-heartedly, playfully, in a smart modern way'. The antithesis between *prisce* and *urbane* throws some light on the Roman conception of *urbanitas* (see on 6. 25); *prisce* evidently conveyed an idea of old-fashioned uncouthness or 'rusticity', in contrast to the up-to-date smartness of 'modern' men-about-town.*

**24. austero:** 'bleak'; the word is used especially of a 'dry' wine (so Cato, *de agri cult.* 126, and often in Celsus and Columella), or of a 'sober' colour or a pungent scent; cf. αὐστηρός. Such an adjective is rarely used with *modo,* which normally has attached to it only demonstratives, numerals, or such words as *par, idem,* etc.; here the collocation with *more* accounts for it; cf. *Verr.* ii. 9 'si humano modo, si usitato more' (N., p. 215).

**ab inferis:** cf. Cic. *Orat.* 85, Quintil. xii. 10. 61 (quoted above), and the famous story of Pompey in Val. Max. vi. 2. 8.

**25. ex barbatis ... non hac barbula:** 'from among those big-bearded men of old, not anyone with a neat little beard as they are now worn'. The older fashion had been for long, full beards; Pliny (*N.H.* vii. 211) states that Scipio Africanus the younger was the first Roman to shave daily. Elegant youths, like Clodius, now wore a carefully trimmed beard, grown after the ceremony of the *depositio barbae,* as may be seen from coins of the period and of the earlier Empire; cf. *ad Att.* i. 14. 5 'concursabant barbatuli iuvenes', Sen. *Epp.* 115. 2 'iuvenes barba et coma nitidos, de capsula totos ('fresh from a bandbox'); see T. Frank, *AJP* xl, 1919, pp. 396 ff. Hadrian brought the full beard back into fashion.

See Mayor on Juv. 16. 31, Daremberg–Saglio s.v. *barba,* Marquardt, *Privatleben,* pp. 579 ff., D. B. Kaufman in *Classical Weekly* xxv, no. 19. The curious would find interest in H. Mötefindt, *Zur Geschichte der Barttracht im alten Orient.* Leipzig, 1923.

Cf. *Sest.* 18, where Gabinius, 'unguentis affluens calamistrata coma', is contrasted with Piso,'unum aliquem . . . ex barbatis illis, exemplum imperi veteris, imaginem antiquitatis, columen rei publicae' (an instructive passage).

**26. horrida:** 'unkempt', not *nitida*.

**2. Caecus ille:** Appius Claudius Caecus, censor in 312, consul in 307 and 296, builder of the Appian Way and the Aqua Appia (Livy ix. 29, Frontin. *de aqu.* i. 5); the speech with which he caused Pyrrhus' peace offer to be rejected was still extant (*de sen.* 16). He was a scholar who interested himself in linguistic problems (cf. Lindsay, *Latin Language*, pp. 6, 105), and the first Roman prose-writer; he has been described as the earliest clear-cut personality in Roman history. Cicero made a good choice of this fine old Roman gentleman to rebuke a flighty descendant, to whom his ways would no doubt seem curiously fusty.

**3. minimum . . . videbit:** a schoolboyish jest, which Caelius must have liked.*

**qui . . . loquetur:** 'if he appears, I imagine (*profecto*) this is how he will treat her, this is what he will say'.

**5. quid . . . Caelio:** 'what business have you with Caelius?' a form of expression from familiar speech, frequent in comedy as well as in Ovid and in Silver Prose (see *Thes. L. L.* s.v. *cum*, col. 1374).*

**adulescentulo:** cf. 36. 25. The word gives no clue to Caelius' age (see L. & S. s.v., and cf. note on 2. 1), but it is certainly a jeer at Clodia's age as compared with his.

**6. familiaris:** *P* adds *huic* (*huius* *Σ*), which Kl. accepts; the omission is due to Severianus (*RLM* 360. 27); probably it should be restored to the text here, as *familiaris* needs a complement, and it offers a pleasant picture of Appius' ghost pointing to Caelius.

**7. ut . . . timeres:** this type of clausula is recommended by Quintil. (ix. 4. 102).

**non . . . videras:** *non* is frequent in a chain of questions like this, when the interrogative tone is clear from the context; see K. II. ii, pp. 503, 516.

**8. patrem . . . atavum:** Cl. adds *abavum non* to complete the genealogy; Kl. reads *non avum proavum abavum atavum* (see his note). W. gives a full family tree (cf. Fra., p. 216).

→ **§ 34. 10. modo:** 'lately' (not to be joined with *non*).

**Q. Metelli:** Clodia's cousin and husband, Q. Metellus Celer, whose sudden death in 59 caused the rumour that she had poisoned him; he was Pompey's legate in Asia in 66, praetor 63, consul 60; as praetor he supported Cicero, and in 60 he vigorously opposed Clodius' transference to the plebs. Clodia and he were on bad terms (*ad Att.* ii. 1. 5 'ea cum viro bellum gerit'; cf. Garrod, *CR* xxxiii, 1919, p. 67). Cicero says of him (*ad Att.* ii. 1. 4) 'est consul φιλόπατρις et, ut semper iudicavi, natura bonus'; cf. *in Pis.* 8.

11. **simul . . . extulerat**: 'the moment he set foot out of doors', quasi-proverbial (cf. Otto s.v. *pes*, 10); Quintil. (ix. 4. 104) quotes *omnis . . . superabat* to illustrate a type of clausula.

15. **cognatus . . . familiaris**: 'was he a relative by blood, a connexion by marriage, a close friend of your husband?'

**quid . . . libido**: 'well then, was there any other reason but sheer wanton passion?' *quid fuit = quid causae fuit*, understood from *cur* above.

16. **nonne te . . . admonebat**: a rather awkward sentence: 'surely, if the images of the male representatives of my family did not induce your respect, did my descendant, the famous Quinta Claudia, not give you counsel either, to rival her family renown in the sphere of womanly honour?' The *imagines* were the busts of the family ancestors, kept in the atrium. *Ne . . . quidem*, as so often when there is no question of gradation between the persons or things negatived = 'also not', 'not . . . either'; cf. *Tusc.* i. 54 '[principium] si nunquam oritur, ne occidit quidem unquam', *de sen.* 27 'ne nunc quidem vires desidero adulescentis', *Acad.* i. 5 'indocti ne a nobis quidem accipient' (see Reid ad loc.), Sen. *ad Helv.* iv. 1, *de brev. vit.* xii. 6 (see Duff ad loc.). *Aemulam . . . esse* is the direct infinitive construction after *admonebat.**

17. **progenies**: perhaps granddaughter; see the story in Livy xxix. 14. 12, Ovid, *Fast.* iv. 305 ff., where see Frazer.

18. **Q. illa Claudia**: note this idiomatic separation of *praenomen* from *nomen*; so too with particles (71. 13 'M. vero Caelius', *de am.* 69 'Q. vero Maximum', Quintil. xii. 11. 23 'M. igitur Cato'; see Du Mesnil on *Flacc.* 104; K. II. ii, p. 135).

19. **Vestalis**: the daughter (perhaps sister, cf. Suet. *Tib.* 2) of Appius Claudius Pulcher, consul in 143; she protected him from attack when the people tried to prevent him from celebrating a triumph (Livy, *Per.* 53, Val. Max. v. 4. 6, Dio Cassius, fr. 74).

21. **cur te . . . moverunt**: 'why was it that you were influenced by your brother's vices rather than by the virtues of your father and of your ancestors, virtues that have appeared constantly ever since my own time, not only in the men but particularly in the women of our family?'

23. **tum . . . feminis**: *tum* introduces what is, for Appius' purpose, the more important point; note that Cicero does not use *mulier* here—*feminis* is not only antithetical to *viris* but bears a complimentary sense (see on 31. 5).

24. **ideone**: 'was it for *this* . . . ?' (anticipatory of *ut*); the triple

repetition makes an effective climax, as the old man contrasts his three great services to the State with Clodia's disgraceful behaviour.

**pacem Pyrrhi:** see on 33. 2; Plutarch (*Pyrrh.* 19) reports the speech, possibly from the original; cf. *Brut.* 61, Quintil. ii. 16. 7.

**amorum . . . ferires:** 'strike the most disgraceful bargains with your lovers'.

25. **aquam:** this, the first Roman aqueduct, was finished in 312; it began some eight miles from Rome, and ran underground for all but sixty paces (Frontin. *de aqu.* i. 5); hitherto the people had been dependent on water from the Tiber or from wells.

26. **munivi:** the t.t. for 'building' a road, which well shows the importance attached to its function; for the methods used, see the interesting passage in Stat. *S.* iv. 3. 40 ff. The Appian Way originally ended at Capua, but was later extended to Brundisium; it was the first road laid down on scientific principles ('regina viarum', Stat. *S.* ii. 2. 12).

**alienis viris:** instrumental abl.; this is normal after *comitatus, stipatus* (but 'stipatum ab his viris', *Sest.* 147); see K. II. i, p. 380, Lebr. pp. 406 ff., Conway on *Aen* i. 312. Cicero, pleased with his idea, repeats it in *Mil.* 17 'quasi Appius ille Caecus viam munierit non qua populus uteretur sed ubi impune sui posteri latrocinarentur'.

§ 35. *'Why have I introduced this austere old man, when he might even begin to condemn Caelius too? But I shall deal with Caelius presently; at the moment, Clodia, I tell you to your face that you will have to explain your intimacy with him.'*

This section provides a transition to Cicero's second prosopopoeia; in it he drops his acting and addresses Clodia in person, with no mercy. It certainly breaks the artistic unity of the two complementary passages, §§ 33–34 and § 36; but it is effective in its own way, for it underlines the real significance of Appius' speech, i.e. that Clodia is so immoral that her evidence is worthless, and it makes clear the important point that Cicero felt so certain of his case that he was willing to risk the danger involved for Caelius by Appius' argument. Norden regards the section as an 'improvisation' (see Appendix VIII); I think it is far more probably an integral part of Cicero's plan to bolster up Caelius; see further Drexler, op. cit., pp. 31 f., H., pp. 233 ff., Reitzenstein, op. cit., pp. 25 ff. And its inclusion certainly gives more point to the frivolity of the line taken by Clodius in § 36, which is really more damaging to Clodia than Appius' criticisms, as Drexler remarks (p. 28).

§ 35. 28. **sed quid . . . induxi:** quoted by Quintil. (ix. 2. 60), in illustration of pretended naturalness, 'quasi paenitentia dicti'. *Inducere* is the t.t. for 'to bring on the stage'.

2. **videro hoc posterius**: 'you will find me attending to this presently'. This use of the future perfect is akin to that found in Plautus and Terence, who employ it commonly with no distinction from the simple future; in the classical period it is retained almost as a formula with *videro*, especially when combined with an adverb of time, but is less common with other verbs. The difference, if any, from the simple future is merely one of tone; *videbo hoc*, 'I shall attend to this', *videro hoc*, 'the time will come for me to attend to it (and you will find that I have not forgotten it)'. See Roby, *Lat. Gr.* ii, § 1593 and p. cvi; K. II. i, p. 148; L.–H., p. 563; Lebr., pp. 200 ff.; Landgraf on *Rosc. Am.* 84, 130.*

4. **tu vero**: a sudden, dramatic turn to Clodia, and an effective use of the figure *apostrophe* (cf. Quintil. ix. 2. 38).

6. **quae facis . . . arguis**: 'your actions, your statements, your charges, your machinations, your allegations'.

**facis . . . arguis**: so *Σ* (see Cl., *An. Ox.*, p. xxxiv; *Descent of MSS.*, p. 268), now supported by *Π*. In *P* the words were omitted by the first hand, but the second hand filled the lacuna with *facis quae dicis quae in sororem tuam moliris quae argumenta* (so also *ge*). The reading preserved by *Σ* was known from the fifteenth-century cod. Mon. 15734 (cf. on 24. 19), but was rejected by Halm as a 'pannus intolerabilis', and even Müll., though he prints it, regards it as 'coniectura non nimis plausibilis'; Cl.'s research gave it eighth-century authority. See further Kl., *Rh. Mus.* lxvii, 1912, pp. 364 f. and his preface of 1919, p. x. Cf. *de fin.* ii. 74 'te . . . quae facis, quae cogitas, quae contendis, quo referas . . . non audere . . . dicere'.

7. **probare cogitas**: 'have an intention of proving'; note the important distinction between *cogito* ('I have thoughts') and *puto* ('I have an opinion').

**rationem . . . necesse est**: 'it is imperative that you should give a clear account of this close intimacy, this association, this connexion'.

9. **libidines . . . navigia**: 'orgies, flirtations, misconduct, trips to Baiae, beach-parties, dinner-parties, drinking-parties, musical entertainments and concerts, boating-picnics'.

10. **Baias**: a colloquial usage (cf. 38. 11). See Sen. *Epp.* 51. 4 for a vivid picture of the place: 'videre ebrios per litora errantes et comissationes navigantium et symphoniarum cantibus strepentes lacus', ibid. 12 'ut praenavigantes adulteras dinumeraret et tot genera cumbarum variis coloribus picta et fluitantem toto lacu rosam, ut audiret canentium nocturna convicia'; cf. Suet. *Nero* 27.

**actas**: cf. *Verr.* v. 94 'tum istius actae commemorabantur, tum flagitiosa illa convivia' (*actae* there is the conjecture of Philippson, *PhW* 1924, col. 938, and is adopted by Klotz in his second edition). Less probably 'a house on the front' is meant (cf. *ad Att.* xiv. 8. 1 'tu me iam rebare . . . in actis esse nostris', where Tyrrell and Purser explain *actae* as 'marine residence'), in which case *Baias* above will be parallel ('visits to the villa at Baiae,' cf. 38. 11). Verres once *in acta cum mulierculis iacebat ebrius* (*Verr.* v. 63). Such beach-parties were evidently a feature of social life; cf. the interesting *ficta controversia* based on such a picnic in Quintil. vii. 3. 31 'iuvenes, qui convivere solebant, constituerunt ut in litore cenarent', etc. Plutarch quotes the expression σήμερον ἀκτάσωμεν (*Quaest. Conv.* iv. 2).

11. **symphonias:** rich persons kept *symphoniaci* to perform band-music; Milo's wife had a troupe (*Mil.* 55), and Verres gave a present of six to a friend (*Verr.* v. 64); cf. Sen. *Epp.* 12. 8, *Verr.* v. 92 'curritur ad praetorium, quo istum ex illo praeclaro convivio reduxerant paulo ante mulieres cum cantu atque symphonia'; see Marquardt, *Privatleben*, p. 151.

**navigia:** cf. *navigatione* in a similar context (49. 8); fleets of pleasure-boats were a feature of Baiae (Sen. *Epp.* 51. 4, Juv. 12. 80). Strabo (xvii. 1. 17) has a like description of Canopus in Egypt: πᾶσα γὰρ ἡμέρα καὶ πᾶσα νὺξ πληθύει τῶν μὲν ἐν τοῖς πλοιαρίοις καταυλουμένων καὶ κατορχουμένων ἀνέδην μετὰ τῆς ἐσχάτης ἀκολασίας, καὶ ἀνδρῶν καὶ γυναικῶν, etc.

**idemque . . . dicere:** this certainly suggests that Clodia's relations with Caelius had been mentioned.

12. **quae tu . . . fateare:** either false charges have been brought, or Clodia's own character makes her statement invalid; here is Cicero's real line of attack.*

§ 36. '*Now, let me introduce someone more refined than that rude old man. What about your dear young brother? He will tell you not to worry about losing this handsome young man whom you have tried so hard to catch; why, he will say, there are plenty of good fish in the Tiber.*'

Cicero now acts a second impersonation, this time of Clodius himself (not the P. Clodius of § 27—see Appendix VI, p.155); the virtuous austerity of Appius has given way to the cynical and amused realism of a profligate brother, and Clodia is damned anew in an even more deadly fashion.

§ 36. 16. **urbanius:** old Appius is too rustic and uncouth for modern standards; Clodius will have all the proper polish and smartness.

**sic agam tecum:** cf. *Verr.* v. 164 'sic tecum agam: Gavium

... ostendam'; sometimes a dependent clause with *ut* follows (*Rosc. Am.* 73, where see Landgraf).

**17. ex his:** modern young men, not the *barbati* of Appius' time; Kl. reads *ex his igitur tuis* (*P²*), 'from among your present-day relatives'; but the more general *ex his* gives the proper antithesis to *illum senem*.

**18. qui ... urbanissimus:** 'whose taste is perfect in that kind of thing'.*

**20. credo:** ironical, like οἶμαι (K. II. i, p. 711; cf. Landgraf on *Rosc. Am.* 46, p. 106); this, not *ut credo*, is usual when irony is intended.

**21. pusio:** 'a little fellow'; a low word, yet, as Quintil. remarks in referring to the passage, 'vim rebus aliquando verborum ipsa humilitas adfert' (viii. 3. 22); cf. W. Heraeus, *Kleine Schriften*, p. 168, R. Fisch, *Archiv für lat. Lex.* v., p. 82. There is an echo of the passage in St. Jerome, *Epp.* 50. 5. 5.

**22. putato:** mock-solemn, as the form shows.

**24. quid ... facis:** trochaic septenarius; the author is unknown (see Ribbeck, *Com. Frag.³*, p. 145), but Spengel attributed the line to Caecilius.

**25. vicinum:** cf. § 18; possibly the intimacy only began after Caelius had moved house (cf. Friedrich, *Catullus*, p. 68, note). *Aspexisti* = 'you caught sight of' (a frequent sense of this compound).*

**candor ... pepulerunt:** 'his beauty, his fine, upstanding figure, his face and eyes attracted you'; *candor* implies radiance of appearance; cf. Dio Chrys. xxi. 1 (p. 500 R.) ὡς ὑψηλὸς ὁ νεανίσκος καὶ ὡραῖος.*

**27. fuisti ... hortis:** 'sometimes you found yourself with him in your park'; cf. 27. 9. *Idem* is similarly used in 57. 20; cf. Virg. *Aen.* iv. 165 'speluncam Dido dux et Troianus eandem deveniunt', Ovid, *Met.* iv. 328 'thalamumque ineamus eundem'. *Horti* is used of the grounds of a villa, here presumably Clodia's; see Mayor's note on Juv. 1. 75, with much interesting description; for Roman gardens in general see P. Grimal, *Les Jardins romains* (Paris, 1943).*

**1. patre ... tenaci:** cf. *parum splendidus*, 3. 11; the epithets suggest the *senex* of comedy (cf. Caecilius' lines quoted in *de nat. deor.* iii. 72).

**3. tanti:** a sneer at Clodia, better suited to Cicero than to Clodius.

**confer te alio:** 'try another quarter'; cf. Ter. *Eun.* 449 f. 'metuit semper quem ipsa nunc capit fructum ne quando iratus tu alio conferas'.

**4. ad Tiberim:** a river-bank was a favourite site for such *horti* (see Grimal, op. cit., p. 315).

E

**paratos**: so Cl., with *Σ*; *parasti* Kl., with *PΠ*. Decision is difficult. *Habes hortos ad Tiberim* is perfectly possible Latin for 'you have grounds by the Tiber', and *ac...paratos* follows naturally (*paratos* = 'set'), although *atque eos* or *atque eos quidem* would be more usual; with *parasti* the meaning will be 'you bought'. Possibly an adjective has fallen out after *ad Tiberim*, as Kl. suggests; see, however, Schönb., p. 41.

5. **condiciones**: 'matches', as often in the intrigues of comedy; cf. *Phil.* ii. 99 'filiam eius . . . eiecisti, alia condicione quaesita', Suet. *Aug.* 69. 1; see *Thes. L. L.* s.v., col. 129. 71, S.–M. on *de am.* 34, p. 246, Mayor on *Phil.* l.c. and *JP* xxx, 1907, p. 209.

**§§ 37–38.** *'To return to Caelius: if I treat him after the style of some stern old man in Caecilius, he has a clear answer, that all this is mere tattle; if I am indulgent, like the father in Terence, he has an easy defence. And in fact, could anyone blame him for his gallantries to a lady of such easy manners?'*

Cicero now sets off his prosopopoeiae by a σύγκρισις representing a pair of fathers from comedy. At its conclusion, he makes another personal attack on Clodia, like that in § 35, developing the line indicated by the speeches of Appius and Clodius. He argues that no charge of misconduct can lie against Caelius, since Clodia is nothing but a *meretrix* and therefore her complaints are meaningless. Just as § 35 explains and supports the first pair of speeches, so § 38 explains the argument of the second pair: each passage has its separate function, and the repetition involved is deliberate. See Drexler, op. cit., p. 32, for a useful discussion.

**§ 37. 7. redeo . . . vicissim:** 'I come now to you, Caelius, in your turn'; *redeo* is used like *revertar* in 6. 12 (see note), of passing to a connected topic: the two sermons read to Clodia must have their counterpart in a like treatment of Caelius, if Cicero's case is to be complete.

9. **Caecilianumne aliquem:** Caecilius seems to have specialized in surly old men; cf. *de sen.* 36, *de am.* 99, *de nat. deor.* iii. 72, *Rosc. Am.* 46 (a reference to the *Subditivus*; see Landgraf ad loc.). See Zillinger, *Cicero und die altrömischen Dichter*, pp. 38, 146, for a discussion of Cicero's use of Caecilius; Z. points out (pp. 66 f.) that the speeches delivered between 56 and 54 are those which contain most quotations from early poets, a fact which (together with the publication of the *de oratore* in 55) throws light on Cicero's literary interests at this period.

Caecilius died *c.* 166; see Schanz–Hosius, *Gesch. der röm. Lit.* i, pp. 101 ff.

11. **nunc . . . ira:** trochaic octonarius (quoted also in *de fin.* ii. 14). *

# COMMENTARY

**14. o . . . sceleste:** Cl. follows the MSS. in retaining this as a
fragment not immediately related to the passage *egone . . . velim*,
thus separating *ferrei . . . patres* from *vix ferendi*: this is possible, as
Cicero often quotes spasmodically and elliptically (cf. Zillinger,
op. cit., p. 81). He treats the lines *egone . . . velim* as iambic senarii,
accepting Spengel's deletion of MSS. *egone* before *quid velim*.
Ribbeck views the passage similarly (*CRF³*, Caecil. 231 ff.), but
reads *egone quid dicam? egon quid velim? quae tu omnia*, etc.

Kl. follows Baehrens in transposing *ferrei . . . patres* to precede
*vix ferendi*, and, though he prints it as prose, assumes that the quotation ran thus:

> o infelix, o sceleste, egone quid dicam ? egone quid velim ?
> quae tu omnia tuis foedis factis facis ut nequiquam velim,

treating the lines as iambic octonarii, with hiatus after *sceleste*.

Fra. (p. 219) also makes a fusion, and arranges the lines as
trochaic septenarii:

> o infelix, o sceleste, egon quid dicam, quid velim,
> quae omnia tu tuis foedis factis facis ut nequiquam velim.

He would delete *vix ferendi*, but the words are obviously sound.

The problem is one for a metrical expert to decide. I can see no
good reason for ejecting *egone* before *quid velim*. The 'figura
etymologica' in *foedis factis facis* seems possibly to favour a 'long
line' rather than senarii. But Kl.'s treatment as octonarii seems to
me somewhat forced, and his critical note suggests that he himself
was not entirely convinced. Fra.'s arrangement is at first sight
easier, but scansion *ō infelix* is doubtful.

*Viderint peritiores!* It is, of course, perfectly possible that Cicero
has not made a continuous quotation. As the text stands, *quae
omnia* is very loosely attached to what precedes; something may
well have been omitted after *quid velim*, and even perhaps after
*omnia*. The possibility makes me doubt Kl.'s transference of
*ferrei . . . patres* from the MSS. position, tempting though it is. I
cannot myself see how any certain metrical arrangement of the
passage can be reached. I am grateful to Professor E. Fraenkel for
his guidance in this problem.

**sceleste:** the word is common in comedy; Cicero would
normally use *sceleratus*: he uses *scelestus* only in *Rosc. Am.* 37
(where see Landgraf), *Sest.* 145; *sceleste* (adv.) occurs *ad Att.* vi. 1. 8.*

→ **18. cur te . . . refugisti:** fanciful attempts have been made
(e.g. by Ribbeck) to arrange these words metrically: they should
certainly be kept as printed here (note the iambic rhythm of *diceret
talis pater!*).

**21. cur alienam . . . meae:** Cl. adopts Fra.'s arrangement as trochaic septenarii, with *tibi* and *non mihi* added *metri gratia*. But I cannot see why words should be inserted to make the passage fit a particular metrical theory. Kl., with greater probability, leaves the whole as it stands in the MSS. He accepts, however, Ribbeck's view that *si egebis . . . meae* form two senarii, the first being truncated; Zillinger (op. cit., p. 149, note 1) takes *cur alienam . . . nosti* and *si egebis* as Cicero's own words, the rest being senarii. Here again I should prefer to make no attempt to reduce any part of the passage to form a continuous metrical excerpt.

**dide ac dissice:** 'scatter and squander'. Kl. reads *disice* (*disce PΠ*); cf. Fra., pp. 219 f.; but in nearly every passage where the word occurs, the form is equally uncertain, and no safe distinction is possible as between a compound of *iacio* and one of *seco*, although the two do exist independently (see Keil, *GL* iii, p. 56, 21-22; Neue–Wagener, *Formenlehre* ii, pp. 920 f.; *Thes. L. L.* s.v. *disicio*, col. 1381. 52 ff.).

**22. tibi dolebit:** a quasi-impersonal use, very frequent in comedy (see *Thes. L. L.* s.v., col. 1827. 65 ff.); normally a neuter pronoun, or a phrase with *cum, quod, quia, si* acts as subject, but cf. *Mur.* 42 'cui placet obliviscitur, cui dolet meminit', where the parallelism with *placet* explains the purely impersonal use.

**non mihi:** added by Fra. (see above); cf. Plaut. *Men.* 439 'mihi dolebit, non tibi, si quid ego stulte fecero'.

**23. qui:** adverbial (the old form of the ablative), 'whereby'.

**§ 38. 25. huic . . . seni:** 'to this glum and blunt old gentleman'.

**26. de via decessisse:** 'had left the straight path', equivalent to *virtutem deseruisse* (see S.–M. on *de am.* 61).

**quid signi:** note the partitive use, although the noun is predicative; it is found as early as Cato, *de agr. cult.* 38. 4; see Landgraf on *Rosc. Am.* 83.

**27. iactura:** 'expense', 'waste' (literally 'a throwing overboard'); cf. *Flacc.* 13 'quae iactura, qui sumptus, quae largitio', *ad Att.* vi. 1. 2 'exhaustam esse sumptibus et iacturis provinciam'. The more usual meaning is 'loss'; the word is no doubt chosen deliberately for the paronomasia with *versura* (see on 17. 9); see Wölfflin, *Archiv für lat. Lex.* i, pp. 381 ff., iii, pp. 457 ff., for similar examples of assonance (cf. 77. 19, 78. 6).

**quotus quisque:** *quotus* is the adjectival counterpart of *quot* ('one of how many'); cf. Hor. *Epp.* i. 5. 30 'tu quotus esse velis rescribe' ('let me know what fraction of the party you want to be'. i.e. 'how big a party you would like'); *quotus quisque effugere potest* = 'what proportion of men can escape?' (lit. 'each being one in how many'), i.e. 'how few'.

1. **quisque:** a fragment of the Turin palimpsest begins here, extending to 42. 15 (other fragments contain 54–56, 66–69).

→ **praesertim:** transposed here by Cl. from its position preceding *effugere* in *Σ* where it is meaningless; Kl. omits it, with *PΠ*.

2. **male audisse:** 'gained a bad reputation' (cf. κακῶς ἀκούειν); a conversational phrase, and, if a Grecism, hardly a conscious one; cf. Laur., p. 114.

4. **patre:** so Cl., Kl. (a conjecture of Schwarz for MSS. *patri*, which involves a difficult change of subject in *defenderet*).*

5. **fores ecfregit:** from Ter. *Ad.* 120–1, where a kind father is indulgent to his son's wild ways (see the whole context); cf. *de sen.* 65 'quanta in altero diritas, in altero comitas!' of the brothers in the play.

7. **Caeli:** a correction (made by Angelius, the editor of the first Juntine edition, 1515), for MSS. *fili*; on the whole, it is preferable, as it makes the position parallel to that in 38. 25: Kl. retains *fili*, which continues the fictitious picture.

8. **nihil . . . dico:** cf. 48. 1; cf. Appendix VIII.

9. **si esset:** in the parallel passage, § 50, Cicero has the primary sequence throughout; here he pretends that such a supposition is impossible, there it is an open hypothesis and only too likely. Note his change of tactics from § 35 ('iam enim ipse tecum nulla persona introducta loquor'), where he addresses Clodia directly; the jury would be entertained by his pretence of anonymity here.

10. **decretum:** 'told off', to be her current lover.

11. **cuius . . . commearent:** 'a woman to whose grounds, house, estate at Baiae, there was an automatic right of way for every lecherous person'. For *Baias* see on 35. 10; here it plainly means a residence (cf. *ad Att.* xi. 6. 6 'Lentulus . . . sibi et Caesaris hortos et Baias desponderat'). *Commearent* suggests a regular flow of traffic. *Libidines omnium* = *omnes libidinosi* (cf. Nisbet on *de domo* 25. 4).

13. **sustineret:** as presumably in Caelius' case; Cl. compares Livy xxxix. 9. 6 'maligne omnia praebentibus suis meretriculae munificentia sustinebatur'. Kl. reads *sustentaret* (so *P*, and possibly *Π*), which seems more usual in the connexion (see Schönb., p. 42); but *sustineret* (*Σ*) gives a better clausula.

**si vidua . . . salutasset:** 'just suppose a widow were living unconventionally, a saucy widow living shamelessly, a rich widow living riotously, a wanton widow living whorishly—well, should I really imagine a man to have committed misconduct if he had been rather free with his gallantries to her?' For the antithetical mannerism cf. 13. 22, note. Quintil. quotes the passage to illustrate the figures *amplificatio* and *minutio*: 'nam et impudicam meretricem vocavit, et eum, cui longus cum illa fuerat usus, liberius salutasse'

(viii. 4. 2); the more developed passage in § 49 lacks the amusing antitheses, and is in some ways less effective for that reason.

**§§ 39–42.** '*So this is my way of bringing up young men. That is what people will say, no doubt. Of course, I recognize an ideal of virtuous conduct; but, really, the strictness of the past is obsolescent, and it is only reasonable that a young man should have his fling, provided he does not carry enjoyment to excess.*'

Cicero now dramatically changes his tone from gay and wicked wit to grave sobriety, as he introduces some more solid reflections, designed to lead up to a picture of Caelius as an earnest, hardworking young man who knew how to put pleasure in its place (§§ 44 ff.; cf. his promise in 35. 2 f.). Such generalities were quite in the spirit of Roman oratory (cf. *Orat.* 45); Herennius had clearly used the same technique (cf. § 25), and in fact Cicero especially prided himself on his skill in enlarging his cases from a consideration of a particular issue to that of general principles. He might have had this very speech in mind in *Brut.* 322 ff.: 'nemo erat . . . qui memoriam rerum Romanarum teneret, ex qua, si quando opus esset, ab inferis locupletissimos testis excitaret, nemo qui breviter arguteque illuso adversario laxaret iudicum animos atque a severitate paulisper ad hilaritatem risumque traduceret, nemo qui dilatare posset atque a propria ac definita disputatione hominis ac temporis ad communem quaestionem universi generis orationem traducere'.

I do not now hold my former view that Cicero did not deliver the whole passage from § 39 to § 50 as it stands (cf. Appendix VIII); for although much of it seems rather dreary moralizing to us, a Roman jury would have found it perfectly natural and even congenial, and in spite of some curious repetitions which these sections involve, it is not likely that any part was in fact omitted; in any case, it is much more likely to have been part of Cicero's original draft than to have been added *en bloc* later on publication, as Heinze and Opperskalski hold.

Cicero uses here what was no doubt as familiar in the rhetorical schools of his day as it certainly was under the Empire, a *locus de indulgentia*; cf. Juv. 8. 163 ff., and note the various arguments in Sen. *Contr.* ii. 6, especially § 11 'concessis aetati voluptatibus utor et iuvenali lege defungor; bona ego aetate coepi; simul primum hoc tirocinium adulescentiae quasi debitum ac sollemne persolvero, revertar ad bonos mores. id facio quod pater meus fecit, cum iuvenis esset.'

**§ 39. 17. dicet aliquis:** a 'potential future' (L.-H., p. 556;

# COMMENTARY §§ 39-40

Roby, *Lat. Gr.* ii, pp. ci ff.). Quintil. (ix. 2. 15) quotes the passage as an example of *ficta interrogatio*.

20. **conlocaret**: 'occupy'; there may be an underlying idea of 'investing' one's early years in *voluptates*.

21. **ego**: 'my reply is . . .'; see N., p. 745, where similar examples are given of this use of *ego*, *ego autem* at the beginning of a long sentence to indicate that a reply is being made to a question or objection.

**hoc robore . . . continentiae**: 'endowed with such power of will, such natural gifts of goodness and self-control'.*

1. **aequalium studia**: 'the amusements of his friends' (cf. 72. 21); *aequales* often means 'contemporaries' in age, rank, etc.

2. **ludi**: see on 28. 16 ('love-affairs').

**convivium delectaret**: so Cl.; *convivia delectarent* Kl., with *P* (the singular noun has the authority of the Turin palimpsest; hence Cl. changed the verb to suit).

4. **mea sententia . . . puto**: for the pleonasm, cf. *prov. cons.* 18 'ego mea sententia C. Caesari succedendum non putarem', and other examples quoted by Kl. ad loc.; Quintil. (viii. 3. 53) disapproves of the mannerism ('est et πλεονασμός vitium, cum supervacuis verbis oratio oneratur: "ego oculis meis vidi", satis enim "vidi" '). For pleonasm as a feature of Latin style see Löfstedt, *Synt.* ii, ch. 9; K. II. ii, pp. 567 ff.

6. **Camillos**: the regular 'saints' gallery' of Roman rhetoric; their names must have worn thin with time, yet we must remember the Roman passion for *exempla*, 'precedents', which made 'history' an essential part of rhetoric. Similar lists of grand old men are frequent in Cicero, and are part of the regular *supellex* of later rhetorical writers (e.g. Quintil. vii. 2. 38, xii. 2. 30, Pliny, *Pan.* 13, Sen. *Contr.* ii. 1. 8, *Suas.* 7. 6, Juv. 2. 3, 154, even Apul. *Apol.* 10); see de Decker, *Juvenalis Declamans* (Ghent, 1913), pp. 34 ff., and cf. Otto s.vv.*

M. Furius Camillus was Dictator in 396 and 390; C. Fabricius Luscinus showed himself an incorruptible general in the war with Pyrrhus, and was censor in 275; M'. Curius Dentatus ended the Samnite war as consul in 290, and as consul again in 275 he defeated Pyrrhus.

**haec**: = *hoc imperium*, as often; cf. Landgraf on *Rosc. Am.* 50, du Mesnil on *Flacc.* 104, N., pp. 213 f.

**§ 40. 7. verum**: a strong contrast; the Romans had been going to ruin (in rhetoric) at least ever since old Scipio Aemilianus expressed his horror at seeing more than fifty Roman boys and girls at a dancing-school (Macrob. *Sat.* xiii. 14. 7): they continued steadily to do so (in rhetoric), cf. Sen. *Epp.* 95. 23 'in rhetorum

103

ac philosophorum scholis solitudo est; at quam celebres culinae sunt', etc.

10. qui . . . sumus: 'who have followed this path and manner of life not so much in theory as in practice'.

13. facere . . . loqui: corresponds to *re magis quam verbis* above; cf. Quintil. xii. 2. 30 'quantum enim Graeci praeceptis valent, tantum Romani, quod est maius, exemplis'. For the Roman attitude to Greek philosophical theory, see Kroll, *Die Kultur der Ciceronischen Zeit*, ii, pp. 120 ff.

§ 41. 15. voluptatis causa: cf. Sen. *Contr*. ii. 6. 2 'quidam summum bonum dixerunt voluptatem et omnia ad corpus rettulerunt'. Cicero alludes to the Epicurean theory of 'pleasure', which he so heartily disliked (see Reid's *Academica*, pp. 21 ff.): this conceived *voluptas* in terms of ἀταραξία and ἀπονία, a view whose true meaning was often misunderstood and misrepresented; see Bailey, *Lucretius*, i, pp. 60 ff., for a discussion of Epicurean moral theory, and cf. A. H. Armstrong, *Introduction to Ancient Philosophy*, pp. 130 ff.

16. hac . . . turpitudine: 'this disgusting statement'.

18. dignitatem: 'virtue'; cf. *Tusc*. v. 85 'voluptatem cum honestate Dinomachus et Callipho copulavit, indolentiam autem honestati Peripateticus Diodorus adiunxit', *Acad*. ii. 131 'voluptatem autem et honestatem finem esse Callipho censuit'. The Academics and Peripatetics held a mid-path between Stoicism and Epicureanism, considering that the chief good lay in joining virtue to bodily pleasure (see Holden's references on *de off*. iii. 119).

19. dicendi facultate: 'by an opportunist argument'.*

20. illud . . . relicti: Cicero means the Stoics, who are 'left nearly high and dry in their lecture-rooms'; cf. Petron. 3. 2 'nam nisi dixerint [*sc*. doctores] quae adulescentuli probent, ut ait Cicero, soli in scholis relinquentur' (cf. Buecheler, *Rh. Mus*. xxxviii, 1883, p. 638). They held the supreme good to be *honesta actio*, the rational selection of things in themselves agreeable to nature (τὰ πρῶτα κατὰ φύσιν), i.e. to reason. Cicero follows their doctrines in the *de officiis*, but without entirely committing himself to their position. The original extreme Stoic harshness, however, had been toned down by Panaetius of Rhodes, who came to Rome with Scipio Africanus in 143, and later by the Syrian Greek Posidonius (see Armstrong, op. cit., pp. 143 ff., and Holden on *de off*., pp. xxxi ff.); Cicero presumably has this in mind in the next sentence (cf. H., p. 238, note). See the interesting discussion in Aul. Gell. xii. 5.

All that this little sketch of philosophical theory amounts to is a rhetoricized statement that the good old ideals of morality have been abandoned: Nature herself has done her part.

22. blandimenta . . . interdum: 'Nature of her own accord has

COMMENTARY §§ 41–42

given rise to many alluring things, such as can lull virtue to rest at
times and cause her to droop her eyes'; *quibus* is instrumental abl.
(not dative after *coniveret*, which is not a classical construction);
cf. Aul. Gell. xiii. 28. 4 'animus atque mens viri prudentis . . . esse
debet erecta . . . iam sollicitis nunquam conivens'.

23. **lubricas:** 'slippery'; cf. Sen. *Contr.* ii. 6. 4 'fuit adulescens
temperatissimus et lubricum tempus sine infamia transiit'.*

24. **quibus:** ablative, cf. *Verr.* iii. 172, *de or.* iii. 33; but see Reid
on *de fin.* ii. 3 (p. 105).

26. **haec aetas . . . conroborata:** 'these early years . . . full
maturity'.

§ **42.** 28. **qui . . . suavitatem:** a good Ciceronian embellishment
for 'scornful of all pleasurable sensation'; sight, smell, touch, taste,
hearing are all neatly catalogued, with *oculis pulchritudinem
rerum . . . auribus omnem suavitatem* framing the rest.

→ 1. **ego . . . pauci:** said no doubt with an understanding glance at
the virtuous jury; these are poor times for such few idealists as are
left.

2. **ergo . . . relinquatur:** 'it is only logical, then, to abandon
this path, forsaken as it is, untrodden, a tangle of branches and
undergrowth'.*

4. **detur . . . aetati:** so Cl., with *T* (now supported by *Π*); cf.
28. 16: *detur aliquid aetati* Kl., with *P* (better, for it suits the generalities that follow, and avoids a lame repetition in line 14 below).
The passage is parallel with § 28 (cf. Appendix VIII).

5. **non omnia:** see K. II. i, p. 191 for this use of *non* in a jussive
sentence, attached to a particular word.

6. **vera:** Kl. adopts Baehrens's *severa*; Sydow (*Rh. Mus.* xci,
1942, p. 358) objects that this epithet is not found elsewhere with
*ratio*; he proposes *vera illa et derecta via* (*Σ* has *via et ratio*), comparing *de fin.* i. 57 'beate vivendi et apertam et simplicem et derec-
tam viam' (*v.l.* vitam). I cannot see that the text needs emendation;
cf. *part. or.* 130 'aequitatis autem vis est duplex: cuius altera derecta veri et iusti . . . ratione defenditur.'

7. **dum modo . . . teneatur:** 'provided that the following (*illa*)
rule and limitation is observed in such matters'.

8. **parcat . . . alienam:** 'a young man should be scrupulous concerning his own repute, and do no violence to that of others'; cf.
Sen. *Contr.* i, pr. 9 'expugnatores alienae pudicitiae, negligentes
suae'.

10. **trucidetur:** 'be crippled'; cf. Livy vi. 37. 2 'nec faenore
trucidandi plebem alium [*sc.* modum] patribus unquam fore', *de
off.* ii. 89, where *faenerari* is made equivalent to *occidere*.

11. **ne probrum . . . inferat:** 'he must not bring vileness upon

105

the pure, a stain upon the virtuous, disgrace upon the honourable';
note the antitheses.

14. **ad ludum aetatis**: see note on 28. 16.

17. **satietate . . . experiendo**: note the variation from noun to
gerund; cf. *de am*. 61 'benevolentiam civium, quam blanditiis et
adsentando colligere turpe est', and S.–M. ad loc.

§§ **43–47.** '*I could mention many men of the highest integrity and
distinction who sowed plenty of wild oats when they were young.
But Caelius is young, and in him you will find no unbridled
extravagance, no disgraceful amours; his own speech, his whole
career shows his steady character. Do not believe what is said
against him: it is Clodia in her infamy who is responsible for
these wild charges.*'

§ **43. 21. defervissent**: 'had simmered down'; cf. Ter. *Ad*. 152
'sperabam iam defervisse adulescentiam'. The word is a vintage-
metaphor; see Sandys on *Orat*. 107 for its application to oratorical
style (cf. *Brut*. 316). Kl. reads *deferbuissent* (so *deferbuerint*,
77. 16): *defervissent* (so also *Π*) is a correction by the second
hand in *P*; the first hand reads *deferuuissent*. See Svennung,
*Untersuch. zu Palladius*, pp. 129 f., for a discussion of these
forms.

22. **ex quibus . . . recordamini**: cf. *Phil*. ii. 1 'nec vero necesse
est quemquam a me nominari; vobiscum ipsi recordamini.' *Libet*
(*Σ*) was conjectured by Madvig (*liquet P*).

24. **ne . . . quidem**: the negative is part of the general negation
already expressed in *nolo*; this is common when a subdivision of a
preceding general negative (*nihil, nemo*, etc.) is introduced by
*neque*, less common when the subdivision is marked by *ne . . .
quidem*, as here; cf. *de sen*. 46 'non intellego ne in istis quidem ipsis
voluptatibus carere sensu senectutem', *de fin*. ii. 30 'neget se posse
ne suspicari quidem'; see K. II. i, p. 827.

27. **praedicarentur**: the verb means 'to make public', often
with the idea of advertisement or boasting.

**partim**: originally an accusative form of *pars*, and often used
with a partitive genitive or *ex*+abl. as subject or object of a clause
(e.g. *de off*. ii. 72 'eorum autem ipsorum partim eius modi sunt ut
ad universos cives pertineant, partim singulos ut attingant', Livy
xxvi. 46 'partim copiarum ad tumulum expugnandum mittit,
partim ipse ad arcem ducit'): see K. II. i, p. 433, L.–H., p. 385.
Here it is a very loose adverb of reference ('in connexion with some
of whom could be mentioned excessive wildness in their young days,
in connexion with others gross profligacy, enormous debts, lavish
expenditure, sensuality of all kinds').

1. **adulescentiae . . . excusatione:** cf. 30. 7 'deprecari vacationem adulescentiae'.

§ **44.** 1. **at vero:** a strong adversative; *Caelius* has no such youthful vices.

3. **quaedam:** Caelius' weaknesses, of which Cicero is not afraid to speak (§ 14, cf. § 77).

5. **nulla . . . libido:** 'no passion for guzzling and debauchery'; *lustrum* is properly used of a morass, then of a wild beast's wallowing-place; cf. *Mur.* 13 'nullum turpe convivium, non amor, non comissatio, non libido, non sumptus ostenditur'.

6. **vitium ventris et gurgitis:** 'this vice of gluttony and gormandizing'; *gurges* strictly means a gluttonous man (cf. Pliny, *N.H.* x. 133 'Apicius . . . nepotum omnium altissimus gurges'), but the lack of co-ordination with *venter* is more apparent than real, and disappears if *ventris* can be taken as in Lucil. fr. 75 M 'vivite lurcones comedones vivite ventres'.

8. **deliciae:** ' "affairs" ' (cf. note on 27. 1); Kl. reads *hae deliciae* (so *P*, and perhaps *Π*).

10. **deflorescunt:** 'flower and fade'; such compounds imply an action that is carried through to its natural end (so *defervescere, desaevire, debellare, desaltare, destertere*, etc.; L. & S. are misleading).

**impeditumve:** so Cl. (*Σ* has *ne impeditumque*); *impeditumque* Kl., *P.* Sydow, *Hermes* lxv, 1930, p. 320, proposes *ne implicatum quidem impeditumve*; cf. Schönb., p. 44.

§ **45.** 11. **cum pro se diceret:** Caelius himself opened the defence. This use of *cum* is followed by the subjunctive even when the tense is present, e.g. *de or.* i. 129 'soleo audire Roscium cum ita dicat'; see Nisbet on *de domo* 93, K. II. ii, p. 333.

12. **accusaret:** his accusation of Antonius, or perhaps of Bestia. Cicero himself had trained Caelius, but pretends that he does not wish to boast.

13. **genus . . . perspexistis:** 'sensible men as you are, you have clearly realized his style, his ability, his fluent thought and expression'. For Caelius' style of speaking, see p. xiv.

14. **quae . . . est:** a compression for *ea prudentia quae vestra est*; see K. II. ii, p. 314; the idiom is frequent (particularly in the letters) in connexion with such qualities, the relative clause being in a loose form of apposition to the idea contained in the verb: it belongs especially to the Ciceronian age, but there are a few later examples (L.–H., p. 711).

17. **nisi me . . . fallebat:** a regular type of formula (see K. II. ii, p. 413), the verb being used impersonally (*Thes. L. L.* s.v., col. 187. 54 ff.); see also Landgraf on *Rosc. Am.* 48.

**ratio ... elaborata:** 'theoretical knowledge, implanted in him by liberal studies and brought to perfection by practice and constant hard work'; in other words, Caelius showed *ars* as well as *ingenium*, a common antithesis of Roman literary criticism (cf. my note on Quintil. xii. 10. 6). *Ratio* = 'science', from the point of view of principle and method; *cura* = μελέτη (cf. *meditatio, meditari*).

**22. desiderio:** so Cl., with MSS.; *desidia* Kl. (see Lehmann, *Hermes* xiv, 1879, p. 216); cf. 76. 28 'sermo deliciarum desidiaeque', *Verr.* ii. 7 'nulla desidia, nulla luxuries, contra summus labor', etc. The emendation is not needed: cf. *Tusc.* iv. 16, where *desiderium* ('desire') is classed with *indigentia* ('insatiate desire') among the subdivisions of *libido*, in the Stoic classification of irrational emotions, and is later defined (ib. 21) as 'libido eius qui nondum adsit videndi'.

**24. quoquo ... agendo:** the words *modo facimus non (Σ)* strikingly confirmed Madvig's conjecture (*Opusc. Acad.*, p. 321), and the editors of *Π* remark that the papyrus probably agreed with *Σ*; see *An. Ox.*, p. xxx (Cl.'s facsimile contains this passage). Cicero is being modest after his manner; he does not wish to say in so many words that oratorical distinction is a thing to boast of.

**25. agendo ... cogitando:** the physical and mental aspects of oratory.

**an:** frequent in argument, when a possible line of thought is anticipated and repelled or contradicted, hence often ironical.

**§ 46. 1. tam sint pauci:** the theme of the early part of the *de oratore* (i. 6-16; Cicero concludes 'quid enim quis aliud in maxima discentium multitudine, summa magistrorum copia, praestantissimis hominum ingeniis ... amplissimis eloquentiae propositis praemiis esse causae putet, nisi rei quandam incredibilem magnitudinem ac difficultatem?').

**2. obterendae ... deserendus:** contrast Sen. *Contr.* i, pr. 8 'torpent ecce ingenia desidiosae iuventutis, nec in unius honestae rei labore vigilatur. somnus languorque, ac somno et languore turpior, malarum rerum industria, invasit animos, cantandi saltandique obscena studia effeminatos tenent', etc. In Cicero's time the *tirocinium fori* ensured hard and careful training, and its reduction to a formality under the Empire had serious consequences.

**3. ludus:** see on 28. 16; *iocus* is used similarly (cf. Catull. 8. 6).

→ **5. labor offendit:** *Σ* again vindicated Madvig (*Opusc. Acad.*, p. 323), and is supported by *Π* (*labore fiendi P*).

**a studioque:** this is the normal position of *-que* when attached to prepositional phrases with *a, ab, ob, sub, apud*, and frequent also when attached to those with *de, ex, in*; see Landgraf on *Rosc. Am.* 114, K. II. i, p. 583.

6. **ingenia:** plural, because the reference is to more than one person (a single person's 'talents' — *ingenium*).

**doctrina puerilis:** 'training in boyhood'; cf. *de or.* iii. 48 'praecepta Latine loquendi quae puerilis doctrina tradit'.

**§ 47. 7. dedidisset:** so Cl. (from Arusianus, Keil, *GL* vii. 465. 14); *dedisset* Kl. (so *ΣΠΡ*), cf. *BPhW* 1914, col. 958. There is a like divergence in 28. 13.

**consularem hominem:** i.e. Antonius (cf. 78. 24).

**admodum adulescens:** 'quite a stripling' (*admodum* is very common with words expressing age); on Pliny's reckoning, Caelius was then 23.

9. **hac in acie:** the 'battleground' of the courts (a frequent metaphor, cf. *pugna*, *certamen*).

10. **subiret . . . capitis:** 'would expose himself to proceedings in a criminal trial' (by his enemies, as Atratinus had now attacked him). Halm oddly punctuates with the comma after *ipse* (cf. Schönb., p. 45).

12. **nihilne . . . redolet:** 'does not a whiff of anything come from that notorious neighbourhood ?' As always, Cicero leads his argument back to the hidden hand of Clodia.

14. **illae vero . . . laetetur:** 'why, Baiae does not simply talk, it rings with the tale that one single woman's lusts have reached such depths, that far from seeking isolation and darkness and the normal cloaks for depravity, she revels in the most disgraceful behaviour, courting the most open publicity and the brightest light of day'.

15. **personant:** cf. *Planc.* 86 'furialis illa vox . . . secum et illos et consules facere acerbissime personabat'.

17. **haec:** cf. note on 25. 8, and see Schönb., pp. 43 f.

**§§ 48–50.** '*But really, when a lady of easy virtue is concerned, what reason is there for complaint ? Such amours worry no one. I will be quite explicit about her conduct, and you can draw your own inferences: and if the cap should happen to fit Clodia, there is obviously no case against Caelius.*'

Cicero now brings his *praemunitio* to a blunt and triumphant conclusion: Clodia is a *meretrix*, and a *procax meretrix* at that. The passage is closely parallel to § 38, but the scheme of argument used there is now developed more fully, and is carried to its logical conclusion in the dilemma which Cicero puts before Clodia (50. 24 ff.). It is certainly curious, as H. remarks, that the fiction of anonymity is now repeated; but it would be much more curious if Cicero had really added the whole of §§ 39–50 in editing the speech for publication, as H̦. believes. The whole passage is an integral part of his line of defence, by which his case stands or falls, and

forms an artistic and impressive climax to the solemnity of his plea
for Caelius as a man of sterling worth.

**§ 48. 20. meretriciis amoribus:** Cicero now takes Clodia's
character for granted; he has explained above that Caelius has
never concerned himself with *amores et deliciae*; he now makes it
plain that an affair with a *meretrix* counts for nothing whatsoever.
To the Romans there was no stigma in such a connexion; cf. Schol.
ad Hor. *Sat.* i. 2. 31 'cum vidisset [*sc.* Cato] hominem honestum e
fornice exeuntem, laudavit . . . postea cum frequentius eum exeuntem de eodem lupanari vidisset, dixit: Adolescens, ego te laudavi
tamquam huc interdum venires, non tamquam hic habitares', St.
Aug. *Serm.* 153. 6 'quis enim ad iudicem ductus est quia meretricis
lupanar intravit ?', Ter. *Ad.* 101.

**24. quando enim...liceret:** Ciceronian theatricality in full dress.

**26. ipsam rem:** so Cl., with Halm; *iam rem P²*, Kl. (*iam
definiam rem Σ*), which seems to me unobjectionable; cf. 38. 8
'nihil iam in istam mulierem dico'—there Cicero was only half-
hinting, here he is ready to be more explicit.

**1. tantum:** 'just so much'; Kl. adopts Koch's *totum*, which I
cannot understand unless one is also to accept Müll.'s needless
conjecture *nullam* for *iam* above, as W. does.

**§ 49. 2. non nupta:** 'without a husband', i.e. *vidua* (cf. 38. 13);
cf. Apul. *Apol.* 27 'quasi non magis mirandum sit quod tot annos
non nupserit' (where *non nupserit* = 'was a widow'). W., following
Fra., wrongly deletes *non*.*

**domum . . . conlocarit:** cf. 38. 11 ff.

**6. incessu:** 'bearing'; the word takes its colour from its context;
Clodia in this respect was far from resembling that Claudia who
was *sermone lepido, tum autem incessu commodo* (*CIL* i. 2. 1211);
it implies not simply 'walk' but the whole demeanour (cf. Reid on
*de fin.* ii. 77); cf. Sen. *Epp.* 66. 5 'modestus incessus et compositus
ac probus voltus et conveniens prudenti viro gestus'. Contrast the
picture in Sen. *Contr.* ii. 7. 3 'matrona . . . ferat iacentis in terram
oculos; adversus officiosum salutatorem inhumana potius quam
inverecunda sit; etiam in necessaria resalutandi vice multo rubore
confusa sit . . . in has servandae integritatis custodias nulla libido
inrumpet. prodite . . . tantum non ultro blandientes, ut quisquis
viderit non metuat accedere: deinde miramini si, cum tot argumentis inpudicitiam praescripseritis, cultu, incessu, sermone, facie,
aliquis repertus est qui incurrenti adulterae se non subduceret ?'*

**7. flagrantia oculorum:** Clodia was nicknamed βοῶπις (*ad Att.*
ii. 9. 1, etc.); cf. *har. resp.* 38 'ne id quidem sentis, coniventes illos
oculos abavi tui magis optandos fuisse quam hos flagrantes sororis ?'
She and Caelius must have made a striking pair.

**sermonum:** so Cl., Kl., with Σ; *sermonis P*; the plural generally = 'gossip', and Schönb. suggests (p. 46, an interesting note) that it is used here for the sake of the homoeoteleuton (cf. *de am.* 66 'accedat huc suavitas quaedam oportet sermonum atque morum').

8. **actis . . . conviviis:** the ablatives are local, and form a separate group from the rest; Schöll needlessly deleted the words (see Kl. ad loc.). For the meaning of *actis*, see on 35. 10.

9. **proterva . . . procax:** 'lascivious . . . lewd'. The words *sed etiam proterva meretrix* (Σ) are omitted in *P*; they were probably in Π (see edd. ad loc.); here again the reading preserved by Σ was known to early scholars (see Graevius' note), but its authority was not realized (cf. *An. Ox.*, p. xxxiv).

11. **expugnare pudicitiam:** but Clodia had no *pudicitia*. Cf. *Verr.* i. 9 'non enim furem sed ereptorem, non adulterum sed expugnatorem pudicitiae', and see Page on Virg. *Aen.* x. 92.

12. **libidinem:** i.e. Clodia's.

§ 50. 13. **iniurias:** Cicero magnanimously pretends to overlook the behaviour of Clodius and his family towards his own family during his exile (see *de domo* 62, *post red. in sen.* 18, *Sest.* 54). His sudden naming of Clodia is dramatic and effective, as he proceeds to put to her in person the question that he has postponed from § 35 and § 38.

15. **ne sint . . . dixi:** 'pray do not imagine that what I have said was meant against *you*' (cf. H., p. 243, note 2). Cicero still maintains his elaborate pretence.

16. **abs te:** characteristic of Cicero's earlier style; he tends later to prefer *a te* (see Landgraf on *Rosc. Am.* 12, Parzinger, op. cit., pp. 57 f.).

17. **sit:** but *esset* in 38. 9 (see note).

18. **paulo ante:** 'a moment ago' (not a reference to § 38, as W. thinks).

**descripsi:** 'painted'; no English word quite gives the meaning of *describere* in such a context, where an evil picture is meant; cf. *in Pis.* 68 'non . . . contumeliae causa describam quemquam, praesertim ingeniosum hominem atque eruditum', Sen. *Epp.* 86. 13 'descripturus infamem et nimiis notabilem deliciis Horatius'; it is particularly used of a repulsive appearance or of wicked morals. See *Thes. L. L.* s.v., col. 659. 65 ff.

19. **cum hac . . . rationis:** 'that a young man should have had some dealings with her'.

20. **perturpe . . . perflagitiosum:** see note on 25. 2.

22. **sin . . . te . . . esse:** 'but if by such a person they mean *you*'.

24. **aut enim . . . dabit:** 'for either your sense of decency will

III

uphold the statement that Caelius has not acted immorally in any way, or your utter indecency will provide both him and all the rest with an excellent means of excusing their conduct'.

25. petulantius: *petulantia* = 'viciousness', in the sense that an animal shows 'vice', and it is often coupled with *libido* (e.g. *Phil.* iii. 35 'libidinosis petulantibus impuris impudicis', *de sen.* 36 'ut petulantia, ut libido magis est adulescentium quam senum', Quintil. v. 10. 26 'ducitur enim frequenter in argumentum species libidinis, robur petulantiae'); cf. Reid on *de fin.* i. 61. Dryden sometimes turns *libido* by 'petulancy'.

26. ceteris: all the rest of her lovers, who may expect like experience.

defendendum: the words *et ceteris magnam ad se* are found only in *Σ*; *P* has *et huic defendendum* (*ei sui defendendi* Madvig, *Op. Acad.* p. 324, *ad hunc defendendum* Müll.). The reading preserved by *Σ* was known already to Manutius (who comments 'haec non leguntur in Erfurtensi'); it involves the rare use of the gerund after *ad* and followed by a direct object (found in Varro and occasionally in Silver Prose—the text of two passages in Livy is uncertain): see L.–H., p. 596; K. II. i, p. 735. Cf. Planc. ap. Cic. *ad Fam.* x. 23. 3 'ut spatium ad colligendum se homines haberent', where, however, emendations have been attempted; both there and here the idea of individual action is uppermost, while *huic* eases the construction considerably in this passage. See Tyrrell and Purser on *ad Fam.* l.c.

## §§ 51–69. ARGUMENTATIO

Cicero now feels himself free to begin the *argumentatio* (cf. note on § 3), since he has effectually disposed of the various defamatory statements and implications brought against Caelius. He begins with a *narratio* of the 'crimen auri', the facts of which seem to be (1) that Clodia lent Caelius some gold ornaments, to help him, as he said, to pay for some games that he was producing; she gave them with no witnesses, and did not ask for them back; (2) that Caelius really wished to use the gold as a bribe to Lucceius' slaves to murder Dio, their master's guest. Cicero makes it as mysterious and improbable as he can, yet there must have been some truth at the back of it; possibly Caelius wished to ingratiate himself with Pompey (see notes on § 23, and cf. H., pp. 248 ff.).

§§ 51–55. '*Now it is all plain sailing. There are two charges, one concerning some gold, the other concerning some poison. On the first, either Clodia gave Caelius the gold with full knowledge of why he needed it, or, if he did not dare to tell her, she cannot have given it him. But I had better call on Lucceius himself, with whom Dio was staying at the time of the alleged attack: the truth will then be obvious.'*

**§ 51. 28. vadis:** 'shallows'; contrast the use of *vadum* as a place of safety (e.g. Ter. *Andr.* 845 'omnis res est iam in vado'); so Quintil. says (vi. 1. 52), with reference to the *peroratio*, 'e confragosis atque asperis evecti tota pandere possumus vela' (see G. Assfahl, *Vergleich und Metapher bei Quintilian*, pp. 66 f., for a discussion of sailing-metaphors in Latin).

**scopulos:** 'reefs'; cf. St. Jerome, *Epp.* 14. 10 'quia e scopulosis locis enavigavit oratio et inter cavas spumeis fluctibus cautes fragilis in altum cumba processit, expandenda vela sunt ventis et quaestionum scopulis transvadatis, laetantium more nautarum, epilogi celeusma cantandum est'.

**2. summorum facinorum: a** qualifying genitive (= *facinerosis-sima*); cf. *de domo* 50 'omnium facinorum et stuprorum hominem'; see note on 64. 24. Cicero repeats here what he had said in § 30, where he pretended to begin his *argumentatio.**

**5. aurum:** *ornamenta* (§ 52), which he would presumably sell.

**6. Luccei:** Cicero's old friend, perhaps best known through the letter (*ad Fam.* v. 12, cf. *ad Att.* iv. 6. 4) in which Cicero begged him to interrupt the chronology of his History of Rome by composing a monograph on the events of 63. He died some time after 45.

**Dio . . . necaretur:** this does not refer to the actual murder (cf. note on 24. 21), but to an alleged attempt made by Caelius; possibly Cicero deliberately stresses the friendship between Dio and Coponius in § 24, to prevent the impression that Dio removed there because he no longer felt safe in Lucceius' house.

**7. magnum crimen:** 'a dreadful charge'; both *legati* and a *hospes* should have been sacrosanct.

**8. insidiandis:** although the verb is not transitive, the gerundive is used in co-ordination with *sollicitandis* (see K. II. i, p. 104).

**§ 52. 11. ob:** so Cl., with *Σ*; *ad* Kl., with *P²* (*in II*): *ad* appears to suit Latin usage better (see Schönb., p. 47, a helpful note).

**12. dixit:** sc. Caelius; *dedit*, sc. Clodia.

**conscientiae scelere:** W. deletes *conscientiae*, on the ground that the *scelus* in question was not *conscientia* ('complicity'), following Schwarz (progr. Hirschberg, 1883, p. 10); Kl. (*Rh. Mus.* lxvii, 1912, p. 380) proposed *conscientia*, but did not admit it to his text. The genitive defines Clodia's part in the alleged crime, that she would have been an accessory before the act; *eodem* is used to mean that she and Caelius were 'together' (cf. 36. 27 'fuisti . . . in isdem hortis', and note): tr. 'she involved herself with him in the crime of her complicity'.

**13. armario:** a safe or chest, such as may be seen in houses at

113

Pompeii (cf. Overbeck–Mau, *Pompeii*, pp. 248, 425, etc.); it would stand near the entrance to the atrium; cf. *Clu.* 179 'cum esset in aedibus armarium in quo sciret esse nummorum aliquantum et auri', Petron. 29. 8.

14. **Venerem:** Clodia's tutelary deity; Cicero suggests that the statue was adorned with spoils taken from Clodia's other lovers (cf. *ceteris*, 50. 26).

15. **spoliatricem:** perhaps a mock cult-title, like *Venus victrix*, etc.; but cf. Martial iv. 29. 5 'sic spoliatricem commendat fastus amicam'.

**ceterorum:** so *Σ*, thus vindicating Madvig's conjecture (*Opusc. Acad.*, p. 324), based on a quotation from the codex S. Victoris by Gulielmius (see *An. Ox.*, p. xxxi); Orelli's note ad loc. makes curious reading now.

17. **labem . . . sempiternam:** 'an indelible stain of guilt'; a man who was *integerrimus* should have had no stain; he should have remained *integer vitae scelerisque purus*.

18. **huic facinori . . . debuit:** 'that generous heart of yours should never have known complicity in such a ghastly deed, that open house of yours should never have abetted it, no, that famous hospitable Venus of yours should never have lent herself to it'. Note the balance and assonance of this elaborate sentence, and its malice.

§ **53. 20. vidit hoc Balbus:** Herennius had foreseen the point and provided an explanation of it. *Vidit* = 'took into consideration' (cf. Nisbet on *de domo* 68).

21. **ita . . . attulisse:** 'gave this as his excuse'; *ita* anticipates the clause *se . . . quaerere*; for this use of *adfero* cf. *Clu.* 127 'illud adferant, aliquid eos . . . de ceteris comperisse', *de div.* ii. 36.

22. **ludorum:** not *ludi publici*, for Caelius held no office to give him such responsibility; he may have wished to help a friend who was a candidate for office at the time.

**si tam . . . aurum:** 'if he was as intimate with Clodia as you make out that he is, in your wordy harangue about his profligacy, then I am quite sure that he told her for what purpose he wanted the gold'; for *velle* = 'mean', 'assert', cf. 50. 22, 58. 24; for the meaning of *profecto* see on 1. 2. In *tu* Cicero suddenly turns to Herennius; supply *eum* with *esse* (cf. 58. 4, note), cf. Ter. *Hec.* 215–16 'an, quia ruri crebro esse soleo, nescire [*sc.* me] arbitramini, quo quisque pacto hic vitam vostrarum exigat?'

26. **o immoderata mulier:** 'you undisciplined woman!'; one would give much to have heard Cicero pronounce these words. Note the use of *o*, in a passage of deep emotion or excitement (Cicero would not say *o patres conscripti*).

28. **quid ego . . . resistam?:** a formula of *praeteritio*, in which

COMMENTARY §§ 53-54

the speaker states that he will not speak of something and, in denying, does so. Here, after the elaborate repetition of *possum dicere*
...*possum*...*possum*, Cicero cheerfully remarks (54. 16) 'brevitatis
causa relinquo omnia'.

3. **credendum ... credendam**: cf. note on 3. 16; but the sentence lumbers somewhat.

5. **alia:** so Cl., with Σ; *illa ΠP* (so Kl.), a preferable reading
(see Schönb., p. 48): *illa* = 'those familiar questions' (see note on
*haec* ... *propria*, 54. 12), of which an excellent illustration is *Rosc.
Am.* 74 'quo modo occidit? ipse percussit an aliis occidendum
dedit? si ipsum arguis, Romae non fuit, si per alios fecisse dicis,
quaero quos, servosne an liberos', etc.

9. **omnis ... peragrare:** 'draw all the coverts of suspicion'; cf.
Quintil. xii. 9. 3 'si iuris anfractus aut eruendae veritatis latebras
adire cogetur'.

10. **non causa ... reperietur:** Cicero follows the traditional
method of the rhetoric schools; see *Rhet. ad Herenn.* ii. 3 ff., where
the writer deals in turn with *causa, vita hominis* (cf. *mores* ...
*disiunctos* above), *signum* (subdivided into *locus, tempus, spatium,
occasio, spes perficiendi, spes celandi*); cf. ibid. iv. 53 'spatium
conficiendi longissimum sumptum est, non sine maxima occultandi
et perficiendi malefici spe'.

**conscius:** substantival, with other substantives; cf. *Clu.* 125
'ministris consciisque damnatis', *Verr.* iv. 143 'illi ipsi tui convivae
consiliarii conscii socii verbum facere non audent'.

**§ 54. 12. haec ... propria:** 'artificial' proofs, ἔντεχνοι πίστεις,
deduced by the orator from within the case itself, as opposed to
ἄτεχνοι πίστεις, 'inartificial' proofs, i.e. facts which do not depend
on the orator's own powers of discovery; the classification goes back
to Aristotle (*Rhet.* i. 2; cf. *de or.* ii. 116, *part. or.* 48 f.). The latter
include decisions of previous courts (*praeiudicia*), evidence given
under torture, documentary evidence, oaths, witnesses; the former
consist of *signa, argumenta* ('deductions'), *exempla*, i.e. what Cicero
has just listed. See Quintilian's fifth book, which is entirely devoted
to these two kinds of proof, and is of much interest. In § 66 below,
Cicero distinguishes between *argumenta, coniectura, signa* (ἔντεχνοι
πίστεις) and *testes* (ἄτεχνοι); cf. 22. 26. See Laurand, pp. 86 ff., for
discussion and parallels, and cf. Schönb., p. 48.

13. **non propter ingenium ... dicendi:** Cicero disclaims any
special skill of his own in such matters; they are the stock-in-trade
of any trained orator.

15. **a me ... proferri:** 'worked up on my own responsibility and
adduced as evidence'; so in *de or.* ii. 116 the ἄτεχνοι πίστεις are
termed 'quae non excogitantur ab oratore'.

115

16. **habeo . . . testem:** after this elaborate pretence of omitting 'artificial proofs', Cicero now turns to an ἄτεχνος πίστις; his attitude towards a favourable witness differs considerably from his line elsewhere, e.g. §§ 22, 66.

17. **religionis:** the binding duty of the oath; cf. *Brut.* 293 'sin adseveramus, vide ne religio nobis tam adhibenda sit quam si testimonium diceremus'; see the valuable analysis of uses of *religio* by Nettleship, *Contributions to Latin Lexicography* s.v.

20. **a M. Caelio:** Kl. brackets the words, following Damsté, perhaps rightly; his grounds for agreeing with Fra. in adding *auditum* after *neglexisset*, and removing *neque tulisset*, are not clear, although his text certainly gives a better clausula.

21. **an ille . . . hospitem:** 'is it likely that such a man, gifted with such sensibility, with the advantage of such literary interests, such accomplishments, such learning, could have ignored the peril of that very friend to whom he was devoted for precisely those very interests? Could he have taken no steps to deal with a crime committed against a guest, such as he would view with the greatest sternness if he heard of it as committed against a total stranger?' Cf. § 24, where Cicero uses similar language about Dio and the Coponii (see notes there).

25. **in hospitem:** so *T*, confirming a conjecture of Garatoni (sc. *intentum*); *P* reads *in hospite*, which gives less good balance.

26. **si comperisset:** *si* Cl., Kl., with *ΣT* (see app. crit.); W. reads *cum*, in pursuance of his view that Dio's murder took place in Lucceius' house (cf. 24. 21, note).

27. **servis:** omitted in *P*; Schönb. (p. 50) agrees with Madvig in deleting it.

2. **agrestis . . . eruditus . . . doctissimi:** cf. note on *urbanitas*, 6. 25.

§ 55. 5. **ipsius . . . cognoscite:** 'he has himself given evidence on oath; mark the solemnity of his affidavit; take in with great care every word of his statement'. *Auctoritas* (cf. 55. 17) is here used of a written statement, a sense for which the plural is more normal; cf. *Flacc.* 15 'quae recitantur psephismata non sententiis neque auctoritatibus declarata non iure iurando constricta', *de or.* iii. 5 'quod in auctoritatibus perscriptis exstat'; see Lebr., p. 65. *Religionem auctoritatemque* is virtually a hendiadys.

7. **L. LVCCEI TESTIMONIVM:** this would take the form of a *testimonium per tabulas datum*, which was always voluntary (Quintil. v. 7. 2); unlike the personal evidence, such testimony was read in court during, and not after, the *actio*. The deposition had to be given on oath (cf. Strachan-Davidson, *Problems of the Roman Criminal Law* ii, p. 116, note; see also H., p. 251, note). Greater

importance was naturally attached to a personal deposition, since a witness's demeanour in court was often the ultimate test of his reliability (Quintil. v. 7. 1). See further Greenidge, *LP*, p. 488; Mommsen, *Strafrecht*, p. 411, and *Juristische Schriften* iii, p. 501.

Presumably Lucceius had examined his slaves and could get no confirmation of the story; he evidently thought it unnecessary to produce the slaves themselves to give testimony, and they could not be so produced without his consent.

Kl. punctuates and reads as follows: *recita L. Luccei testimonium.* ⟨*TESTIMONIUM L. LUCCEI*⟩. He considers that *recita* by itself is too brusque an order (*Rh. Mus.* lxvii, 1912, p. 362, note); but *Verr.* ii. 24, iii. 26, 83, *Flacc.* 79, show that this was a normal custom in addressing the clerk of the court. His repetition in *testimonium L. Luccei* (so *P*, but without the praenomen) is based on an apparent lacuna in *Π*: an ingenious reconstruction, but unnecessary (*Π* and *T* agree here in reading *L. Luccei testimonium*; see Kl., *BPhW* 1914, col. 957).

**8. vocem ... mittere:** cf. *Clu.* 88 'veritas vocem contra invidiam ... miserit', Demosth. *Ol.* i. 2 ὁ μὲν οὖν παρὼν καιρὸς ... μόνον οὐχὶ λέγει φωνὴν ἀφιείς.

**9. haec est ... veritatis:** 'why, here is a defence of the innocent, here is a plea put forward by the case itself, here is the single utterance of Truth'; Pluygers proposed *viva vox* (*Mnemosyne* NS, ix, 1881, p. 142), comparing *leg. agr.* ii. 4 'non tabellam vindicem tacitae libertatis, sed vocem vivam prae vobis ... tulistis' (where *unam* is a variant)—attractive, but not necessary.*

**11. suspicio:** 'ground of suspicion'; Cicero means in this sentence that there are no ἔντεχνοι πίστεις of any sort (see note on 54. 12) nor yet any ἄτεχνοι πίστεις to support Clodia.

**13. totum crimen ... domo:** 'the entire charge proceeds from a hostile, disreputable, savage, crime-ridden, lust-ridden family'; note the triumphant climax, and the totally unexpected *domo* for *muliere*; cf. Tac. *Ann.* xiii. 20. 5 'nec accusatores adesse, sed vocem unius ex inimica domo adferri'.

**15. domus autem illa:** the juxtaposition with *domo* is effective, as well as the solemn repetition in *ex qua domo* below. Cicero's tone would be quite changed in this sentence.

**16. dicitur:** here the passage contained in *Ox. Pap.* x. 1251 (*Π*) ends.

**17. iure iurando ... auctoritas:** 'a sworn affidavit' (see on 55. 5).

**19. utrum ... videatur:** 'whether you think, on the one hand, that an irresponsible, wanton virago of a woman has preferred a false charge, or, on the other, that a responsible, scholarly, temperate man has given conscientious evidence'.

The disjunctive question is one in form only, and the answer to both parts is affirmative (cf. *Verr.* iii. 83, *Caec.* 29, *de domo* 7). I see no reason for accepting *irreligiose* (so W.), which was proposed independently by Schwarz (progr. Hirschberg, 1883, p. 10) and Fra. (p. 225), not so much because Cicero nowhere uses this adverb, but because the rhythm would be upset, and because *religiose* so admirably completes the picture of Lucceius. J. L. Heller (*CP* xxix, 1934, pp. 141 ff.) proposed *non finxisse*, a better proposal if a change is needed, but I cannot see that it is.

§§ 56–58. '*There remains the allegation of poisoning. Why should Caelius have wanted to poison Clodia? How could he have expected to do it? There is nothing consistent in the story, nothing to suggest its possibility.*'

The second part of the *argumentatio* now begins, with some general reflections on the *crimen veneni*, the details of which are left to §§ 61 ff.; Cicero's method of approach must have been familiar to anyone who remembered his defence of Cluentius ten years previously (e.g. *Clu.* 169 ff.).

§ 56. 25. **ne crimen haereret:** 'to prevent a charge from lying against him' (i.e. the charge of an attack upon Dio); cf. 15. 17.

1. **verbo:** 'in a single word'; cf. Ter. *Ph.* 197 'id, si potes, verbo expedi', *Verr.* iv. 35 'quod verbo transigere possum', [Quintil.] *decl. mai.* 12. 23 'sat erat verbo negare quod verbo ponitur'; see Mayor on Juv. 1. 161, and cf. note on 10. 12.

3. **tantum facinus:** the alleged poisoning of Clodia.

5. **sceleris maximi crimen:** 'a charge involving a most terrible crime'; this is the alleged attempt upon Dio, which Cicero says is being trumped up to account for the *alterum scelus*, the alleged attempt upon Clodia.

§ 57. 6. **commisit:** sc. *rem*; to discredit the ἔντεχνοι πίστεις, Cicero fires off seven questions that all mean the same thing—whose agency did Caelius employ?

10. **ingenium:** contrasted with what is implied in *demens*; the stupid story is inconsistent with what would be expected of a man whom even his opponents (*vos*) admitted to be clever.

**etiam si . . . detrahitis:** 'even though in every other point you belittle him in malevolent terms'.

12. **quibus servis ?:** 'what sort of slaves ?' they were nominally slaves, says Cicero, but actually Clodia's agents and associates in debauchery.

16. **mater familias:** see note on 32. 10.

19. **versentur:** 'are rife'; cf. *Verr.* iv. 83 'Dianae simulacrum

virginis in ea domo conlocabit in qua semper meretricum lenonum-
que flagitia versantur ?'

20. **qui . . . voluptatibus:** 'who play their part with her in her
profligacy'; for *isdem* in this sense see on 36. 27, 52. 12.

21. **ad quos . . . redundet:** 'who get a good many perquisites
even from the everyday expenditure and extravagance of the house-
hold'; *redundare* implies an overflow, here into the pockets of the
slaves (cf. *Verr*. iii. 155 'necesse est, si quid redundarit de vestro
frumentario quaestu, ad illum potissimum per quem agebatis
defluxisse').

§ **58. 24. voltis:** cf. 53. 23 (*vos* means the prosecution, as in 57.
10).

1. **ipsius . . . fingitur ?:** 'but as to the actual poison—what
theory is invented about *that* ?' Cicero again asks the familiar type
of question (cf. 53. 5) in connexion with the ἔντεχνοι πίστεις.

4. **vimque . . . venenum:** 'that he had tested its efficacy upon a
slave whom he got specially for this very purpose; the man died in
a few seconds, whereupon Caelius regarded the poison as satisfactory.' The subject of *expertum* is Caelius; *eum* must be supplied
with *habuisse* above (for the omission, which belongs to conversational style, see K. II. i, p. 701, Landgraf on *Rosc. Am.* 59, Lebr.,
pp. 376 ff., and cf. 53. 23, 68. 8).

It is significant that Cicero takes for granted such an act towards
a slave; cf. Tac. *Ann.* iv. 54, where Agrippina, suspecting poisoned
fruit, 'intacta ore servis tramisit'. The emperors employed slaves
as *praegustatores*, 'tasters' (see Mayor on Juv. 1. 70, p. 118); cf. the
story of Cleopatra and Antony in Pliny, *N.H.* xxi. 12, where the
queen, to prevent Antony from taking her at her word and drinking
from a cup containing poisoned flowers, 'inductam custodiam
bibere iussit ilico exspirantem'.

5. **perceleri:** the adjective occurs also in Amm. Marc. **xxix. 6. 1**
(L. & S. give no example apart from this passage).

§§ **59–60.** '*What cruelties the gods overlook in men! Think of the
untimely death of Q. Metellus, that great patriot, Clodia's
husband. Clodia would be wiser to make no mention of quick-
working poisons.*'

Cicero now inserts a malicious and skilful digression on the death
of Clodia's husband, whom she was suspected of having poisoned
(see on 34. 10); note the sudden dramatic change of tone, from a
lively briskness to a funereal gloom and most elaborate periods, a
good example of the artistry that made Cicero so formidable an
advocate. T. Frank, *Catullus and Horace*, p. 49, dismisses the story
as mere rumour.

For cases of poisoning at Rome see Mayor on Juv. 1. 70, Kaufman, *CP* xxvii, 1932, pp. 156 ff.

**§ 59. 7. conivetis:** cf. *har. resp.* 52 'in tot tantisque sceleribus conivebant'. *Praesentis* is genitive.

**8. in diem:** 'for a future day'; cf. Ter. *Ph.* 781 'praesens quod fuerat malum in diem abiit', Q. Cic. *Comm. Pet.* 48 'id, si promittas, et incertum est et in diem et in paucioribus; sin autem neges, et certe abalienes et statim et pluris.'

**vidi enim . . . civitati:** 'I have witnessed, yes, I have witnessed what was perhaps the most bitter sorrow of all my days, and I drained the cup of grief to its depths, on that day when Q. Metellus was ravished from the bosom and the embrace of his dear country: the day when that great gentleman, dedicated from birth (as he considered) to the service of our Empire, was torn from us when but two days since he had been at the height of his powers in the Senate, the courts, the political scene—torn most hideously from every loyal citizen and the entire Roman state, in the prime of his life, in the best of health, and in the utmost vigour of body.'

**9. hausi:** cf. *de domo* 30 'haurire me unum pro omnibus illam indignissimam calamitatem', *Sest.* 63 'luctum nos hausimus maiorem, dolorem ille animi non minorem'.

**11. natum huic imperio:** cf. Sen. *Suas.* 6. 23 'sic M. Cicero decessit, vir natus ad rei publicae salutem', *Sest.* 50 (of Marius) 'divinum illum virum . . . natum ad salutem huius imperi', *Mur.* 83 'M. Cato, qui mihi non tibi sed patriae natus esse videris', Lucan ii. 383 (of Cato) 'nec sibi sed toti genitum se credere mundo'. The rhetorical antithesis of the last two passages seems to go back to Plato, *Epp.* ix, p. 358 a, ἕκαστος ἡμῶν οὐχ αὑτῷ μόνον γέγονεν ἀλλὰ τῆς γενέσεως ἡμῶν τὸ μέν τι ἡ πατρὶς μερίζεται τὸ δέ τι οἱ γεννήσαντες, τὸ δὲ οἱ λοιποὶ φίλοι, a passage which Cicero paraphrases in *de fin.* ii. 45, where see Reid's note.

**12. floruisset:** cf. *de sen.* 42 'invitus feci ut . . . L. Flamininum e senatu eicerem septem annis post quam consul fuisset'; the subjunctive is due primarily to attraction (see K. II. ii, p. 203), but there is a concessive idea also.

**14. bonis omnibus:** cf. note on 14. 7.

**17. cum me . . . civitati:** 'there was I, in tears: and he turned his eyes towards me, and kept stressing, in broken, dying accents, the black tempest that hung above my head, the fierce storm that the State must weather.' Cicero refers to his own approaching exile.

**19. parietem:** the party-wall of the house, which adjoined that of Catulus; cf. T. Frank, op. cit., p. 281.

**20. Q. Catulo:** Q. Lutatius Catulus died in 60, during Metellus' consulship; he had been a leading optimate, and was a man of high principle, not shrinking from opposing Caesar (on the matter of sentencing the conspirators in 63) or Pompey (in 66, on the Manilian Law). His death was a great blow to the optimates, and especially to Cicero; cf. *ad Att.* i. 20. 3 'illud tamen velim existimes, me hanc viam optimatem post Catuli mortem nec praesidio ullo nec comitatu tenere'. See *leg. Man.* 51, 59, Sall. *Cat.* 49.

21. ut . . . doleret: 'in terms that showed his grief to be caused not at his own death, but at the fact that his protection was being removed from his country and, in particular, from me'.

§ 60. 24. furenti fratri: 'his revolutionary cousin', i.e. Clodius, to whom Cicero constantly applies the terms *furens*, *furibundus*, *furia*, etc.; *furere* (cf. 15. 19) is a party expression for 'left' tendencies, used by the *boni* ('constitutionalists') of their opponents; cf. *in Pis.* 47 'quid est aliud furere? . . . non cognoscere leges, non senatum, non civitatem?' and see Clark on *Mil.* 3.

The MSS. add *patrueli* after *fratri suo*; but *frater* alone can mean 'cousin' (so too *soror*); and in any case Metellus and Clodius were cousins on the mother's side, *consobrini*. See Nisbet on *de domo* 7. 23.

25. consul: Clodius was already planning his adoption into the plebs in 60, and Cicero may refer to this.

26. tonantem: so Cl., for MSS. *conantem*, comparing *Mur.* 81 'intonuit vox perniciosa designati tribuni'; the conjecture was later confirmed by cod. Oxon. Canonici 226 (see his preface to O.C.T. *pro Quinctio*, etc., p. xii). Kl. objects that *tonantem* is inconsistent with *incipientem*; and the parallel from *Mur.*, l.c., is not in fact wholly convincing (note also, as Schönb. observes, p. 53, that Cicero does not use *tonare* elsewhere in this metaphorical sense, except in *Orat.* 29, where he is translating from Greek). There is a further point, raised by Kl. (*PhW* 1934, col. 827), that *atque tonantem* involves a noticeable hexametric rhythm before the pause. On the whole, I am inclined to retain *conantem*; it could mean 'making efforts', 'starting up' trouble; cf. *in Cat.* i. 15 'nihil adsequeris, neque tamen conari ac velle desistis'; Schönb., l.c., quotes two instances where *conatus* appears in a closely similar context (*Phil.* iii. 5 'nisi unus adulescens illius furentis impetus crudelissimosque conatus cohibuisset', ib. x. 11 'nisi incredibilis ac divina virtus furentis hominis conatum atque audaciam compressisset', where *conatus* is made clear by the adjacent nouns, just as *incipientem furere* here helps to explain *conantem*).

27. domo . . . celeritate: surely a play on the name Metellus Celer; cf. *leg. agr.* ii. 59 'volitat enim ante oculos istorum Iuba . . . non minus bene nummatus quam bene capillatus', *Rosc. Am.* 124

'venio nunc ad illud nomen aureum Chrysogoni'; see Laur., pp. 240 ff.

**28. nonne ipsam . . . impedivit:** 'will she not feel terror at the very house, lest it cry out against her, will she not shudder at those walls which share her secret, will she not tremble at the memory of that night of death and lamentation? But I come back to the indictment before us; indeed, my reference to this distinguished and gallant patriot has brought tears to enfeeble my voice, sorrow to cloud my mind.'

**ipsam domum . . . eiciat:** cf. *Marcell.* 10 'parietes, medius fidius, . . . huius curiae tibi gratias agere gestiunt', Aesch. *Ag.* 37 οἶκος δ' αὐτός, εἰ φθογγὴν λάβοι, σαφέστατ' ἂν λέξειεν, Eur. *Hipp.* 1074.

**2. revertor:** so Cl., Kl., with Σ; *revertar* P (Schönb. shows, p. 51, that the future is far more common).

**§§ 61–69.** '*Well, how was the poison got? We are asked to believe that it was given to P. Licinius, to be handed over to Clodia's slaves at the baths; that the slaves double-crossed Caelius and told their mistress; that it was Clodia who had herself arranged this curious rendezvous, so that Licinius could be caught actually delivering the poison. And then in some strange manner Licinius got away! The whole thing is a farce, with no coherent plot about it. No wonder Clodia so mysteriously manumitted her slaves, no wonder she was the victim of a revolting practical joke!*'

Cicero, after this skilful piece of acting, riddles the story of the prosecution in his most light-hearted manner. Yet there is method behind his apparent fooling; the tale of the rendezvous at the baths is too circumstantial to be entirely false; something must have happened there, for the whole affair was obviously all over Rome; and Cicero's purpose is to confuse the jury's minds and entertain them at the same time. The clue to the whole story may well lie in the *obscenissima fabula* of 69. 10, of which we have no solution. The passage is masterly, and it would be hard to find anything in Cicero that is better done; note the somewhat similar story of a poisoning plot in *Clu.* 46 ff.

**§ 61. 6. huic:** Licinius (of whom nothing is known) was present in court (cf. 67. 15); it is odd that no attempt was made to call him as a witness.

**7. constitutum:** so Cl., following Naugerius; *constitutum pactum* Σ, *constitutum factum* P; Kl. deletes *constitutum* and reads *pactum esse cum servis* (see *Rh. Mus.* lxvii, 1912, p. 381; he thinks it more probable that *constitutum* was a gloss on *pactum* than vice versa). The simple narrative style makes for one or the other, not both: otherwise *constitutum pactumque* would be possible (cf. *in*

*Cat.* i. 24 'cui sciam pactam et constitutam cum Manlio diem'). With Cl.'s reading cf. *Clu.* 53 'constitutumque inter eos alia de re fuisse, ut medicamentum, non venenum Diogenes adferret'.

**8. balneas Senias:** probably baths run as a private speculation (cf. *de or.* ii. 223), such as one often reads of in Martial; the adjective may conceal the name of the manager or builder of the baths (see Jordan, *Hermes* ii, 1867, p. 79), just as the *balneae Pallacinae* (*Rosc. Am.* 18) may have been built or run by a Pallacius or Pallacinus; for such establishments see Platner and Ashby, *Topographical Dictionary of Ancient Rome*, pp. 381 f., and cf. Mayor on Juv. 7. 4.

**9. pyxidem:** a small case of boxwood, used for unguents of all kinds, and particularly for poisons; cf. Sen. *Suas.* 2. 21 'inter pyxides et redolentis animae medicamina constitit mitrata contio', Sen. *ap.* Lactant. *Inst.* iii. 15. 13 'medicos quorum tituli remedia habent, pyxides venena', Suet. *Nero* 47 'sumpto a Locusta veneno et in auream pyxidem condito'; hence in Juv. 13. 25, *pyxis* itself = 'poison'. The Greek πυξίς is similarly used of a medicine-box (Lucian, *Philops.* 21).*

**10. ferri:** *fieri* P (see Cl.'s app. crit.). Kl. rightly remarks (*Rh. Mus.* lxvii, 1912, p. 381, note) that the actual bringing of the poison to the assignation is the point; Schönb. (p. 54) defends *fieri*, taking *constitutum* with it ('that an appointment should be made to go to that place'), which seems very doubtful Latin (cf. Kl., l.c.). Ernesti deleted *constitutum* as a gloss on *eum*, which Kl. thinks may be right; but the sentence loses point to some extent without it.

**14. sin autem ... nimirum:** 'if, on the other hand, jealousy was already latent, if their intimacy had been brought to an end, if a rupture had occurred, well, well—then the cat is out of the bag'.*

**16. hinc illae lacrimae:** a proverb, from Ter. *Andr.* 126 (cf. Hor. *Epp.* i. 19. 41); see Otto, p. 184. Cicero continues to treat Clodia as behaving like a common *meretrix* who felt herself slighted.

**17. scelerum atque criminum:** see note on 1. 10.

**§ 62. 17. immo:** 'oh no'; for the use of *immo*, a word especially connected with dialogue, see L.-H., p. 669. The subject of *inquit* may be Herennius (cf. *Clu.* 92); more probably it is quite vague ('we are told'); see Reid on *de fin.* ii. 78.

**21. manifesto:** often with *comprehendere, deprehendere,* of catching 'red-handed'.

**23. traderet:** note the tense. For a somewhat parallel situation cf. *Clu.* 47 'venenum diebus paucis comparatur; multi viri boni cum ex occulto intervenissent, pecunia obsignata, quae ob eam rem dabatur, in manibus Scamandri liberti Fabriciorum deprehenditur.'

**25. reprendendi:** 'refutation', a common meaning in rhetoric.

27. **togatis:** wearing outdoor dress (cf. *calceati et vestiti* below).

**posset:** the tense would have been the same if the verb had not been in a dependent question (it is part of a conditional clause with suppressed protasis), and so is unaffected by the tense of *invenio*; cf. *Verr.* v. 139 'omnia quae dicam sic erunt inlustria, ut ad ea probanda totam Siciliam testem adhibere possem', *Rosc. Am.* 92 'video igitur causas esse permultas, quae istum impellerent'. See K. II. ii, p. 193; Lebr., p. 252.

1. **sin ... vellent:** 'but if they wanted to stow away in the inner part'.

2. **calceati et vestiti:** cf. *Phil.* ii. 76, where Cicero compares his own return to Rome *cum calceis et toga* with Antony's disgraceful *négligé*. They ought to have been *excalceati* (like actors in a mime, cf. Sen. *Epp.* 8. 8).

3. **nisi forte:** ironical, as always in Cicero (see L.–H., p. 779).

**nisi ... balneatori:** 'unless, naturally, that influential lady, doing the usual farthing deal, had turned into a crony of the bathman'. It would have been interesting to have watched the faces of the jury at this point. Cicero means that she had paid the usual bath-charge, but for the men's bath (see below); and he implies further, in *permutatione*, that Clodia had first received the fee in payment herself.

Cicero is playing up to a jest made by Caelius, who had dubbed Clodia a *quadrantaria Clytemnestra* (Quintil. viii. 6. 53), with reference both to the story that she had killed her husband and to the legend that she admitted her lovers for a *quadrans*; he gives it a fresh turn by linking *quadrantaria* with this tale of the bath. Frazer's note on Ovid, *Fasti* iv. 133 suggests yet another facet to the witticism. Cf. Antiphon i. 17 (with reference to a case of poisoning) ἔδοξεν οὖν αὐτῇ βουλευομένῃ βέλτιον εἶναι μετὰ δεῖπνον δοῦναι, τῆς Κλυταιμνήστρας τῆς τούτου μητρὸς ταῖς ὑποθήκαις ἅμα διακονοῦσα.

The meaning of *quadrantaria* is clear from Plutarch, *Cic.* 29 Κλωδίαν δὲ Μέτελλος ὁ Κέλερ εἶχεν, ἣν Κουαδρανταρίαν ἐκάλουν ὅτι τῶν ἐραστῶν τις αὐτῇ χαλκοῦς ἐμβαλὼν εἰς βαλάντιον ὡς ἀργύριον εἰσέπεμψε· τὸ δὲ λεπτότατον τοῦ χαλκοῦ νομίσματος κουαδράντην ἐκάλουν. There is a curious echo of the passage in St. Ambrose, *Exp. Ev. Luc.* vii. 157–8 'quadrantaria enim permutatio velut quaedam est compensatio cum aliud redditur et aliud significatur solutum . . . quadrantem autem in balneis dari solere reminiscimur' (cf. Migne ad loc.).

A *quadrans* was the usual price of admission to the men's baths (cf. Sen. *Epp.* 86. 9), and from Juv. 6. 447 it is clear that in his time the women paid more; this is supported by the post-Hadrianic Lex Metalli Vipascensis (Bruns[7] 112, p. 291, 23), which gives a charge

of $\frac{1}{4}$ *as* for men and 1 *as* for women. The *conductor* of the bath took
the money; at Pompeii a box was found at the entrance-hall to a
bath, perhaps a receptacle for these fees.

Friedrich (*Catullus*, p. 66) takes *quadrantaria* to mean little more
than *vilis*, comparing *semissis homo* (*ad Fam.* v. 10 a. 1), *non esse
sextantis* (*de or.* ii. 253), *homo dipundiarius* (Petron. 74. 15) (cf.
St. Jerome, *Epp.* 40. 2 'quadrante dignam eloquentiam'); but this
tones the nickname down too much, and a better parallel is *scorta
diobolaria* (Plaut. *Poen.* 270) or δυοῖν ὀβολοῖν ἑταιρίδιον (ps.-Plut.
*pro nobilitate* xiii. 3). *

**5. balneatori:** Quintil. (ix. 4. 63 f.) uses this and a passage from
*Verr.* v. 70 to illustrate a criticism levelled against Cicero's use of
certain structures in his clausulae; he remarks that Demosthenes
incurred no criticism for such clausulae as τοῖς θεοῖς εὔχομαι πᾶσι καὶ
πάσαις and κἂν μήπω βάλλῃ μηδὲ τοξεύῃ, yet except that these rhythms
are *severiora* they are essentially the same as Cicero's *familiaris
coeperat esse balneatori* (a quotation from memory) and *archi-
piratae*, which were objected to. He continues: 'est in eo quoque
nonnihil, quod hic singulis verbis bini pedes continentur, quod
etiam in carminibus est praemolle', comparing such verse-endings
as *fortissima Tyndaridarum* (Hor. *Sat.* i. 1. 100), *Appennino*
(Pers. i. 95), and others. He concludes 'quare hoc quoque vitandum
est, ne plurium syllabarum verbis utamur in fine'.

The point of this criticism is obscure, and Quintilian's own conclusion is hardly intelligible unless *plurium* is specifically narrowed
in meaning. Cicero does, of course, use pentasyllabic words of this
structure, like *balneatori*, in his clausulae; yet they are not common
(e.g. ten only in this speech, 9. 27, 20. 6, 27. 6, 29. 23, 40. 10, 45. 18,
50. 23, 62. 5, 63. 12, 69. 17), and it looks as though his critics,
realizing this, were attempting to seize upon something that they
thought, mistakenly, to have some special significance, and as
though Quintilian was similarly mistaken. Cf. Norden, *Antike
Kunstprosa* ii, p. 927; Laur., p. 205.*

**§ 63. 5. atque equidem . . . impetravisset:** 'I assure you, it
was with much excitement that I kept waiting to hear who those
stout fellows could possibly be, who were alleged to have witnessed
the discovery of this poison in Licinius' hands; you see, we have
heard no names so far. But I am quite certain that they are emi-
nently responsible persons: why, to begin with, they are intimates of
so excellent a lady; secondly, they accepted the duty of being stuffed
away in the baths, a job that she could never have got them to do,
be she ever so influential, had they not been the soul of honour and
men of unimpeachable worth.'

**6. manifesto:** lit. 'on the spot' (cf. 62. 20), i.e. just as Licinius was handing it over; normally it would be the delinquent who would be 'caught red-handed'.

9. **talis feminae:** Cicero uses the complimentary *femina* here with cheerful irony (cf. 31. 5, note).

11. **quam velit sit potens:** cf. 67. 18 *quam volent . . . faceti . . . sint.* In such expressions the normal *quamvis*, i.e. *quam vis*, is replaced by *quam* + another form of *volo*, so that the original verbal aspect of this conjunction retains its full force; so *Verr.* v. 11 'facinus quam vultis improbum', *Phil.* ii. 113 'quam volent illi cedant otio consulentes'; see L.–H., p. 737, K. II. ii, p. 443.

14. **in balneis . . . temperantis:** ' "They lurked in the baths": what outstanding witnesses! "Then they incontinently jerked themselves out": sober fellows, to be sure !'*

The homoeoptoton in *delituerunt . . . prosiluerunt* is deliberately amusing; for a similar 'rhyme' cf. *Scaur.* 45 'domus tibi deerat ? at habebas. pecunia superabat ? at egebas' (quoted in *Orat.* 223 as an example of 'quae incisim efferuntur'); cf. Laur., p. 138, and for the whole subject of 'rhyme' in Cicero see Polheim, *Die lateinische Reimprosa*, pp. 183 ff.; Marouzeau, *Traité de stylistique appliquée au latin*, pp. 54 ff. There may be a word-play in *temere . . . temperantis*; they were 'on the water-wagon' and yet behaved so unsedately: cf. *Phil.* xiii. 26 'quem tamen temperantem fuisse ferunt Pisauri balneatorem'.

15. **sic . . . coniecisse:** the changes of tense throughout are important. There must have been some truth behind the ridiculous tale.

21. **o magnam . . . defendat:** Muretus compares Aeschin. *in Timarch.* 84 οὕτως ἰσχυρόν ἐστιν ἡ ἀλήθεια, ὥστε πάντων ἐπικρατεῖν τῶν ἀνθρωπίνων λογισμῶν.

**§ 64.** 23. **velut . . . exitum potest:** 'for example: take this wholy pretty little drama, the work of a lady-poet who is an old hand at the game and has many romances to her credit—how devoid of plot it is, how utterly lost for an ending !'*

*Velut* is used here (like *ut, sicut*) to adduce an illustration; cf. Plaut. *Merc.* 225 'miris modis di ludos faciunt hominibus . . . velut ego nocte hac . . . in somnis egi satis', *de nat. deor.* ii. 124 'est etiam admiratio nonnulla in bestiis aquatilibus iis, quae gignuntur in terra; velut crocodili . . . aquam persequuntur'. See K. II. ii, p. 450, L.–H., p. 676.

24. **veteris:** in a bad sense; cf. Landgraf's valuable note on *Rosc. Am.* 17.

**plurimarum fabularum:** *fabula* here has several implications; it implies that Clodia wrote plays, but it could suggest a farce or trick (cf. *ad Att.* iv. 2. 4 'ad suam veterem fabulam rediit',

Livy iii. 44. 9 'notam iudici fabulam petitor, quippe apud ipsum auctorem argumenti, peragit'), and could also hint at the tales that were told about Clodia, with special reference to the *fabula* of § 69 (cf. G. Giri, *Rivista Indo-Greca-Italica* vi, 1922, p. 163, note).* The genitive is qualitative, as in 51. 2 'muliere summorum facinorum'; cf. *Brut.* 286 'Charisius multarum orationum', *Rosc. Am.* 17 'plurimarum palmarum vetus ac nobilis gladiator', where see Landgraf, *ad Att.* xiii. 28. 4 'Cornificiam . . . vetulam sane et multarum nuptiarum', *ad Fam.* ix. 26. 3 'non multi cibi hospitem', Cic. *ap.* Macrob. *Sat.* iii. 16. 4 'acipenser iste paucorum hominum est'; cf. note on 77. 18.

This genitive is often a means of avoiding compound adjectives of a kind that belongs to the Greek genius, but is unsuited to Latin: see Wölfflin, *Archiv für lat. Lex.* xi, p. 207 (but note comments in L.–H., p. 398). For a discussion of the genitive in relation to the ablative of quality, see Löfstedt, *Synt.* i, ch. 10; E. Vandvik, *Genetivus und Ablativus Qualitatis* (Oslo, 1942, cf. *CR* lxi, p. 22); Edwards–Wölfflin, *Archiv für lat. Lex.* xi, pp. 197–211, 469–90.

25. **argumento:** a coherent plot; Cicero is leading up to his comparison with a mime (§ 65); cf. *de nat. deor.* i. 53 'ut tragici poetae, cum explicare argumenti exitum non potestis, confugitis ad deum'.

8. **ante tempus:** 'too soon'; cf. *Tusc.* i. 93 'ante tempus mori miserum esse'; so *post tempus* 'too late', cf. Phaedr. iv. 19. 1 'qui fert malis auxilium post tempus dolet'; see Landgraf on *Rosc. Am.* 128. The story of the prosecution, as represented by Cicero, is certainly very lame; possibly Licinius had upset their case by refusing to come forward with evidence.

**fuerant . . . conlocati:** such 'double' pluperfects usually denote a state which had ceased to exist at some moment in the past; here Cicero means 'their original instructions, their original stationing had been for this one purpose', stressing the length of time for which the scheme had stood. See Lebr., pp. 203 f.; K. II. i, p. 166.

**ad hoc:** so *Σ* (as Lambinus had conjectured); *hoc* Kl. (with *P*), less well.

§ **65. 11. tempore:** ἐν καιρῷ; they were not premature, but chose the proper moment, and yet failed.

15. **imploraret . . . pernegaret:** 'he would have been found begging for protection, roundly denying that it was he who had delivered that box to them'. The imperfect in the apodosis marks the possibility of an event in past time, contingent on another action; cf. *Tusc.* iii. 54 'nec, si aliquot annis post idem ille liber captivis missus esset, vulneribus mederetur'. See K. II. ii, pp. 396 f.; the imperfect implies continuing action (cf. Dougan on *Tusc.* i. 27).

§ 65                    COMMENTARY

*Imploraret hominum fidem* is equivalent to 'protesting his inno-
cence'.*

16. **reprehenderent?** ... **dicerent?**: past deliberatives ('how
were they to refute him? Were they to say ...?'); in the next
sentence there is an ellipse of *quod si fecissent* or the like.

17. **ad se vocarent**: so Cl.; *ad se revocarent* Kl., with *P*. Cl.'s
emendation does not seem needed; *revocarent* = 'they would be
bringing upon their own heads' the suspicion that had previously
fallen on Licinius, i.e. that they themselves had handed over the
poison (cf. Schönb., p. 57; Busche oddly conjectures *ad visa
revocarent*, *BPhW* 1917, col. 1388).

20. **expediret**: cf. *conaretur tradere*, 63. 16; Cicero deliberately
stresses the ludicrous position of Licinius, fumbling for the box;
note also the way in which he repeats the man's name, to make him
ridiculous (eight times on this page alone).

21. **mimi ... tollitur**: 'as a result we have the finale of a mime,
not of a straight play; the kind of thing where, when a proper
ending cannot be devised, someone wriggles away, clatter go the
clogs, and—curtain!'
Mimes were notable for their grotesque improbabilities, and for
their inconsequent style; cf. *Phil.* ii. 65 'exsultabat gaudio persona
de mimo, modo egens, repente dives'; in *Rab. Post.* 35 Cicero speaks
of *praestigiae* and *fallaciae* in association with them; note Demetrius, π. ἑρμ. 153 ἡ δὲ τοιαύτη ἀνακολουθία καλεῖται γρῖφος, ὥσπερ ὁ παρὰ
Σώφρονι ῥητορεύων Βουλίας· οὐδὲν γὰρ ἀκόλουθον αὐτῷ λέγει. But the
reference to a mime here has a further point, in that the women's
parts in them were often played by *meretrices* (cf. Lactant. *Inst.* i.
20. 10); and, as part of an Oxyrhynchus mime-fragment (*Ox.
Pap.* iii. 413) represents a poisoning-scene, this aspect too may be
suggested.
See Schanz–Hosius, *Gesch. der röm. Lit.* i, pp. 253 f.; Friedländer,
*Sittengeschichte Roms*[9] ii, pp. 113 f.; Reich, *Der Mimus*, pp. 50 f.;
Allardyce Nicoll, *Masks, Mimes, and Miracles* (London, 1931);
Beare, *The Roman Stage*, ch. xviii.

22. **clausula**: here the conclusion of a play; cf. Macrob. *Sat.*
ii. 7. 13 'cum canticum quoddam saltaret Hylas cuius clausula erat
τὸν μέγαν Ἀγαμέμνονα', Sen. *Epp.* 77. 20 'quomodo fabula, sic vita
non quam diu, sed quam bene acta sit refert. nihil ad rem pertinet,
quo loco desinas. quocumque voles desine; tantum bonam clausu-
lam impone', Suet. *Nero* 39. 3.

23. **scabilla**: a diminutive of *scamnum* (see L.–H., p. 155; cf.
Varro, *L.L.* v. 168, Quintil. i. 4. 12), used to mean a clapper which
was attached to the feet like a shoe; this was employed in marking
the time for the pantomimist or the dancers, and from this passage

128

it appears that a special *scabillarius* had the duty of signalling to the man who worked the curtain (Beare, op. cit., p. 161). Cf. Suet. *Cal.* 54 'repente magno tibiarum et scabellorum crepitu ... prosiluit ac desaltato cantico abiit', St. Aug. *de mus.* iii. 1 'symphoniaci scabella et cymbala pedibus feriunt'. The Greek κρούπεζα was similar; see Westermann, *Journal of Egyptian Archaeology* 1924, pp. 134 f. (The words *dein scabilla concrepant* look like an iambic quotation; they occur in the Glossary of Placidus, see Lindsay and Pirie, *Glossaria Latina* iv, p. 33).

aulaeum tollitur: for the working of the Roman drop-curtain, see Beare, op. cit., pp. 259 ff. This is the first mention of the *aulaeum* in literature: it was raised when the stage was to be concealed, lowered (*aulaeo misso*, Phaedr. v. 7. 23; *aulaea premuntur*, Hor. *Epp.* ii. 1. 189) for the performance to begin. It was embroidered with painted figures (Virg. *G.* iii. 25; Ovid, *Met.* iii. 111 ff.). Beare infers that it was introduced precisely because of the formless nature of the mime, in which only an external device could indicate that the show was over. Remains of Roman theatres show a slot under the stage-floor, near the front of the stage, into which the curtain was dropped; see Beare, p. 261 (he holds that after the age of Tiberius the curtain worked like a modern curtain).

§ 66. 24. quaero ... expresserint: 'I fail to understand why those woman-inspired commandos let Licinius give them the slip, when he was stumbling, tripping, backing, struggling to get away; why they did not grab hold of him; why they did not use his personal confession, the full publicity, the cry of the deed itself, to give full shape to a charge involving such a horrid crime.' Cicero draws a vivid and amusing picture of the surprised and stupefied Licinius.

25. mulieraria: a rare word; the sense is plainly shown by *fortis viros ab imperatrice ... conlocatos* (67. 10); note the word-play in *manus ... manibus*.

26. emiserit: but *amiserunt* in 64. 1; cf. *Verr.* iii. 32 'cum ... rem de manibus amisisses', ibid. iv. 44 'praeda ... de manibus emissa' (*v.l.* amissa).

1. expresserint: 'express' in English has lost the colour of *exprimere*, which is properly used of statuary.

an: 'perhaps', ironical; note the antitheses.

3. argumentum ... suspicio: i.e. no ἔντεχνοι πίστεις will be found; only the witnesses are left—ἄτεχνοι πίστεις—*if* they appear.

5. coniectura: 'inference', drawn by comparing facts with one another (see Nisbet on *de domo* 15).

§ 67. 8. praegestit ... conlocatos: 'I am simply agog to see, to start with, those young sprigs of fashion who are intimate with a rich and high-born lady, and then again those intrepid fellows who were posted by their female commandant in the ambush and entrenchment of the baths'.

**praegestit**: the word suggests physical excitement (cf. Catull. 64. 145 'animus praegestit apisci'; Virg. *G.* i. 387 'studio incassum videas gestire lavandi').

10. **praesidio**: suggests both the protection that the baths afforded and that it was the 'station' that the men had to occupy as 'garrison'.

12. **alveus**: a bath-tub (πύελος), used for the warm baths in the *caldarium*; originally a small slipper-bath, but later the word was applied to the warm swimming-bath itself.

**equus Troianus**: cf. *Phil.* ii. 32 'in huius me tu consili societatem tanquam in equum Troianum cum principibus includis', *Verr.* iv. 52, *de or.* ii. 94 (*Mur.* 78 'intus, intus, inquam, est equus Troianus', of a sudden, hidden danger).*

14. **illud . . . respondere**: 'reply to this'; cf. *in Vat.* 18 'illud volo uti respondeas', *Mur.* 28 'quae consuluntur autem, minimo periculo respondentur'.

17. **se . . . explicabunt**: 'disentangle themselves' from questioning; they will be so 'tied up' by their story; cf. *Flacc.* 10 'quem ad modum se explicent dicendo'.

**in istum locum**: the witness-box.

18. **quam volent**: see note on 63. 11.

**faceti, dicaces**: 'humorous and witty'; cf. *Orat.* 87 '(sales) quorum duo genera sunt, unum facetiarum, alterum dicacitatis. utetur utroque; sed altero in narrando aliquid venuste, altero in iaciendo mittendoque ridiculo' (see Sandys's helpful note); with *dicax* cf. *dictum*, 'a *mot*'. Cicero uses the adjectives deliberately: they can be smart and fashionable men-about-town (cf. note on 6. 25) at dinner-parties, but in the witness-box they will look like silly country bumpkins.

19. **ad vinum**: 'over their bottle'; so Pliny (*N.H.* x. 117) says that the parrot is *in vino praecipue lasciva.* For *diserti*, see note on 15. 18.

**alia fori . . . lychnorum**: 'a court-room and a dining-room have a very different signification; the witnesses' bench is not the same thing as a dining-couch; jurymen and junketers look entirely dissimilar; in short, daylight and candle-light do not in the least resemble each other.'*

20. **subselliorum**: the benches of the court, occupied either by the jury or by counsel or by the litigants and witnesses.

**ratio**: much like *vis* above, 'idea', 'meaning'.

21. **lux**: i.e. the publicity of the court; cf. Quintil. xii. 6. 4 'est

tamen proprius quidam fori profectus, alia lux, alia veri discriminis facies' (of a real trial as opposed to a school-exercise).

**22. alia lychnorum:** *et lychnorum P, ac lychnorum T.* Schönb. (pp. 58 f.) objects that *longe alius . . . alius* in such a context is rare, and found nowhere else in Cicero (*longe alius . . . atque* or *ac, Caec.* 3, *ad Att.* xi. 10. 2). But the parallel structure of *alia fori vis est,* etc., makes an overwhelming case for *alia* here, whether unusual or not. (See Schönb., l.c., for a useful list of passages in Cicero where *alius* or *aliter* is followed by *ac* or *et.*) For the quasi-proverbial flavour of the phrase, see Otto s.v. *sol.*

**excutiemus:** 'shake out', 'knock away'; cf. *Sull.* 24 'excutient tibi istam verborum iactationem'.

**23. delicias:** 'affected ways' (cf. note on 27. 1); cf. *Orat.* 39 'longissime . . . a talibus deliciis vel potius ineptiis afuerunt'.

**sed . . . deserviant:** 'but let them take my advice: let them turn their energies elsewhere, curry favour in some other way, show off in some other line, cut a dash with their lady in their elegance, play the great man in their extravagance, be inseparable from her, lie at her feet, be her devoted slaves.' For *navent aliam operam* cf. **21.** 17, note; *venustate* is deliberately chosen to suit the picture (cf. note on *dignitas,* 8. 13); *dominentur* is used with reference to possible rivals, not to Clodia.

**27. capiti . . . fortunisque:** a regular legalistic formula (note the invariable plural *fortunae*), to denote the civil and material 'life' of a man: sometimes *fama* is added (e.g. *Quinct.* 8 'caput alterius, famam fortunasque defendam'); see Landgraf on *Rosc. Am.* 5.

**§ 68. 28. at:** *occupatio*; the slaves are those mentioned in §§ 61-62.

**de cognatorum sententia:** it was normal for a family council to be held where a decision affected the family interests (cf. Landgraf on *Rosc. Am.* 27); Cicero suggests that Clodia found their approval a novelty. Note the assonances here and in the next sentence (*cognatorum, nobilissimorum et clarissimorum, suorum propinquorum, fortissimorum virorum*): Cicero was much enjoying himself.*

A woman, being theoretically *in tutela,* could not manumit of her own right; Clodia would be under the *tutela* of her *agnati* unless her husband had expressly named a *tutor* in his will. In practice, however, by means of the legal fiction *coemptio fiduciae causa,* a woman could obtain a *tutor* of her own nomination, and thus be practically independent (cf. *Mur.* 27).

In this formula Cicero always uses *de,* not *ex* (Landgraf, l.c.).

**2. propinquorum:** cf. [Quintil.] *decl. mai.* 2. 14 'exheredaturus filium pater non advocat propinquos?'

4. **cupio**: ironical; cf. *Caec.* 33, *Phil.* ii. 84 (with *audire*), *Caec.* 37 (with *discere*), *Phil.* v. 6 (with *videre*).

**quid . . . argumenti**: 'what is the drift of'; cf. *de off.* ii. 84 'tabulae vero novae quid habent argumenti?'

5. **in qua . . . persolutum**: 'it means either that a charge had been engineered against Caelius, or that a possibility of examination was removed, or that a richly deserved reward was paid to slaves who knew so many of her secrets'.

**crimen . . . Caelio quaesitum**: i.e. that the slaves had helped Clodia to trump up a charge.

**quaestio sublata**: i.e. so that the slaves could not be forced to give evidence under torture; cf. *Mil.* 57 'cur igitur eos manu misit? metuebat scilicet, ne indicaretur, ne dolorem perferre non possent, ne tormentis cogerentur occisum esse a servis Milonis . . . P. Clodium confiteri.'

7. **inquit**: 'I am told' (cf. 62. 17, note); *inquis* or *inquit* is often added in such an *occupatio* (see *Thes. L. L.* s.v. *at*, col. 996. 53 ff.).

9. **deferre**: for the omission of *te* cf. note on 58. 4. Presumably Clodia did not tell her relatives that it was a put-up job; but the point made by Cicero is obscure without further detail.

**§ 69. 10. commenticiam**: 'bogus'; the word is used of something 'fabricated' (cf. *comminiscor*), often equivalent to 'imaginary', 'ideal' as opposed to real.

**obscenissima . . . fabula**: cf. Quintil. *decl. min.* 300 (p. 184 R) 'nihil mihi obiectum est in aetate prima, nulla fabula ante partum secuta est'. No satisfactory explanation of the allusion is available, and it is obviously the clue to much of the mystery of the preceding sections. But some practical joke must have been played on Clodia; cf. Quintil. vi. 3. 25 'facto risus conciliatur interim admixta gravitate . . . interim sine respectu pudoris, ut in illa pyxide Caeliana, quod neque oratori neque ulli viro gravi conveniat' (perhaps a reference to Caelius' own speech, as Kl. suggests). For some highly coloured attempts at explanation, see Maggi ad loc.; van Wageningen in *Mnemosyne* xxxvi, pp. 183 ff. (cf. Juv. 2. 141); Fra., p. 229; Harnecker in *BPhW* 1884, col. 225. Heinze discusses the passage with admirable caution (p. 252); Cicero himself gives timely warning, *percipitis . . . quid nolim dicere*.*

Schöll oddly connects Prop. ii. 32. 23 ff. with this episode (*Jahrb. für kl. Phil.* xxvi, 1880, pp. 481 ff.); cf. Harnecker, *Philologus* xli, 1882, p. 470, note 5.

12. **cadere**: 'to suit', 'to fall into line with'.

16. **non tam insulso**: like *non infacetum* below, the expression suggests that whatever the jest was, it at least had some *urbanitas* about it, but it was too *inverecundum* for a sensitive young man like

Caelius (Harnecker, *BPhW*, l.c., thinks that the *adulescens* was Catullus!). Busche (*BPhW* 1917, col. 1388) suggests transposing *est enim . . . inverecundo* to follow *mendacium* below: but then what is to be supplied with *est*?

21. **quadrare apte**: 'to tally nicely' with Clodia's reputation; it is just possible that *quadrare* is meant to play upon *quadrantaria*.

**§§ 70–80. PERORATIO.** '*My ·case is finished. You see the gravity of the issue, and the way in which Caelius has been victimized. He is an honourable and hard-working young man, as his whole life shows; I beg you to preserve him for the State and for his unhappy father; and you will reap a rich and lasting reward from his services.*'

Cicero now begins his peroration, leaving the case quite suddenly, wrapped in mystery, with the jury rocking in inextinguishable laughter. His inclusion of a detailed *vita* here (cf. §§ 10 ff.) shows the importance of the need to leave the jury quite clear that Caelius' character was exemplary, and that his promise was exceptional. The elevated style is all the more noticeable for the easy manner of so much of the rest of the speech.

→ **§ 70. 24. quae lex . . . exstinxit**: see note on 1. 7 for the identity of this law (*tulit* below seems to preclude Mommsen's theory that Catulus had the law carried by a tribune). The repetition in *quae lex . . . hac nunc lege* is a mannerism fairly frequent in Cicero, though especially common in Caesar (Parzinger, op. cit., pp. 7 f.).

26. **Q. Catulus**: this dates the law to 78–77 B.C.

27. **quaeque . . . exstinxit**: 'the law which stamped out the smouldering embers of the conspiracy, after that conflagration which took place when I was consul'.

1. **libidines et delicias**: 'depraved caprice'.

**§ 71. 2. Camurti . . . Caeserni**: a case, otherwise unknown, presumably quoted by the prosecution as a precedent for extending the *Lex de vi* to cover a case of immorality; Clodia had been concerned in it, and Cicero intends to deplore the imprudence of its mention in the present context, with all that it implied about her.

The fragment of the Ambrosian palimpsest begins at *Caeserni*, and continues to *infelici* in 75. 20.

5. **audetis**: so Cl., with *Σ*; *audetisne* Kl., with *P*; Schönb. (pp. 61 f.), who supports Cl., has an interesting note on the repetition of *-ne*.

7. **crimine**: see note on 1. 10.

8. **perierunt**: 'were condemned' (cf. *periculum*, of a criminal trial; see on 16. 2).

**dolorem et iniuriam . . . persecuti**: 'they avenged the spite and resentment'. Nothing is known of the connexion of the Vettius referred to here with Clodia or with the case of Camurtius and Caesernius; it is pure conjecture that he was the author of the trick played upon Clodia in Plutarch's story (62. 4). There is a Vettius named in *in Vat.* 24 ff. (see Pocock's edition, pp. 183 ff.).

9. **Vettiano**: deleted by Kl.; *nefario* was deleted by Schöll. But it seems necessary to retain *Vettiano*, to lead up to *Vetti nomen* in the next sentence; the removal of *nefario* would then improve the sentence, but it is difficult to account for its presence at all if it is not genuine; on the whole Cl.'s text may be regarded as sound, with *Vettiano stupro* taken as a single concept, though the word-order is strange.

10. **illa vetus ... fabula**: 'that old penny dreadful': presumably there is a play on *vetus*, *Vetti* (cf. *Flacc.* 66, where there is a play on *auri* and *gradibus Aureliis*). The *fabula* is unknown, unless there really is a reference to Plutarch's story (see above, 62. 3); *aeraria* was conjectured by Garatoni, and confirmed by Σ (cf. Kl. in *Rh. Mus.* lxvii, 1912, p. 373).*

12. **quamquam ... tenebantur**: this illustrates the tendency to enlarge the scope of the *Lex de vi* (cf. H., p. 203).

§ 72. 14. **M. vero Caelius**: cf. note on *Q. illa Claudia*, 34. 18. The particle is strongly adversative.

15. **cui ... coniunctum**: 'no charge is brought against him that is pertinent to this court, nor in fact a count that is germane to your powers of stricture though unconnected with the law *de vi*'; i.e. there is absolutely no parallel with the case just quoted.

The Ambrosian palimpsest reads *proprium quidem crimen quaestionis*, whence Halm conjectured *proprium quoddam cr. qu.*; Sydow (*Hermes* lxv, 1930, p. 321) proposed *ne proprium quidem*; neither is an improvement on the text as shown.

20. **eis autem ... videretur**: 'again, he made friends with such older men as afforded him the most desirable examples of hard work and self-control, he was attracted by such of his contemporaries' interests as could make it plain that he aimed at the road to honour with the finest and the best'.

**autem**: not adversative, but continuing the argument a stage farther (see K. II. ii, p. 95).

21. **maxime vellet, eis studiis**: *maxime velitis, is aequalium studiis* Kl. (see app. crit.); Madvig (*Adv. Crit.* iii, p. 144) inserts *eum* after *quorum*, reading *velitis*. The parallel structure makes *vellet* much more probable; Cicero is not addressing the jury or some hypothetical persons, but speaking of Caelius' own predilections. Cf. Schönb., p. 63.

§ 73. 24. **Q. Pompeio ... contubernalis**: 'as an aide to Pom-

peius'; he was a member of Pompeius' *cohors*, just as Catullus went
to Bithynia with Memmius. Q. Pompeius Rufus was praetor in 63,
when he was stationed at Capua to prevent a slave-rising in support
of Catiline (Sall. *Cat.* 30); as proconsul in 61 he was governor of
Africa. He is not to be confused with the Pompeius Rufus who was
tribune with Caelius in 52, whom the latter afterwards prosecuted
(introd., p. ix).

2. **possessiones paternae:** this is the only evidence that the
elder Caelius was a man of property, even though *parcus ac tenax*.

**tum etiam . . . tributus:** 'and, what is more important, there
was available the kind of experience of provincial administration
that has traditionally, and with reason, been regarded as essential
for a young man'. Kl. marks a lacuna after *provincialis*; W.
supplies *parabatur* after *tributus*. The sentence is certainly a little
awkward, but there is no reason to suppose it corrupt. Cicero
means that Caelius had both personal grounds and 'career' reasons
for wanting to go to Africa.

5. **adulescentium exemplo:** cf. note on 3. 11, and see further
on 78. 2.

**§ 74. 8. vellem . . . detulisset:** cf. § 18 'mihi quidem molestam,
sibi tamen gloriosam victoriam'.

11. **benefici . . . malefici:** Antonius' services in defeating the
Catilinarians at Pistoria (as official commander) is contrasted with
his suspected treason (see Appendix VII); in *Sest.* 8 Cicero shows
him clearly as a trimmer ('nunquam illum illo summo timore ac
periculo civitatis neque communem metum omnium nec propriam
nonnullorum de ipso suspicionem aut infitiando tollere aut dissimu-
lando sedare voluisse').

13. **negotiis:** 'court-cases' (see on 1. 4), in which Caelius would
act as *advocatus* to his friends (cf. note on 10. 14).

15. **quae . . . consecutus:** cf. 45. 21 ff.

**§ 75. 17. flexu:** 'critical turn'; a metaphor from the race-course,
which had a low fence (*spina*) running down the middle, with the
*metae* ('posts') at either end: it was in turning at these *metae* that
a fall was most to be feared, since the riders kept as close to them
as possible (cf. Soph. *El.* 720, 744); cf. καμπή, κάμπτειν βίον, etc.;
Lycophron, *Alex.* 286 τὴν πανυστάτην δραμὼν . . . βίου βαλβῖδα.

18. **fretus . . . vestra:** 'being assured of your sympathy and
common sense'; *humanitas* is the feeling that one man has for
another.

19. **haesit ad metas:** cf. Ovid, *Tr.* iv. 8. 35 'nec procul a metis,
quas paene tenere videbar, curriculo gravis est facta ruina meo'.
Cicero means that Caelius was on his way to make his reputation,
when his good name was nearly wrecked at the post, and for the

moment he 'came a cropper', as it were, when he went to live near
Clodia. He draws a pleasant picture of the innocent youth being
swept off his feet in high life 'owing to his recent acquaintance with
this lady, his disastrous proximity to her, the novelty of the gay
world'. *Nova eius* is Cl.'s emendation (*novae Σ, nova P*, which Kl.
retains); but it is some time since Clodia has been mentioned, and
*eius* seems unlikely (and 'a lady' is more pointed).

20. quae ... universae: 'such dissipations, after they have been
rather long hedged in, controlled and checked in early days, quite
often suddenly work themselves up and burst out in a mass'.

22. se ... profundunt: cf. 28. 17, and note.

23. vel dicam: cf. *Phil.* ii. 30 'stuporem hominis vel dicam
pecudis attendite' (see Mayor ad loc.); Reid, on *de fin.* i. 10,
observes that it is not a common formula in Cicero. It acts as a
corrective, and so has no effect upon the construction: the connecting relative *quo* is repeated from the original *qua*, as if the sentence
were still beginning (cf. note on 32. 16). Tr. 'but from this way of
living—no, here is a better way of putting it—from this kind of
gossip'.

24. loquebantur: see note on 11. 29.

25. verum ... propulset: Cicero pulls himself up and makes a
third start: 'well, from whatever it was, he came up to the surface
from it and completely forced his way out and cleared himself; he
is so far from disgracing himself by friendship with her that it is
her enmity and loathing against which he is now defending himself.'

eiecit: so Cl., with *P*; *erexit* Kl. (an emendation by Karsten,
*Spicilegium Criticum*, p. 15, on the analogy of *Planc.* 33, *leg. agr.*
ii. 87). But *eiecit* exactly suits the picture, and should not be
changed: see Löfstedt, *Synt.* ii, p. 446, *Peregr. Aeth.*, p. 266 (he
well compares Pliny, *Epp.* viii. 17. 3 'Anio ... se super ruinas eiecit
atque extulit'). In his preface of 1919, p. lxi, Kl. retracts his view
and supports the MS. reading.

§ 76. 28. ut ... moreretur: 'to scotch all the tattle that was
getting in his way, about his loose living and idle habits'; the objective genitive after *sermo* is like that after *fama*.*

1. amici mei: Bestia.

2. quem ... revocat: 'Bestia was acquitted; Caelius returned to
the charge and indicted him a second time.'*

4. cadit in: 'is suited to' (cf. 69. 12).

6. in his ... nostris: 'in men who are at our particular time of
life' (cf. 18. 17).

8. herbis ... fruges: for the illustration cf. Quintil. i. 3. 3 ff.
'illud ingeniorum velut praecox genus non temere unquam pervenit
ad frugem ... non subest vera vis nec penitus inmissis radicibus

nititur, ut quae summo solo sparsa sunt semina celerius se effundunt et imitatae spicas herbulae inanibus aristis ante messem flavescunt'.

9. etenim ... inserenda: 'why, brilliant young men have always had to be reined back from distinction rather than be spurred towards it: more pruning than grafting is needed at that age if mental gifts show a mass of blossom.'

Cf. *de fin.* v. 61 'indicant pueri, in quibus ut in speculis natura cernitur. quanta studia decertantium sunt! quanta ipsa certamina! ut illi efferuntur laetitia, cum vicerunt! ut pudet victos! ut se accusari nolunt! quam cupiunt laudari! quos illi labores perferunt ut aequalium principes sint!'*

11. amputanda: this compound retains the original sense of *putare*, to make neat and clean (so Virg. *G.* ii. 407); it is from this meaning that the more familiar uses of *putare* develop (*putare rationes*, to balance accounts > in general, to reckon up > to count as good, bad, etc. > to judge, hold an opinion). For the metaphor cf. *de or.* ii. 88 'facilius sicut in vitibus revocantur ea quae sese nimium profuderunt quam, si nihil valet materies, nova sarmenta cultura excitantur; item volo esse in adulescente unde aliquid amputem; non enim potest in eo sucus esse diuturnus, quod nimis celeriter est maturitatem exsecutum.'

§ 77. 14. vis, ferocitas, pertinacia: 'energy, spirit, obstinacy'.

minimorum horum: with reference to what follows; Cicero seems to be supporting Caelius' own plea (Quintil. xi. 1. 51) 'ne cui vestrum atque etiam omnium, qui ad rem agendam adsunt, meus aut vultus molestior aut vox immoderatior aliqua aut . . . iactantior gestus fuisse videatur'. Caelius must have been an objectionable young man.

15. purpurae genus: presumably he used too rich a shade of purple, probably of Tyrian or Tarentine dye; cf. *Sest.* 19, where the ordinary shade is termed *paene fusca*, and Plutarch, *Cat. min.* 6. 3 ἐπεὶ πορφύραν ἑώρα τὴν κατακόρως ἐρυθρὰν καὶ ὀξεῖαν ἀγαπωμένην, αὐτὸς ἐφόρει τὴν μέλαιναν. Augustus and Nero after him restricted the wearing of the Tyrian purple to magistrates. The prosecution must have instanced this to show how Caelius had lived above his station (cf. 3. 11); it is amusing to see how Cicero could adapt himself to circumstances, by comparing this passage with *Clu.* 111, *in Cat.* ii. 5, 22.

16. splendor . . . nitor: 'his glitter and glamour'; cf. Quintil. viii. 5. 34 'sicut in cultu victuque accessit aliquis citra reprehensionem nitor'. Caelius was full of show and swagger; cf. the young Disraeli (A. Maurois, *Disraeli*, p. 62 ): 'He went to Caroline Norton's in a coat of black velvet, poppy-coloured trousers broidered

with gold, a scarlet waistcoat, sparkling rings worn on top of white
kid gloves.'

→     **deferverint**: see note on 43. 21; the future perfect is like
*videro* in 35. 2; 'you will presently find that all this has mellowed,
soon his added years, events themselves, the days as they pass will
tone it all down.' Cicero uses vintage-metaphors: cf. *Mur*. 65 'te . . .
animi quodam impetu concitatum et vi naturae atque ingeni
elatum . . . iam usus flectet, dies leniet, aetas mitigabit', *de sen*. 45
'sed erat quidam fervor aetatis, qua progrediente omnia fiunt in
dies mitiora'.

18. **conservate . . . virorum**: 'I beg you then, gentlemen, to
preserve for the body politic a Roman citizen of virtuous principles,
a loyal citizen, a constitutional citizen'. Cicero is at pains to stress
Caelius' intense political loyalties; note the deliberate repetition *rei
publicae . . . rei publicae . . . rei publicae . . . rem publicam . . . in re
publica . . . res publica*. His solemn words resemble the close of the
*pro Archia* (31).

**bonarum artium**: the innate qualities which Cicero has so
consistently upheld to the jury.

19. **bonarum partium**: see notes on 13. 13, 14. 7; Caelius was no
revolutionary 'wild man'. The idea is continued in *bonorum virorum*.*

**bonorum virorum**: Kl. inserts *studiosum* after *civem* (but he
retracted this in his 1919 preface, p. lxi), Müll. adds it after *virorum*,
which gives a bad clausula (cf. Zielinski, *Das Clauselgesetz in
Ciceros Reden*, p. 208), Weiske proposed *bonorum morum*. These
proposals were made on the assumption that *bonorum virorum* is
impossible as a qualitative genitive. But in spite of them, I feel that
the MSS. have preserved what Cicero wrote: it is too artistic a
parallelism to be faulty.

*Bonorum virorum* is certainly troublesome grammatically if it
is considered in isolation from the other two genitives; *civis bonarum
artium* = 'a citizen characterized by *bonae artes*', *civis bonarum partium* = 'a citizen belonging to *bonae partes*'; but *civis bonorum
virorum* does not fit in with such a category, and it is hard to see in
the genitive anything really analogous to such expressions as
*hominem multorum hospitum* (*Clu*. 163), *perpaucorum hominumst*
(Ter. *Eun*. 409). But if *bonorum virorum* is regarded as a mere
extension of the thought in *bonarum partium* (from which it cannot
be dissociated, and which explains its meaning), then it can surely
stand: Cicero has been at pains to devise a striking parallelism of
expression and structure at the opening of his final bid to save
Caelius, and his chief concern is with the rhythmic effect (which the
proposed emendations would destroy) of a triple structure, in pursuance of which he has used a phrase which cannot stand by itself

but which is intelligible and justifiable when fused with its whole context.

Vandvik (*Genetivus und Ablativus Qualitatis*, p. 83) appears to take *civem* as equivalent to *virum*; I should prefer to regard *virorum* as equivalent to *civium*, if such a method of interpretation would ease the problem. But it is simpler to regard *bonorum virorum* as a restatement of *bonarum partium*. However the genitive is explained, it seems to me certain that the text is sound.

21. **a nostris rationibus:** 'from my own way of thinking', i.e. Cicero's own political party, the *boni*.

23. **se ipse:** cf. note on 11. 23; Caelius has undertaken this for himself, no one else has done it for him.

**§ 78.** 24. **hominem consularem:** Antonius; cf. 47. 7.

26. **ambitu:** this appears to be the only passage in Cicero where *absolvere* is used with an ablative of the charge; the usual construction is a genitive (e.g. *Clu.* 116 'maiestatis absoluti sunt permulti', *Verr.* i. 72 'non te absolutum esse improbitatis'); for the ablative cf. Livy ii. 8. 1 (*suspicione*), viii. 22. 3 (*crimine*), Tac. *Ann.* i. 74 (*criminibus*). *Solvere*, however, is used with such an ablative; cf. Reid on *Mil.* 9 (he remarks that *ambitu* here is 'doubtless an error').

1. **largitor:** with reference to the charge *de ambitu et de criminibus sodalium ac sequestrium* (§ 16): note the 'professional' implication of this class of noun.

2. **obsides periculi:** 'hostages against dangerous behaviour'; cf. 73. 5, and see note on 3. 11; for such accusations see Landgraf on *Rosc. Am.* 55 (p. 122), *de off.* ii. 49; Quintil. uses similar language (xii. 7. 3 'creditique sunt etiam clari iuvenes obsidem reipublicae dare malorum civium accusationem'). Apuleius (*Apol.* 66) has a long and inaccurate list of such cases, remarking 'quippe homines eruditissimi iuvenes laudis gratia primum hoc rudimentum forensis operae subibant, ut aliquo insigni iudicio civibus suis noscerentur'.

**pignora voluntatis:** cf. *in Cat.* iv. 9 'habemus enim a Caesare ... sententiam tanquam obsidem perpetuae in rem publicam voluntatis'.

3. **qua in civitate:** taken up by *in ea civitate* below. This attack on Sex. Clodius, even though his trial would be fresh in the jury's minds, is only relevant in so far as it served to remind them of Clodia's power and Caelius' very different character. The reference helps to date the speech (see Appendix IV). Milo had prosecuted Sex. Clodius at Pompey's instance, and his acquittal shows the confused state of parties at the time. Cicero describes him always as deeply depraved (cf. *de domo* 25, etc.); see *Q.F.* ii. 4. 6 for mention of his trial.

4. **per biennium:** since P. Clodius' tribunate in 58.

5. **sine re ... sine sede:** note the assonance; cf. *de domo* 142, and see Wölfflin, *Archiv für lat. Lex.* i, p. 386, Otto s.v. *res*; cf. note on 38. 27.*

7. **aedis sacras:** the *aedes Nympharum*; cf. *Mil.* 73 'qui aedem Nympharum incendit, ut memoriam publicam recensionis tabulis publicis impressam exstingueret', where see Clark. The records of the censors were kept there (*census, memoria publica*).

9. **Catuli monumentum:** the portico built by Q. Lutatius Catulus, the victor of Vercellae in 101. It adjoined Cicero's house on the Palatine (*ad Att.* iv. 3. 2), and in 58 P. Clodius destroyed both house and portico, while in 57 he burned Q. Cicero's house in the same district; cf. *de domo* 102-3, 114, and see Appendix V in Nisbet's edition. Cicero seems to attribute these disturbances to either Clodius indifferently.

12. **absolutum ... condonatum:** 'acquitted by a woman's favour', . . . 'sacrificed to a woman's lust'; note the elaborate chiasmus, and the adversative asyndeton.

**§ 79.** 16. Cicero now begins a short *miseratio* ('appeal to pity'), a form of oratory in which he excelled; see *Orat.* 130 'quid ego de miserationibus loquar? quibus eo sum usus pluribus, quod, etiam si plures dicebamus, perorationem mihi tamen omnes relinquebant; in quo ut viderer excellere non ingenio sed dolore adsequebar', a statement which does much to explain Cicero's success. Other examples of *miserationes* occur in the *pro Sulla, pro Sestio, pro Milone*. See Quintil. vi. 1. 21 ff.; he lays down the rules for their delivery in xi. 3. 170; they need 'flexum vocis et flebilem suavitatem, qua praecipue franguntur animi, quaeque est maxime naturalis'. It must have needed some superb acting on Cicero's part to carry off the thing with such constant súccess; his whole manner would have been that of chief mourner at a funeral (cf. Quintil., l.c. 'nam etiam orbos viduasque videas in ipsis funeribus canoro quodam modo proclamantes').

**quod cum ... serviatis:** 'but as you set the picture of this young man before you, I beg you to keep before your eyes as well the afflicted father here, bowed down with age: Caelius is his only son, his prop and stay; on Caelius' brilliant promise his peace depends; Caelius' ruin is the one thing that he dreads. Here he is, gentlemen, a suppliant for your compassion, subservient to your power; see him prostrate before you—I will not say, prostrate at your feet, but before your instincts, your sensibilities; raise him up, I beg you, impelled either by the memory you still possess of your own fathers or by the joy you take in your own children, that in consoling another's misery you may indulge your filial affection, or, it may be, your parental kindness.'

# COMMENTARY §§ 79–80

**17. huius miseri:** the elder Caelius, present in court (but *huius* in 16 and 18 is the son). Cicero would point to father and son, with magnificently moving gesture.

**23. pietati . . . indulgentiae:** a reference to *recordatio parentum* and *liberorum iucunditas* respectively.

**nolite . . . velle:** cf. *Balb.* 64, and see K. II. ii, p. 569.

**24. hunc:** the father (but *hunc* in the next line is the son).

**25. exstingui volnere vestro:** the necessary pause after *extingui* breaks what would otherwise be a marked hexameter rhythm. Such pauses, if properly observed, generally destroy the illusion of verse-rhythms in classical prose (see some interesting remarks by Laurand, pp. 146 f., and Reid's notes on *de sen.* 2 and 47). Tacitus' ear was different; yet even with him caution is needed in judging such apparent rhythms (cf. Furneaux's introd. to the *Annals*, ch. v, § 79). I venture to note here, for its preservation, in this context, a good alcaic verse in [Quintil.] *decl. mai.* 2. 10, *post caecitatem carior est pater*. See the discussion in Quintil. ix. 4. 72 ff.*

**§ 80. 27. conservate . . . capietis:** 'Save, I implore you, a son for his father, a father for his son; never let it be thought that you have flung aside an old man whose hopes are well-nigh done, or that you have failed to sustain—nay, have stricken down and utterly crushed—a young man in whom hope and promise are high. Gentlemen, if you restore Caelius in safety to me, to his family, to the body politic, I promise that you shall find him your bounden servant, devoted to you, pledged to you and to your children; yes, and you more than all others shall reap a rich and lasting fruit from all his exertions and his toils.'

**29. spei:** *B* has *spes*, which Kl. thinks may possibly be accepted as a genitive form (see Kl. 1919 preface, p. li; cf. *Sest.* 28, where the genitive *dies* is vouched for in Aul. Gell. ix. 14. 6).

Cicero ends on a high note; Caelius is a young man who has much to give the State; he, Cicero, will be responsible for this.

In reading a speech of Cicero, it is essential to remember the part that voice and gesture would play in its delivery. The evidence comes mainly from Quintilian, but he certainly represents the tradition of an earlier age, although in his time a somewhat more theatrical manner had developed (cf. Quintil. xi. 3. 184). Cicero would not simply be speaking *for* Caelius: in a certain sense, he would *be* Caelius, just as a great actor assumes the character of his part. And the whole scene would have an animation which it is hard for us to picture.*

The true orator will possess, says Cicero (*de or.* i. 128), 'vox tragoedorum, gestus paene summorum actorum' (elaborated ibid.

141

# COMMENTARY

iii. 213–27). Quintilian (xii. 5. 5) thus describes a contemporary speaker: 'ea corporis sublimitas erat, is ardor oculorum, frontis auctoritas, gestus praestantia, vox quidem . . . super omnis quos ego quidem audierim tragoedos'; the elder Seneca ascribes to Cassius Severus (*Exc. Contr*. iii, pr. 3) 'corporis magnitudo conspicua, suavitas valentissimae vocis, . . . pronuntiatio quae histrionem posset producere nec tamen quae histrionis posset videri'; and we may be sure that Cicero himself had all these qualities in a superlative degree. To fit him for the necessary command of *pronuntiatio*, 'delivery', the orator had to undergo a strenuous course of voice-production and physical training: not only the voice but the eyes (*de or*. iii. 222), hands, and in fact the whole body had to be brought into play, 'est enim actio quasi sermo corporis, quo magis menti congruens esse debet' (ibid.). Without such training, oratory was useless: 'adfectus omnes languescant necesse est, nisi voce, vultu, totius prope habitu corporis inardescunt' (Quintil. xi. 3. 2).

Quintilian treats the subject in great detail in book xi, dealing first with the manner appropriate to various types of case (ch. 1, with several illustrations from the *pro Caelio*), and then (ch. 3) with the rules for control of voice and gesture; these chapters should be read by all who wish to gain some idea of what Roman oratory demanded. The orator must keep himself physically fit, by walking, simple living, good digestion; he must take great care of his throat, and exercise his voice in every possible way so that it will not be strained, for example, on a windy, wet, or hot day; he must learn proper control of breath, and how to vary his tone (see xi. 3. 47 ff. for an analysis of the proper tones and pauses in delivering the beginning of the *pro Milone*). Careful attention must be paid to the carriage of the head, the expression of the eyes, the movement of the eyebrows, the action of the lips (e.g. 'they must not be twisted sideways till they nearly reach the ear'), the bearing of neck, chin, and shoulders, and above all to the motions of the hands and arms. Quintilian lays down a complicated set of careful rules for the fingers, describing the gestures appropriate to different parts of a speech and to differing tones of expression; his examples of exaggerated and faulty gesture are often amusing. The stance of the speaker also has its rules, and he must be careful not to walk about too much: an orator was once asked how many miles he had spoken. The decorous arrangement and control of the toga is of almost equal importance. The *exordium* is best suited by a quiet delivery; the *narratio* is less sedate, with the hand extended farther, the toga allowed to fall back, the tone still conversational but more emphatic; *argumentatio*, *digressio*, and *peroratio* each have their appropriate gesture and tone. The whole topic is of immense

# COMMENTARY

interest, for these careful and detailed rules were taken over whole-sale as a basis of rhetorical delivery in Elizabethan England: see B. L. Joseph, *Elizabethan Acting* (Oxford, 1950), with special reference to John Bulwer's *Chirologia* and *Chironomia*, published in 1644 (the plates illustrate finger-movements similar to those prescribed by Quintilian to suit particular emotional expressions; the writer has, however, scarcely realized how largely his various authorities have drawn on Quintilian).

The three traditional functions of the orator were *docere, delectare, movere*. The third of these was especially associated with the 'grand style', and the importance of this emotional aspect of ancient oratory should always be remembered. Quintilian remarks of such a speaker (xii. 10. 61) that he will 'carry the judge off his feet even though he struggle against him', he will 'breathe wrath and pity into his audience', and as he speaks, 'the judge will turn pale and shed tears and be swept through the whole gamut of emotion'; to achieve such a result the orator had himself to experience these passions, not merely to simulate them (cf. note on 79. 16). This function has little place in the *pro Caelio*, except, naturally, in the peroration, and in the digression on the death of Metellus (and even in these passages Cicero is comparatively restrained). The *officium docendi* is seen chiefly in the early part of the speech (§§ 1–24), where Cicero is giving a matter-of-fact account of Caelius' life and habits. He concentrates much more on the *officium delectandi*. He had before him a jury of tired and potentially irritable men, who were deprived of a holiday owing to the tactics of the prosecution (as Cicero represents the matter); and with the greatest skill he set himself to combat their restiveness in case it should tell against Caelius. His method is resourceful and bewilderingly varied, and the whole speech is notable for its swift and subtle changes of mood and manner: the student will find it profitable to detect these for himself. It would be an interesting exercise to apply some of Quintilian's rules for gesture to different parts of the speech; but nothing will ever give us the tone of Cicero's *o immoderata mulier*, or the expressive glance that accompanied his gibes at Clodia, or the gaiety of his prosopopoeiae, or the sheer fun of his picture of the unfortunate Licinius and his band of stalwarts, 'stowing away', in outdoor dress, in the baths. The *pro Caelio* explains so much of Cicero's success as an advocate; in many ways it is a masterpiece of what Cornelius Severus called, in a later age, *Latiae facundia linguae*.

# APPENDIX I

## DATE OF CAELIUS' BIRTH

CAELIUS was born, according to Pliny (*N.H.* vii. 165), on 28 May 82 B.C.: 'C. Mario Cn. Carbone III coss. a. d. quintum kalend. Iunias M. Caelius[1] Rufus et C. Licinius Calvus eadem die geniti sunt, oratores quidem ambo, sed tam dispari eventu.'

Nipperdey[2] and most succeeding scholars rejected this date. Caelius was tribune in 52 (*Mil.* 91; Appian, *B.C.* ii. 22); hence Nipperdey concluded that he was quaestor in 55, and so could not have been born later than 85; Pliny, he thought, either meant some other orator (e.g. Curio, coupled with Calvus in *Brut.* 280) or else had confused the third with the first consulship of Carbo. Wegehaupt[3] argued that Caelius was born in 88, as he was praetor in 48 (Caes. *B.C.* iii. 20) and according to the law should then have been 40. It seems, however, desirable to show that Pliny has been wrongly discredited.[4]

All arguments for an earlier date than 82 are based on the assumption that the *leges annales* can be strictly applied to Caelius' career. This is quite unwarranted. Nipperdey rests his theory on the quaestorship; but no writer tells us when Caelius was quaestor. He certainly cannot have held the office in or before 56, for Cicero must then have mentioned it in the very detailed biography at the end of this speech. Nor can we assume from the mention of *ambitus* in § 16 (see note) that Caelius was standing for the quaestorship for 55. Wegehaupt argues from the year of his praetorship; but Caesar probably appointed him quite arbitrarily, and no justifiable inference can be made as to Caelius' age. The *cursus honorum* gives a false scent altogether.

The only reliable evidence is given by Cicero himself in §§ 9–11. Here he is defending Caelius against *impudicitia* in connexion with Catiline during the period of his *tirocinium*. We are told that Caelius was put in Cicero's care on assuming the *toga virilis*, and never left him from 66 to 64, but in 63 did at last incline towards Catiline. Cicero implies that by then Caelius had had an unusually long *tirocinium*, so that no suspicion of immorality could attach to him when at length he did support Catiline. Now it is only reason-

---

[1] For the text see Mayhoff ad loc., and cf. Appendix VI, p. 157, note 2.
[2] *Rh. Mus.* xix, 1864, pp. 289 f.
[3] pp. 4 f.; similarly Gröbe, *Hermes* xxxvi, 1901, p. 612.
[4] Nipperdey's date is accepted by van Wageningen, Tyrrell and Purser, and others.

# APPENDIXES

·able that the first actual date mentioned by Cicero (66) is the year in which Caelius assumed the *toga virilis*; then, on Pliny's dating, he would have been 16, a very usual age for that ceremony. Cicero therefore defends his *pudicitia* between the ages of 16 and 19, to which years such charges as those implicit here were much more likely to apply than to the years from 19 to 22 or from 22 to 25. The key to the whole question, in fact, lies in the *tirocinium*, not in the *leges annales*; Nipperdey would make this probationary period too long, Wegehaupt absurdly so. Pliny's date exactly fits Cicero's evidence.[1]

Arguments have further been based on the relative ages of Clodia and Caelius, who on Pliny's calculation would have been more than ten years younger than his mistress.[2] But it was her attractions, not her age, that counted; 'für einen Bürgerlichen ist eine Marquise immer 30 Jahre alt' (Friedrich, *Catullus*, introd., p. 64; he offers a learned and entertaining list of similar *amores*)—and Clodia was Juno herself. But if anything can be based on this, it is more probable that Caelius' connexion with her began at the age of about 23 than at 26 or 29 (cf. § 75 *in hoc flexu quasi aetatis*, referring to the period immediately following 59). In other points also the tenor of the speech supports Pliny; minor evidence is noted in the commentary.

If, then, we accept Pliny's statement that Caelius was born in 82, when was he quaestor ? There are two possibilities. (1) As an interval of one year only was customary at this time between the quaestorship and the tribunate (Mommsen, *Staatsrecht* i, p. 534), he may have been quaestor from December 55 to December 54, by eluding the technicalities of the law as regards his age (cf. H., p. 194, note 3); or the date may even be put a year later (it is to be noted that in May of 53 he would have entered his thirtieth year), and there would still be an interval of four days between his demitting office as quaestor on 5 December 53 and entering on his tribunate on the 10th. Either supposition is admittedly difficult, but at that period of political upheaval neither can be said to be impossible without further evidence. (2) Caelius may never have been quaestor at all, but have made the tribunate his first important magistracy. This

[1] H., p. 194, note 3, supports Pliny's date. It might be argued that Caelius spent some time with Crassus before becoming 'adsiduus' with Cicero in 66; but this still makes the *tirocinium* too long, and in any case Cicero's language in § 9 does not suggest anything but a joint tutelage between himself and Crassus.

[2] e.g. by Wegehaupt, who imagines such disparity to be psychologically impossible. Schwabe (*Quaestiones Catullianae*, p. 59) puts Clodia's birth about 95–94, and suggests 93 for that of Clodius, arguing from his *cursus honorum*.

# APPENDIXES

would at least have been possible in pre-Sullan times (Mommsen, *Staatsrecht* i, p. 551, note 4; p. 553, notes 4 and 5), and Caelius may have revived a former practice in defiance of existing custom, entering the Senate either through the curule aedileship or even as tribune (ibid. iii, p. 863).

The second of these possibilities would seem to me preferable if any analogous example from this period were known; for if Caelius had ever been quaestor, there is every reason to suppose that there would be some mention of his activities in that capacity. In any case I am convinced that Pliny is right in placing his birth in the year 82.

# APPENDIX II

## PLACE OF CAELIUS' BIRTH

THE evidence is in § 5 of this speech: 'quod est obiectum municipibus esse adulescentem non probatum suis, nemini unquam praesenti Praetuttiani maiores honores habuerunt quam absenti M. Caelio'. Here *P* reads *praetoriani* (-*tori*- added by a later hand, over an erasure). *Σ* has *Praestutiani*, which Lambinus knew but rejected; Gruter too knew it, or something like it (from the Cod. S. Victoris), and conjectured *Praetutiani*, which must certainly be the true reading (cf. Barwes, *Quaest. Tull.*, p. 23); but he did not admit his conjecture to his text, nor has any subsequent editor adopted it. Clark first adduced the reading *Praestutiani* from *Σ*, but obelized it, merely recording the emendation. It is now time that Gruter should receive his full due, 340 years after his edition of Cicero was published; in this I have support from Rothstein, *Philologus* lxxviii (1923), p. 18 (his view had Dessau's agreement), and through the kindness of M. Jean Cousin I learn that he too will admit Gruter's conjecture to his prospective Budé edition.

An *ager Praetuttianus* in Picenum is mentioned by Livy (xxii. 9. 5, xxvii. 43. 10), and by Pliny (*N.H.* iii. 110, 112); cf. Polybius iii. 88. 3, with Walbank's note, and see Hofmann in *RE* xxii. 2, s.v. *Praetuttiana regio*. Its chief town was Interamnia, the modern Teramo;[1] inscriptions show, as Mommsen noted (*CIL* ix. 5074–5), that this was both a *municipium* and a *colonia*, with a local senate and *quinquennales* (ibid. 5067, 5076, 5078). Thus, if Caelius was born at Interamnia, Cicero's mention of *municipes* and *amplissimus ordo* is explained.

---

[1] Cf. Thomas, *Revue critique d'histoire et de littérature*, 1906, p. 283; but Interamnia is there confused with the better-known Interamna, on the Nar (the modern Terni).

146

The reading *Praetuttiani* has been questioned on the ground
that the people of the *ager* would have been named 'Practuttii';[1]
but this substantive occurs nowhere, and there is no reason why
Cicero should not be using *Praetuttiani* as a shortened form for
the full title *Interamnates Praetuttiani*,[2] by which the inhabitants
were distinguished from the Interamnates Nartes (Pliny, *N.H.* iii.
113) or from the Interamnates Lirenates (ibid. 64). The scribe of
Σ made his transcripts very carefully, and came very close here to
the true form of an unfamiliar name[3] (which caused confusion also
in the MSS. of Livy, l.c.).

The reading of *P*, with its erasure, caused much useless conjecture, understandable as long as the authority of Σ was not known.
Since the *prae-* of *praetoriani* might well have come from ditto-
graphy, the way was open for almost anything.[4] Beroaldus' *Puteolani* long held the field; but, as Caelius was alleged to have mal-
treated the Alexandrian embassy at Puteoli, surely Cicero would
have said something to brush away the charge if a *laudatio* from
Caelius' native town had given him the opportunity. Baiter's
*Tusculani* had more plausibility (cf. Gröbe, *Hermes* xxxvi, 1901,
p. 612); the *gens Caelia* was a distinguished Tusculan family (*CIL*
xiv. 2622, 2623, 2624, 2627),[5] and the place was near enough to
Rome for Caelius' father to visit the city frequently and ultimately
to migrate there. But cf. note on 5.1.

Clark's recovery of the reading of the *vetus Cluniacensis* has
resulted in a reasonably certain identification of Caelius' birthplace,
not the least of his services to the text: a pity that, with Gruter at
his side, he did not go all the way.

---

[1] Ptolemy (354. 9, 355. 4) calls them Πραιγούττιοι (*sic*); but Stephanus
of Byzantium, s.v., calls the district Πραιτετία, and adds ἧς ὁ οἰκήτωρ
Πραιτετιανός.
[2] Frontinus, *de Controv.* i, p. 18. 10 Lachm. (= *Corp. Agrim. Rom.*
I. i, p. 7. 14); *CIL* ix. 5084; the inscriptions prefer the form *Interamnites*.
Similarly, the *Frentani* of some MSS. in *Clu.* 197 are probably the people
of Anxanum, who appear in *CIL* ix. 3314 as 'Anxates Frentani' (cf.
Rothstein, *Philologus*, l.c.).
[3] The name 'Usidicani' (Pliny, *N.H.* iii. 114) is a possible parallel
form, as suggesting an original 'Usidii'; compare also the 'Caediciani' of
*CIL* i. 1199 with the *campus Caedicius* of Pliny, *N.H.* xi. 241; see
W. Schulze, *Zur Geschichte lateinischer Eigennamen* (Berlin, 1904),
pp. 539, 562, n. 1.
[4] e.g. *Praenestini* (Orelli), *Cumani* (Wegehaupt), *Formiani* (Luter-
bacher), even *Veronenses* (Vollenhoven). Oetling proposed *oppidani*,
Harnecker *populares*!
[5] A Caelius Rufus is elsewhere mentioned only in a late and doubtful
inscription from Aeclanum (*CIL* ix. 1238; cf. Münzer in *RE*, s.v. *Caelius*,
no. 35); *CIL* x. 5961 speaks of a Caecilius Rufus at Signia.

# APPENDIX III

## CAELIUS AND CATULLUS

CAELIUS is generally thought to have been a rival of Catullus for Clodia's affections. This view depends upon two complementary assumptions: (1) that Catullus alludes to M. Caelius Rufus in all or some of the poems in which a Caelius or a Rufus is mentioned, (2) that Catullus' Lesbia was the Clodia of Cicero's speech, i.e. the wife of Q. Metellus. Neither can be proved, but both are highly probable.

1. Catullus names a Caelius in poems 58 and 100. In 58 he tells Caelius of Lesbia's utter depravity, in tones of misery and horror; there is nothing to show his feeling for this man, except the fact that he has made him the recipient of such a confidence. In 100 Caelius is a friend who has stood by Catullus in an unhappy love-affair (Lesbia is not named), and Catullus wishes him good luck in his own love. It is hard not to suppose that both poems are addressed to the same man; and if that is so, then neither can refer to M. Caelius Rufus, for the Caelius of 100 is a Veronese (for Caelii at Verona see *CIL* v. 3441, 3570, 3689)—and our Caelius had no connexion with Verona, unless the evidence adduced in Appendix II is totally misconceived. If they are addressed to different men, it could be claimed that 58 may refer to M. Caelius Rufus: in that case, the situation in this poem has to be reconciled with the evidence of another (77), a proceeding which in my view strains probability.

Catullus names a Rufus in poems 69 and 77 (the text of 59 is uncertain, and nothing can be based upon it). The tone here has nothing in common with that of either 58 or 100: it is futile to attempt to link the two pairs of poems, and so to produce an unimpeachable M. Caelius Rufus.[1] Catullus attacks Rufus in both, but it is improbable that he is addressing the same man in both.[2] The Rufus of 69 is a dirty creature, pilloried for his public nastiness: the Rufus of 77 is a one-time friend, who has done Catullus a private, personal wrong by creeping in and stealing away his

---

[1] There would be, however, no inherent difficulty in the use of two names for the same person. Catullus uses both Calvus (14, 53, 96) and Licinius (50), both Ortalus (65) and Hortensius (95), and he calls the bride in 61 now Iunia, now Aurunculeia. In this speech Cicero addresses L. Herennius Balbus as Herennius (25, 56) or Balbus (27, 53).

[2] Rufus was a very common name, and the dissociation of the two is not far-fetched.

happiness.[1] If either can be identified with M. Caelius Rufus, the subject of 77 is alone a possibility; despite the need to discount much of Catullus' violent coarseness as a temperamental mannerism, the picture in 69 runs clean counter to the *urbanitas* and *nitor* of Cicero's client, and it is far more likely that this Rufus is some *bête noire* who happened to infuriate Catullus.

Poem 77 runs:

> Rufe mihi frustra ac nequiquam credite amice
> > (frustra ? immo magno cum pretio atque malo),
> sicine subrepsti mi, atque intestina perurens
> > ei misero eripuisti omnia nostra bona ?
> eripuisti, heu heu nostrae crudele venenum
> > vitae, heu heu nostrae pestis amicitiae.

Here we have an entirely conceivable situation if the reference is to M. Caelius Rufus. Cicero's speech and the fragments of Caelius' own defence point to the existence of a coterie of Clodia's Young Men, current or obsolete (cf. 38. 10 'quae haberet palam decretum semper aliquem', and the significant *ceterorum* of 52. 15), with their own brand of allusive wit (cf. note on 18. 6, and introd., p. vii). It does not strain credulity or reason to imagine Catullus and Caelius meeting in such a circle (or indeed in any social circle where *homines venustiores* gathered), nor to picture them as becoming friends, for they were close in age and not unlike in temperament and 'style'. But Caelius was the younger and had more staying power than Catullus; Clodia may well have found him more fun; he was cynical and calculating and cool: and it is highly probable that this 77th poem reflects the outcome of a rivalry between them.

If this is accepted, the case for identifying the Caelius of poem 58 with M. Caelius Rufus becomes even more difficult: it involves a change of attitude on Catullus' part amounting apparently to complete forgiveness, which, in a matter so deeply concerning the *foedus amicitiae*, was entirely foreign to his nature.[2]

2. That Lesbia's real name was Clodia[3] is stated by Apuleius (*Apol.* 10). Most scholars have agreed that this Clodia was Metellus' wife, the second sister of P. Clodius, an identification first

---

[1] Catullus' words *omnia nostra bona* (77. 4) surely refer to Lesbia (cf. 68. 158 'a quo sunt primo omnia nata bona'). A false friend is bitterly reproached in poem 73 also, but no name is given, and it cannot safely be adduced in support of 77.

[2] For these problems cf. C. L. Neudling, *A Prosopography to Catullus* (Iowa Studies in Classical Philology XII, 1955), pp. 37 ff. (in an interesting discussion of Caelius, but too highly coloured by inference to be used without much caution).

[3] For the principle involved see Bentley on Horace, *C.* ii. 12. 13, and cf. Fraenkel, *Horace* (Oxford, 1957), p. 62, note 3.

suggested in the sixteenth century by Petrus Victorius (*Var. Lect.* xvi. 1). One of the main points in the argument (see Ellis's *Commentary on Catullus*, pp. lxiii ff. for the full details) is the identification of M. Caelius Rufus as a rival of Catullus, with the result that Cicero's speech becomes valid evidence for the character and personality of Lesbia. The theory has not, however, found unanimous acceptance.[1] Rothstein has maintained[2] that none of the arguments is so definitive that it cannot apply equally well to the Clodia who was P. Clodius' youngest sister, married to Lucullus and divorced by him.[3] G. Giri, in a gloomy paper,[4] dismisses every single one of the usual arguments as proving nothing, and concludes that the 'Clodia' of Apuleius was no relation of P. Clodius but some other member of the *gens*. There is a summary of these dissentient views, with references to earlier discussions, in M. Schuster's article in *RE* vii a (1948), s.v. Valerius, no. 120, cols. 2357 ff., as well as a clear restatement of the grounds for accepting the traditional theory.[5] It seems to me that the plausibility of Victorius' original identification remains unshaken.

To sum up: Catullus probably does refer to M. Caelius Rufus in poem 77, and Lesbia is probably Clodia *Metelli*; Cicero's speech provides a probable document for the reconstruction[6] of the 'social background' of Catullus, and in this way his defence of Caelius is of special importance to the literary historian.

[1] See, for example, the curious remarks of Corradinus de Allio on Catullus 5, in his edition (Venice, 1738).

[2] *Philologus* lxxviii (1923), pp. 19 ff., and lxxxi (1926), pp. 472 f.; cf. P. Maas, *CQ* xxxvi (1942), pp. 79 ff. See also Kroll's introduction to his edition of Catullus, p. v, note 1 (but cf. G. Jachmann, *Gnomon* i (1925), p. 201).

[3] Her disreputable character is hinted at by Plutarch, *Lucull.* 38; for her marriage, cf. Varro, *RR* iii. 16. 2.

[4] *Rivista Indo-Greca-Italica* vi (1922), pp. 161 ff. (see further *Athenaeum* vi (1928), pp. 183 ff., 215 ff.); cf. F. Arnaldi, *Rivista di Filologia* v (1927), pp. 350 ff.

[5] See also H. Rubenbauer, in Bursian's *Jahresbericht über die Fortschritte der klassischen Altertumswissenschaft*, vol. ccxii (1927), pp. 171 ff.; cf. Neudling, op. cit., pp. 97 ff.

[6] This has been a dangerous pastime for many scholars: a good early example of a conjectural biography of Catullus, with some unexpected details, is offered by Corradinus de Allio; a good modern example may be seen in Tenney Frank's *Catullus and Horace* (with *CQ* xx, 1926, p. 200). There is not a shred of evidence for Frank's assertion that Caelius introduced Catullus to Manlius Torquatus, or that Catullus refers to Caelius' house in his 39th poem.

# APPENDIX IV

## DATE OF DELIVERY OF THE *PRO CAELIO*

THE evidence rests on two passages in the speech itself: § 1 'quod diebus festis ludisque publicis . . . unum hoc iudicium exerceatur', and § 78 'qua in civitate paucis his diebus Sex. Clodius absolutus est'.

Sex. Clodius stood his trial towards the end of March 56 B.C. (*Q.F.* ii. 4. 6). Therefore Caelius' trial must have occurred about the beginning of April. Cicero was absent from Rome this year from 9 April to 6 May; he accounts in detail for events at Rome between 6 and 9 April, but does not mention this case (*Q.F.* ii. 5). But in the same letter he speaks of another lately sent; this earlier letter has not been preserved, and it seems as if the trial must have been mentioned in it, for Cicero would not have failed to inform his brother of his triumph over Clodia. It would appear, then, that the case came into court on one of the first four days of April; now the *ludi Megalenses* began on 4 April (§ 1 note; see Sternkopf, *Hermes* xxxix, 1904, pp. 412–14), which must have been the day of Cicero's speech. It is unlikely that the trial was completed in one day, in view of the number of speakers (cf. H., p. 240), and so, as Cicero is speaking last, it must have begun on 3 April.

W. and others assume that the first day of the games could in any case have been the only possible day because it alone was not marked in the Calendar as *nefastus* (Warde Fowler, *Roman Festivals*, p. 22). This is wrong, for criminal jurisdiction was not interrupted by such marks; it was because of the *ludi*, not because a day was *nefastus*, that the courts were closed; so that this trial, as also that of Milo which was held 4–8 April 52 B.C., shows that cases of *vis* could be brought into court even during *ludi*. See Greenidge, *LP*, p. 457, note 6, where other instances are given of trials on *dies nefasti*.

# APPENDIX V

## THE CHARGES

THERE were five formal counts against Caelius: (1) *de seditionibus Neapolitanis*, (2) *de Alexandrinorum pulsatione Puteolana*, (3) *de bonis Pallae*, (4) *de Dione*, (5) *de veneno in Clodiam parato*. Of these, the first three were handled by Crassus, and the remaining two by Cicero.

(1) This was probably some local dispute, such as would normally have been settled in the local courts (cf. H., p. 201).

(2) This charge, although no information is available, must have been connected with the same matter as (4).

(3) The case of Palla (see § 23 note) may have been one of violent dispossession, such as would have given the prosecution the best handle for bringing an action under a law *de vi*,[1] though in other circumstances it too would have been dealt with privately.

(4) Like (2), this concerns the affair of Ptolemy Auletes of Egypt, which had for some time agitated Rome.

Ptolemy's usurpation of the throne was tolerated but not formally acknowledged by Rome; he greatly desired such recognition, especially as the late king had bequeathed Egypt to Rome in his will (*leg. agr.* ii. 41) and although for over twenty years no action had been taken annexation under his will might be expected at any time. In 59 Caesar had Ptolemy recognized, at a price of 6,000 talents (Suet. *Iul.* 54; the act was in Pompey's name as well as his own). But in 58 the king was deposed by his subjects, and he went himself to Rome asking for restoration and specifically naming Pompey as leader of the necessary army. The Senate resisted a proposal which would have given Pompey so much power, and after protracted negotiations the task was given to Cicero's friend P. Lentulus Spinther, then proconsul of Cilicia.[2] Meanwhile the people of Alexandria sent an embassy of a hundred citizens to put their case at Rome, led by Dio, an Academic philosopher (*Acad.* ii. 12). Ptolemy had them waylaid and massacred; it was even hinted that Pompey abetted him.[3] There was much indignation at Rome, but

---

[1] H., p. 201. He thinks that the Lex Plotia dealt with certain cases of the kind, cf. Gaius ii. 45 '[rem] vi possessam lex Iulia et Plautia [prohibet]'. He points out that Quintil. iv. 2. 27 expressly names this charge, classing the rest together as 'tota de vi causa'. As Caelius also dealt with the point (Quintil., l.c.) as well as Crassus, it must have had some technical importance. H. questions the reading of Quintilian, and interprets him as critical of Cicero's methods rather than laudatory.

[2] *ad Fam.* i. 1–7; *Q.F.* ii. 2. 3; for details see Dio Cassius xxxix. 12–16.

[3] Strabo xvii. 1. 11.

# APPENDIXES

when Dio was summoned to give an account of events, Ptolemy prevented him from obtaining a hearing of the Senate, and afterwards had him murdered by one P. Asicius (57 B.C.). The latter was tried in 56 and acquitted on Cicero's defence.

It was alleged by Caelius' enemies that he had been in some way implicated in an attack made on the ambassadors at Puteoli; whether this was the actual ambush set by Ptolemy is impossible to determine. Further, he was said to have been involved in the murder of Dio carried out by Asicius;[1] and another and quite separate accusation was that he had made an independent attempt to kill Dio. The whole story is vague and complicated, and Cicero wraps it up in such additional intricacy that the charges against Caelius appear lost in a maze of words. But there must have been some truth at the bottom of such persistent rumours. It is clear that although the trial of Caelius was not political his opponents were availing themselves of the political situation in trying to represent him as a creature of Ptolemy, and thus to aim a blow at Pompey.

(5) This charge arose out of the last one; it is treated in detail in the speech, though so mysteriously that it is impossible to discover what really happened: here again the story of the prosecution is so circumstantial that there must have been some underlying stratum of truth. Both this and the attempts on Dio and the embassy would normally have come within the competence of the *quaestio inter veneficos et sicarios.*

The accusation was brought under a *lex de vi* (§ 1 note). This law was aimed especially at those who caused seditious tumults by means of armed bands; thus Clodius was accused under it in 57, although he escaped trial (*ad Fam.* i. 9. 15; *Sest.* 89; Dio Cassius xxxix. 7), and Sestius had only recently been defended by Cicero on a like charge. It has been shown that all the formal charges, except perhaps that *de bonis Pallae*, would in normal circumstances have been dealt with in other courts and under different laws. The explanation of the apparent irrelevance of the means used to bring Caelius to justice is twofold: (1) cases of *vis* held precedence, and could be taken even during the games, when the other criminal courts were closed (§ 1 note; cf. *ad Fam.* viii. 8. 1), and (2) the prosecution took advantage of the undoubted tendency of the time to widen the official scope of the law (cf. § 71 note, and see H., p. 203). In this the full importance of the case against Caelius can be seen.

Cicero's speech is remarkable in that two-thirds of it have nothing to do with the technical counts. He focuses attention on what he considers, and what in fact actually was, the real point at issue—

---

[1] § 23; this was not part of the formal indictment, but was dragged in by the prosecution as corroborative detail.

# APPENDIXES

the scabrous charges brought by Clodia on moral grounds, through her own mortification and desire for revenge. Cicero rallies his whole forces to show that Clodia is herself entirely immoral, and that therefore her evidence has no weight at all. He uses this method to counter the deep impression made on the jury by Herennius Balbus who summed up for the prosecution, and does so with complete success; a parallel to his line of argument is suggested by the case of *Ferrar* v. *Mont* in Galsworthy's *Modern Comedy*. It is impossible to assume that the prosecution did not mention Caelius' relations with Clodia[1] in the hope that Cicero would not speak of them either. Rather, the whole case is made to turn on the point, and Cicero skilfully and unexpectedly defends Caelius on the ground that it was the woman who tempted him, thus revenging himself for the wrongs he had suffered from the Clodian *gens* by exposing Clodia as perhaps no great Roman lady had ever been exposed before.

# APPENDIX VI

## THE PROSECUTORS

L. SEMPRONIUS ATRATINUS, the formal initiator of the prosecution, is said to have been only seventeen years old at the time.[2] This is compatible with Cicero's attitude towards him in §§ 2, 3, 15 (cf. Quintil. xi. 1. 68).

Atratinus' father, whose double prosecution by Caelius was the immediate cause of this trial, was on friendly terms with Cicero (§§ 7, 76); the word *beneficium* in § 7 may imply that the latter had defended him in some suit (see note). Yet there is no evidence that Cicero ever delivered a speech on behalf of a Sempronius Atratinus. However, on 11 February 56 B.C. he defended L. Calpurnius Bestia on a charge of *ambitus* (*Q.F.* ii. 3. 6), and Münzer has shown beyond all reasonable doubt that this was none other than Atratinus' father.[3] For an inscription from Hypata in Thessaly runs as follows (Dessau, *Inscr. Lat. Sel.* 9461): ἡ πόλις Ὑπάτα Λ[ε]ύκιον Σενπρ[ώ]νιον Βηστία υἱὸν Ἀτρατῖνον πρεσβευτὰν καὶ ἀντιστράτηγον, τὸν ἴδιον εὐεργέταν. Here we have a Sempronius Atratinus whose father was named Bestia, the family name of the Calpurnii; but as after the patrician holders

---

[1] See § 30 note; cf. H., p. 228; Reitzenstein, p. 32.
[2] St. Jerome, ad Euseb. Chron. Ol. 189 (21 B.C.) 'Atratinus, qui XVII natus annos Caelium accusaverat, clarus inter oratores habetur. ad extremum morborum taedio in balneo voluntate exanimatus heredem reliquit Augustum.'
[3] *Hermes* xliv, 1909, pp. 135 f.

APPENDIXES

of the name in the fifth and fourth centuries there is no other Atratinus known, he may be safely identified with the accuser of Caelius, and his father with the Bestia defended by Cicero. Probably the boy was adopted by some member of the Sempronian *gens* who had himself revived the name of Atratinus and did not wish his branch of the family to become extinct.[1] Now in § 26 of Cicero's speech a Bestia is named; the passage is obscure, but much of its difficulty disappears if Cicero is here really speaking of Atratinus' father; the name occurs so casually that all present must have been familiar with Bestia's identity and his connexion with the case. Nor is there any other Bestia to whom the inscription could conceivably refer.

Nothing is known of Atratinus after the trial of Caelius until he reappears in 40 as augur (*CIL* i², p. 60); Josephus' mention of him as speaking in the Senate on behalf of Herod, then in flight from Jerusalem, must belong to the same year (*Bell. Iud.* i. 284). Shortly before or after this he must have been in Greece with Antony[2] (the inscription from Hypata shows that he was *legatus pro praetore*), and numismatic evidence proves that he commanded a division of the fleet sent by Antony to help Octavian in the war against Sextus Pompeius.[3] In 34 he was consul with L. Scribonius Libo, succeeding Antony who retired in his favour.[4] After this he seems to have supported Octavian; in 21 he triumphed on returning from the proconsulship of Africa (*CIL* i², pp. 50, 77), and Jerome's notice of him in the same year shows that he then had some reputation as an orator. From the *Fasti Augurales* his death can be placed in A.D. 7.[5] Thus Atratinus' accusation of Caelius was but the beginning of a long and honourable career.

Atratinus' *subscriptores* were P. Clodius and L. Herennius Balbus. It is unlikely that the former is Clodia's notorious brother. The contemptuous reference to his speech in § 27 could not possibly stand as it does if Cicero were really speaking of his arch-enemy. Again, Cicero stages an imaginary conversation between Clodius

[1] Cf. Münzer in Pauly–Wissowa s.v. *Atratinus*, no. 26 (suppl., 1923). An inscription from the Acropolis mentions a Λεύκιος Ἀτρατεῖνος who may have been the adoptive father of our Atratinus. His daughter Sempronia Atratina was married to L. Gellius Poplicola, consul in 36; see Münzer s.v., nos. 27, 108, and cf. Köhler, *Hermes* xxx, 1895, pp. 629–30; see note on § 23. 2.
[2] Coins with his portrait and superscription show that he had been in Sparta (Cat. of Gk. Coins in the British Museum, *Peloponnese*, 128. 69).
[3] Coins from Entella and Lilybaeum (ibid. *Sicily*, 61. 8; 95. 4–6).
[4] Dio Cassius xlix. 39. Coins describing him as *augur cos. desig.* date from the Sicilian war, 36 or 35 B.C.; see Münzer, l.c.
[5] *CIL* i², p. 60.

and his sister, in such a way that he must surely have mentioned the former as being a prosecuting *subscriptor* had that been the case. It is true that Clodius could not have been present in court on 4 April, for he was aedile and would have been holding the games; but whether he were present or not, Cicero's prosopopoeia is scarcely compatible with his being one of Caelius' official accusers. It is much more probable that the P. Clodius in question was some less prominent member of the *gens*, whose share in the case would attract less attention to Clodia's part in the proceedings than if her distinguished brother had acted for her (cf. note on § 27).

Herennius Balbus spoke last for the prosecution; he was an old friend of Atratinus' father (§ 56). A man of this name is mentioned by Asconius in his commentary on the *pro Milone*,[1] but there is no evidence to connect them. At one time it was held, from Cicero's peculiar method of using first the name Herennius and then Balbus, that these were actually separate persons; but the whole tenor of the speech shows that this is impossible.

Thus within a few weeks Cicero first defended Bestia against Caelius, and then defended the latter against the former's son. Probably it was due to his own somewhat awkward position that in his speech he did not stress either his own connexion with Bestia or the relationship of the latter to Atratinus. His silence in the letters as to Caelius' part in the Bestia case may well be accounted for by the estrangement between the two men which had arisen since Caelius lent his support to Catiline. Obviously the present charge against Caelius had assumed such proportions that Cicero realized that only he could save him, incidentally recapturing his allegiance. This consideration must have outweighed all his feelings towards Bestia. The latter, it should be noted, had not always been his friend, for he is probably to be identified with that Bestia who as tribune in 63 was to have given the signal for the beginning of the Catilinarian outbreak by attacking Cicero in the comitia;[2] while years afterwards Cicero displays the greatest animosity towards him when he supported Antony after Caesar's death.[3] Nor was this the first occasion on which Cicero had found himself in such a position. When defending Cluentius in 66 he was much

[1] Ascon., p. 30 KS; cf. § 25. 1 note.
[2] Sall. *Cat.* 43; Appian, *B.C.* ii. 3; in *Sest.* 11 'tribunorum pl. novorum, qui . . . res eas quas gesseram vexare cupiebant', Schol. Bob. refer the passage to Bestia and Metellus Nepos; cf. id. ad *Sull.* 31.
[3] *Phil.* xi. 11, xii. 20, xiii. 2, etc. It seems most probable that the Bestia of the *pro Caelio* is to be identified both with the Bestia of these passages and with the Catilinarian. Drumann–Gröbe ii, pp. 79 f., though treating of them separately, admit that there is a case for the identification, which is actually made by Lange (*R.A.* iii, p. 325).

# APPENDIXES

hampered by his previous defence of Scamander, whom Cluentius had himself prosecuted for sharing in an alleged attempt on his life. One may compare also the action brought in 62 by the young Manlius Torquatus against P. Sulla, when Cicero was obviously in a like difficulty about his course.[1]

## Note

The identification of Atratinus' father with Bestia helps to solve another problem. Pliny (*N.H.* xxvii. 4) remarks: 'constat omnium venenorum ocissimum esse aconitum . . . hoc fuit venenum quo interemptas dormientes a Calpurnio Bestia uxores M. Caecilius accusator obiecit. hinc illa atrox peroratio eius in digitum.' Ruhnken's proposal to read here *Caelius* for *Caecilius* (as in *N.H.* vii. 165; cf. Appendix I) was contested by Nipperdey[2] and others, chiefly because only three *acres accusationes* are mentioned by Cicero in *Brut.* 273. This objection will disappear if the accusation brought by Caelius against Bestia is identical with that brought against the father of Atratinus. Pliny's language is exactly suited to Caelius' known oratorical style, while, as Tacitus also implies that the case of Bestia attracted much attention, it is highly probable that a man of Caelius' standing would have brought the accusation.[3] Ruhnken's conjecture is definitely confirmed by the new evidence.[4]

[1] Cf. especially *Sull.* 46. The whole speech offers a parallel to the circumstances of Cicero's defence of Bestia, since both he and Sulla had been implicated in the Catilinarian affair. Sulla must afterwards have become Cicero's enemy, for in 57 he helped Clodius in his attack on Milo's house (*ad Att.* iv. 3). This was Torquatus' second attack on Sulla, so that Caelius' persistence had its precedent. The young Atratinus' action in counter-attacking his father's accuser resembles the case of Q. Gallius and Calidius (*ad Fam.* viii. 4).

[2] *Opusc.*, p. 299; cf. Wieschhölter, p. 4, note 1; Wegehaupt, p. 13, note 8. The MS. error of *Caecilius* for *Caelius* is found also in Appian, *B.C.* ii. 22, and Dio Cassius xvii. 22; cf. also *Q.F.* ii. 4. 6, where Cicero is speaking of the acquittal of Sex. Clodius—*Clodio* has been corrupted to either *Caelio* in the MSS. or *Caecilio*; see Sternkopf, *Hermes* xxxix, 1904, p. 413.

[3] Tac. *Dial.* 39 'satis constat C. Cornelium et M. Scaurum et T. Milonem et L. Bestiam et P. Vatinium concursu totius civitatis et accusatos et defensos'.

[4] For the whole argument, see Münzer, *Hermes*, l.c.

# APPENDIX VII

## THE CASE AGAINST ANTONIUS IN 59 B.C.

THE relevant authorities are as follow:

(1) in *Cael.* § 15 Cicero has the expression *coniurationis accusatione*; in § 74 he says of Antonius: 'cui misero praeclari in rem publicam benefici memoria nihil profuit, nocuit opinio malefici cogitati'; and in § 78 'non enim potest qui hominem consularem, cum ab eo rem publicam violatam esse diceret, in iudicium vocarit, ipse esse in re publica civis turbulentus'.

(2) Dio Cassius xxxviii. 10 οὐ μέντοι καὶ ἐπὶ τούτοις [sc. τοῖς Μακεδονικοῖς] αἰτίαν ἔσχεν, ἀλλ' ἐγράφη μὲν ἐπὶ τῇ τοῦ Κατιλίνου ξυνωμοσίᾳ, ἑάλω δὲ δι' ἐκεῖνα, καὶ ξυνέβη αὐτῷ, ὧν μὲν ἐκρίνετο μὴ ἐλεγχθῆναι, ὧν δ' οὐκ ᾐτιάζετο, κολασθῆναι.

(3) Quintilian (iv. 2. 123) quotes Caelius' famous description of Antonius' debauch before a battle, almost certainly from his speech in this trial (see introd., p. xv, note 1).

(4) Cic. *Flacc.* 5 'condemnatus est is qui Catilinam signa patriae inferentem interemit'; and Schol. Bob. ad loc. 'Gaius scilicet Antonius, collega Ciceronis, M. Caelio Rufo accusante non tantum pecuniarum repetundarum crimine, verum etiam ob hanc coniurationem non ita pridem damnatus fuerat.' Cf. also *Flacc.* 95.

As regards (1), Cicero's language in § 15 need not imply that the main charge was for sharing in the conspiracy; § 74 certainly refers to Antonius' suspected treason (see note ad loc.); § 78 is too generally expressed for any definite conclusion to follow.

(2) Dio's statement is impossibly confused. If Antonius had been accused of one crime, he could not have been condemned for a different one at the same trial.

(3) Quintilian's excerpt shows that Caelius certainly dealt with Antonius' misconduct in Macedonia.

(4) In the *pro Flacco* Cicero is clearly drawing a parallel between the case of Flaccus (accused of *repetundae*) and that of Antonius. He implies that a concerted attack on the *boni* of 63 is in progress; Antonius has already been condemned, and if Flaccus goes the same way there will be little hope for Cicero himself. Now if the main charge against Antonius had been for sharing in the conspiracy, the parallel would be impossible.

In *Flacc.* 95 Cicero speaks of the joy of the Catilinarian remnant at Antonius' condemnation, which they regarded as vengeance for Catiline; Flaccus is now to be the victim to avenge Lentulus. The statement becomes intelligible if Antonius was condemned for misconduct in the very province which was supposed to be the price of his betrayal of the Catilinarians (Sall. *Cat.* 26).

The conspiracy, then, can only have been brought into Caelius' accusation as a side issue, even though it was that which really ruined Antonius. The actual charge must have been one of either *maiestas* or *repetundae*. As criminal offences the two were closely allied; cf. *in Pis.* 50 'exire de provincia, educere exercitum, bellum sua sponte gerere, in regnum iniussu populi Romani aut senatus accedere, quae cum plurimae leges veteres tum lex Cornelia maiestatis, Iulia de pecuniis repetundis planissime vetat'. In the *Digest* (48. 4. 4) a man is guilty of *maiestas* 'cuius dolo malo exercitus populi Romani in insidias deductus hostibusve proditus erit'. These passages cover the acts of which Antonius was said to have been guilty in Macedonia (Dio Cassius, l.c.; cf. Quintilian's excerpt). Since, however, there is every evidence that the conspiracy was introduced in some way into the case, it seems more likely that Antonius was charged with *maiestas*, which would cover that also, rather than with *repetundae*. But the latter may have formed a sub-section of the accusation; thus the statement of the Scholiast can be accounted for as well as the convolutions of Dio.

The fact that Caelius introduced the conspiracy at all shows how far he was estranged at the time from Cicero; yet had that been the main charge, Antonius' condemnation would have been tantamount to an attack on Cicero's own policy such as Caelius could hardly have contemplated.

See du Mesnil's useful note on *Flacc.* 5; he thinks the charge to have been *maiestas*, as do also Heitland (*Roman Republic* iii, p. 132) and Pauly–Wissowa (s.v. *Antonius*, no. 19); Strachan-Davidson (*Problems of the Roman Criminal Law* ii, p. 12, note 1) prefers *repetundae*, likewise T. B. L. Webster (Cic. *Flacc.* 5) and A. Bergmann (*Einleitung in Ciceros Rede für L. Valerius Flaccus*, Schneeberg, 1893, pp. 16 ff.—a very helpful dissertation); H., p. 210, note 3, believes that Antonius was accused before the *quaestio de vi*, in view of the parallel here between him and Caelius—but the inference is not necessary.


# APPENDIX VIII

## NOTE ON THE COMPOSITION OF THE SPEECH

THERE are some curiously parallel passages or 'doublets' in the *pro Caelio* which have been searchingly discussed and varyingly explained by several scholars (see bibliography). These are (*a*) § 28

# APPENDIXES

and §§ 41-43, (b) §§ 35, 38 and §§ 48-50. Here is a summary of opinions:

(1) Norden holds that the impression made by Herennius' speech (cf. § 25) forced Cicero to change his plans, and to introduce, earlier than he had intended, certain passages from his prepared *commentarius*. He regards § 28 as an improvisation from the longer and prepared passage §§ 41-43, and §§ 48-50 as an improvisation from the shorter § 38, with § 35 similarly improvised.

(2) Opperskalski and Heinze both reject Norden's theory. But they take §§ 39-50 as a unit which was added afterwards by Cicero when he edited the speech;[1] H. regards Cicero's motive as being a wish to rehabilitate himself in the eyes of posterity, in case his defence of wild oats should give a wrong impression.

(3) Reitzenstein thinks that the effect of the repetitions has been exaggerated, and that the speech was delivered in much the same form as we possess it.

(4) Humbert regards the first passage in each pair of parallels as a deliberate preparation for the more elaborate later passage.

(5) Drexler sees Cicero as caught up in a 'vicious circle' of argument: the more he showed up Clodia, the more he laid Caelius open to condemnation, so that his own tactics in the defence forced him to repeat just those points which were bound to recur.

I feel sure that Norden's theory of 'improvisations' is untenable; quite apart from any other objections, if Cicero had in fact been forced to anticipate his own arguments, he could have done so without such close verbal repetition. I feel equally sure that §§ 39-50 are not a later addition inserted on publication. I think that Reitzenstein, Humbert, and especially Drexler have looked at the problem in the only reasonable way, even though their methods vary.

In the first place, these 'doublets' do not really jar, and the first of each pair serves a different purpose from the second. In § 28 Cicero is countering Herennius' arguments, in §§ 41-43 he is leading carefully up to a reasoned defence of Caelius' way of living; certainly the earlier passage could be termed an 'improvisation', in the sense that it was introduced at that particular point because of what Herennius had said, but it was done deliberately, not because Cicero was caught off his guard—he saw his opportunity to give a hint of his later argument, and gladly took it. The repetition

---

[1] Cf. the gibe of Calenus in Dio Cassius xlvi. 7. 3 ἢ οἴει τινα ἀγνοεῖν ὅτι μηδένα τῶν θαυμαστῶν σου τούτων λόγων οὓς ἐκδέδωκας, εἴρηκας, ἀλλὰ πάντας αὐτοὺς μετὰ ταῦτα συγγέγραφας;—but this invective cannot be considered an historical document (cf. Laurand, pp. 3 f.). It was not usual, of course, for the complete speech to be written out beforehand, as was the case with the *post reditum in sen.* (*Planc.* 74).

seems more irritating than it really is, owing to the obtrusively moralizing content of both passages. Likewise, § 35 first makes clear the general dilemma before Clodia, and shows the risks that Cicero is willing to take in exposing her (see note ad loc.); § 38 carries the argument a stage farther in connecting an imaginary young man with an imaginary merry widow, while in §§ 48–50 the argument is finally clinched as Cicero makes it plain that the widow in question is Clodia (whom he now takes for granted as a common *meretrix*) and that the young man is Caelius (whom he has proved to be virtuous and steady).

Secondly, as Drexler has shown, there is no real break at § 39, only a change of tone. The whole passage, §§ 39–50, is essential to Cicero's defence; the first part of it may seem dull to us, but the jury would have understood it and have approved of it (see introductory note on § 39)—even more, they would have felt defrauded without something like it.[1] In this part of his speech Cicero's defence gains the necessary *gravitas*, which it needed rather more than do most of his pleadings; without this passage the whole case would have seemed too flimsy. Cicero's audacity and wit may have assured him victory, but a passage of this kind was needed to consolidate it. It should not be forgotten that he was on very dangerous ground. He had to go cunningly, first to hint, then to develop those hints into open exposure; and the grave solemnity of §§ 39–43 is admirably conceived to lead up to the crushing climax of §§ 48–50, after the way has been paved by § 35 and § 38 on the one hand and by §§ 44–47 on the other.

For these reasons I would agree with Drexler in his general view of the composition of the speech. In fact, too much has been made of these 'doublets': Norden's original scrutiny of them was an interesting piece of work, and not without its value, but it is too academic, and puts the problem in a wrong perspective. The matter is, of course, connected with the question of publication. Norden thought that Cicero's attention was turned from the speech by the political events of 56, that he then let it lie for some time, and in the end only partially edited it. But it is much more probable that the speech was published at once; this was Cicero's usual custom (cf. Laurand, pp. 16 ff., an interesting and sober discussion), and he was most unlikely to have delayed putting on record as soon as possible his triumph over Clodia, or to have been indifferent to what is a most brilliant and amusing speech, which some scholars have held to be the best he ever composed. This, then, is an added reason for rejecting the theory of a later addition.

---

[1] In my first edition I took a completely wrong view of §§ 39–43, and was led to an improbable conclusion.

# ADDITIONAL NOTES

## Additions to the Bibliography

DE SAINT-DENIS, E. Le plus spirituel des discours cicéroniens: le 'pro Caelio' (*L'Information littéraire*, x, 1958, pp. 105–13).

DOREY, T. A. Cicero, Clodia, and the *Pro Caelio* (*Greece and Rome*, 2nd series, v, 1958, pp. 175–80).

GARDNER, R. Cicero, *pro Caelio, de provinciis consularibus, pro Balbo*, with an English translation (Loeb Classical Library). London, 1958.

GILLIAM, J. F. The *Pro Caelio* in St. Jerome's Letters (*Harvard Theological Review*, xlvi, 1953, pp. 103–7).

HAURY, A. L'Ironie et l'humour chez Cicéron. Leiden, 1955.

MALCOVATI, H. Oratorum Romanorum Fragmenta (2nd edition). Turin, 1955.

NEUDLING, C. L. A Prosopography to Catullus (Iowa Studies in Classical Philology, XII). Oxford, 1955.

---

(p. xix). Professor Watt has pointed out to me that Gulielmius did not in fact edit Cicero, but died in Germany while collating MSS. for a projected edition (see the preface to Gruter's edition, where his notes were finally published).

§ 1. 9. legem . . . requirat: a better translation of *crimen* . . . *requirat* would be 'he would seek to know the kind of charge that was before the court'.

§ 1. 16. putet . . . existimet: Cicero likes this variation; cf. *post red. in sen.* 13 'etiam si agrestem et inhumanum existimares, tamen libidinosum et perditum non putares', *Sest.* 42 'intenta signa legionum existimari cervicibus ac bonis vestris falso, sed putari tamen'.

§ 3. 7. ac mihi quidem videtur: this idiom ('I think') is a very favourite type of Ciceronian formula; see G. Grossmann, *de particula 'quidem'* (diss. Königsberg, 1880), pp. 38 f., where it is stated that this particular variation, introduced by *ac*, occurs exclusively in Cicero, apart from one passage in Sallust (*Cat.* 3. 2).

§ 3. 9. deformandi . . . gratia: better, 'to disgrace my client and to strip him and despoil him of his good name'; *deformare* with a personal object in this metaphorical sense is rare (cf. *har. resp.* 51 'in qua Pompeium ornat,—an potius deformat ?')—see *Thes. L.L.* s.v., col. 371. 79 ff.

§ 3. 16. hi sic habeant: 'I should like them to realize this, that . . .'; *sic* (like *hoc, illud*, etc.) is a 'sign-post' word, anticipating and facilitating the long object-clause. *Habere* here is equivalent to

# ADDITIONAL NOTES

*scire, sibi persuadere*, and in this sense a jussive form is generally found; cf. *de am.* 10 'de me autem, ut iam cum utroque loquar, sic habetote', ibid. 91 'habendum est nullam in amicitiis pestem esse maiorem quam adulationem' (where see S.-M.), *Tusc.* iii. 13 'illud quidem sic habeto, nisi sanatus animus sit . . . finem miseriarum' nullum fore'; the idiom is especially frequent in Cicero's letters. See *Thes. L.L.*, s.v. *habere*, col. 2449. 7 ff.

§ 4. 23. est . . . existimatio: cf. Reitzenstein in *Hermes* li (1916), p. 622, where this passage is adduced to support the reading *haec et vestra consensio est* in Minucius Felix xi. 5.

Grossmann (op. cit., p. 66) observes that this is the only occurrence in the speeches of the collocation *quidem . . . sed . . . certe*.

§ 4. 25. lacrimae . . . luctusque: Mr. W. M. Calder has drawn my attention to Plato, *Apol.* 34c, where Socrates refuses to have recourse to such emotional tricks (cf. Aristophanes, *Vesp.* 568 ff.).

§ 6. 19. paeniteat: cf. Hor. *S.* i. 6. 89 'nil paeniteat sanum patris huius', and Kiessling–Heinze ad loc.: see Fraenkel, *Horace*, p. 5, n. 6, where it is pointed out that this meaning ('to be dissatisfied') belongs originally to early Latin; he notes a striking example in Cic. *rep.* vi. 16 'iam ipsa terra ita mihi parva visa est, ut me imperii nostri, quo quasi punctum eius attingimus, paeniteret'.

§ 6. 25. urbanitas: see A. Haury, *L'Ironie et l'humour chez Cicéron* (Leiden, 1955), *passim*, for various aspects of *urbanitas*, and cf. E. de Saint-Denis, *Le plus spirituel des discours cicéroniens*.

§ 8. 8. primum . . . existiment: I now prefer my original view of this passage (see the 1933 edition), that *ut . . . existiment* is a parenthetic final clause.

§ 8. 11. ut . . . ne dicas: for *ut ne* cf. J. André, *RÉL* xxxv (1957) pp. 167 ff.

§ 9. 22. nihil dicam . . . me: with Cl.'s punctuation there is no anacoluthon, but Kl. ends the parenthesis at *existimatis*, and puts a period at *deductum*, making a new sentence begin at *nemo hunc*.

§ 12. 5. et quidem: see Grossmann, op. cit., p. 108, Nisbet on *de dom.* 11. 7.

§ 13. 13. civis meliorum partium: this is predicative, parallel with *taetrior hostis*. In the next line, *aliquando* is a variation of *quodam tempore* above.

§ 13. 21 ff. Mr. W. M. Calder well compares Plutarch, *Alcibiades* 23 ἦν γάρ, ὥς φασι, μία δεινότης αὕτη τῶν πολλῶν ἐν αὐτῷ, καὶ μηχανὴ θήρας ἀνθρώπων, συνεξομοιοῦσθαι καὶ συνομοπαθεῖν τοῖς ἐπιτηδεύμασι καὶ ταῖς διαίταις, ὀξυτέρας τρεπομένῳ τροπὰς τοῦ χαμαιλέοντος . . . Ἀλκιβιάδῃ δὲ διὰ χρηστῶν ἰόντι καὶ πονηρῶν ὁμοίως οὐδὲν ἦν ἀμίμητον οὐδ' ἀνεπιτήδευτον, ἀλλ' ἐν Σπάρτῃ γυμναστικός, εὐτελής, σκυθρωπός· ἐν Ἰωνίᾳ χλιδανός, ἐπιτερπής, ῥᾴθυμος· ἐν Θρᾴκῃ μεθυστικός, ἱππαστικός, etc.

§ 13. 22. tristibus: Professor Watt has drawn my attention to

163

# ADDITIONAL NOTES

**Hor. *Epp.* i. 18. 89 f.** 'oderunt hilarem tristes tristemque iocosi, sedatum celeres, agilem gnavumque remissi'.

**§ 14. 8. oculis . . . manibus:** cf. *Clu.* 20 'cum . . . res non coniectura, sed oculis ac manibus teneretur', where Fausset translates 'the matter was not one of inference, but of palpable ocular demonstration'.

**§ 16. 5. cupiditas:** cannot this mean simply 'ambition' (cf. note on 1. 15)? It is in any case incorrect to state, as I have done, that the absolute use is 'not common'. (The word is one of Cicero's favourites: see the interesting table in *Thes. L.L.* s.v., showing the relative frequency of *cupiditas* and *cupido* in prose writers.)

**§ 18. 17. et ex publica causa:** Professor Watt remarks that the form of Clark's critical note shows that he meant to delete *et* (so Kl.).

**§ 18. 24. quo loco:** 'on this topic', 'in this connexion'; cf. *Flacc.* 57 'quo loco etiam atque etiam facite ut recordemini' (cf. Madvig on *de fin.* iv. 73).

**§ 18. 27.** This quotation from Ennius was a great favourite with Cicero: see *de fato* 35, *de inv.* i. 91, *Top.* 61, *de fin.* i. 5, *de nat. deor.* iii. 75, *Tusc.* i. 45; cf. *Rhet. ad Herenn.* ii. 34.

**§ 18. 1. ac . . . quidem:** a collocation not found in Varro, Caesar, or Nepos (Grossmann, op. cit., p. 50).

**§ 19. 10. prudentia:** for *communis sensus* cf. Fraenkel, *Horace*, p. 88, n. 2.

**§ 19. 23.** For the writing up of a speech for publication after delivery cf. *Tusc.* iv. 55 'oratorem vero irasci minime decet, simulare non dedecet. an tibi irasci tum videmur, cum quid in causis acrius et vehementius dicimus? quid? cum iam rebus transactis et praeteritis orationes scribimus, num irati scribimus?', and see Henry ad loc.

**§ 22. 27.** See additional bibliography s.v. Gilliam, and H. Hagendahl, *Latin Fathers and the Classics* (Göteborg, 1958); cf. H. T. Rowell, *Eranos* lvii (1959), pp. 59 ff.

**§ 23. 2. Pallae:** for Gellius Poplicola cf. C. L. Neudling, *A Prosopography to Catullus*, pp. 75 ff.

**§ 23. 3. de quo . . . rex:** my translation of *quod is . . . fatetur* is wrong; *quod* must be causal, not the pronoun (i.e. 'considering that the author of the deed is either unafraid or else actually admits responsibility').

**§ 24. 12.** For *praevaricatio* see *RE* xxii. 2, cols. 1680 ff.

**§ 25. 2. in quo:** more probably neuter ('in this connexion'); cf. note on 15. 17.

**§ 25. 8. esset . . . soleret:** the verbs are in the past tense, because Cicero is referring to a past occasion (*fuit*), and Latin idiom follows the normal principles of tense-relationship even when, as here, a statement is made that still applies as a general truth:

this was Herennius' normal behaviour at the time when he was for the moment speaking so censoriously, and it still is characteristic of him. Examples seem to come mainly from outside the speeches: thus *Brut.* 155 'cum duae civiles artes plurimum et laudis haberent et gratiae, perfecit ut altera praestaret omnibus . . .', ibid. 214 'sed ei tamen unum illud habebant dicendi opus elaboratum, idque cum constaret ex quinque notissimis partibus, nemo in aliqua parte eorum omnino nihil poterat', ibid. 112 (where see Kroll), 254, 276, *de off.* i. 143 'quae erant prudentiae propria, suo loco dicta sunt', ibid. ii. 36 'erat igitur ex iis tribus quae ad gloriam pertinerent, hoc tertium', *Tusc.* i. 26, 51, ii. 43 (where see Dougan). Cf. Lebr., p. 219, K. II. i, p. 123, L.-H. p. 701.

§ **27. 1. deliciarum:** especially love-affairs (as in 44. 8, 76. 28; cf. Catullus 68. 26); in *ad Att.* ii. 8. 2, Cicero calls the Bay of Naples 'Cratera illum delicatum'.

**etiam lenior:** Professor Watt regards Clark's conjecture *et a causa alienior* as brilliant and right; I do not now feel that the arguments brought against it in my note amount to much: from Cicero's point of view, a general sermon *was* 'irrelevant' to Caelius' particular case, but it was more dangerous to his client and therefore 'impressed him more'. Certainly as the years go on I find Clark's proposal very attractive.

§ **27. 4. inflammatus:** for this absolute use cf. *de or.* ii. 190 'nulla mens est tam ad comprehendendam vim oratoris parata, nisi ipse inflammatus ad eam et ardens accesserit'. Cicero's picture of P. Clodius here resembles what he says of Fimbria in *Brut.* 233 'omnia magna voce dicens verborum sane bonorum cursu quodam incitato ita furebat tamen, ut mirarere tam alias res agere populum ut esset insano inter disertos locus'.

§ **27. 8. si licet:** this must be right; Cicero is being mock-solemn: add *de domo* 138 'neque is cui licuit neque id quod fas fuit dedicavit', *Mil.* 43 'ut eum nihil delectaret, quod aut per naturam fas esset aut per leges liceret', *rep.* iii. 33 'huic legi nec obrogari fas est, neque derogari . . . licet', Ovid, *F.* i. 25 'si licet et fas est', Martial xii. 6. 11 'nunc licet et fas est'. (For confusion of *si-* and *sci-* in MSS. cf. Havet, *Manuel de critique verbale*, 1070, p. 255.)

**si fas est:** i.e. 'if it is not forbidden'; cf. *Quinct.* 94 'si fas est respirare P. Quinctium contra nutum . . . Naevi' (see *Thes. L.L.* s.v. *fas*, col. 293. 15). Conway on Virgil, *Aen.* i. 77 observes that *fas* 'has always the notion of a law whose commands are mainly negative'.

§ **27. 10. qui Baias viderit:** Gilliam (op. cit., p. 104) quotes St. Jerome, *Epp.* 45. 4. 1 'Baias peterent, unguenta eligerent. divitias et viduitatem haberent, materias luxuriae et libertatis'. There is a curious correspondence here with one of the fragments

# ADDITIONAL NOTES

of Cicero's speech *in P. Clodium et C. Curionem* (Klotz–Schoell viii, pp. 439 ff.): (frg. 20) 'primum homo durus ac priscus invectus est in eos qui mense Aprili apud Baias essent et aquis calidis uterentur. quid cum hoc homine nobis tam tristi ac severo ? non possunt hi mores ferre hunc tam austerum et tam vehementem magistrum, per quem hominibus maioribus natu ne in suis quidem praediis inpune tum cum Romae nihil agitur liceat esse valetudinique servire. verum ceteris ⟨licitum⟩ sit ignoscere, ⟨ei⟩ vero ⟨qui praedium habeat⟩ in illo loco, nullo modo. "quid homini" inquit "Arpinati cum Baiis, agresti ac rustico ?" ' (See also on 34. 10, 36. 16 below).

This invective was composed by Cicero as a sequel to the events of 61 B.C., when Clodius stood his trial after the Bona Dea scandal of the previous year, and was acquitted. Clodius had been defended by the elder Curio, and Cicero himself had given evidence against him. At a meeting of the Senate on 15 May, Cicero first delivered a set speech against Clodius, and followed this by an *altercatio* (*ad Att.* i. 16. 8, written in 61); Curio seems then to have attacked Cicero in a pamphlet (*ad Att.* iii. 12. 2, written in 58), and in return Cicero concocted this invective: apparently he intended it as a private bit of retaliation, but it got published somehow, to his annoyance (*ad Att.* iii. 12. 2). See Schanz–Hosius, *Geschichte der römischen Literatur*, vol. i (1927), p. 445; Gelzer in *RE* s.v. *M. Tullius Cicero*, cols. 897 f.; and cf. T. A. Dorey, *Greece and Rome*, second series, v (1958), p. 180.

It looks uncommonly as if in this 'speech', whatever the circumstances of its composition, Cicero had treated Clodius in much the same gay and ribald fashion as that in which he attacks Clodia in the *pro Caelio*—almost, in fact, as if in attacking the sister he had deliberately drawn upon the earlier onslaught upon the brother. It is exasperating that the whole invective has not been preserved. Cf. Haury, op. cit., pp. 137 ff.

§ 29. 24. dies . . . deficiat: Virgil dresses up the idea in *Aen.* i. 372 ff. 'O dea, si prima repetens ab origine pergam, et vacat annalis nostrorum audire laborum, ante diem clauso componet Vesper Olympo'; cf. Ovid, *Epp. ex Ponto* ii. 4. 12 'saepe fuit brevior quam mea verba dies'.

§ 30. 6. erat enim meum: the imperfect is used as in *par erat, aequius erat, poteram*, etc.; cf. *Tusc.* iv. 66 'atque erat facile . . . negare unquam laetitia adfici posse insipientem, quod nihil unquam haberet boni. sed loquimur nunc more communi'. In such expressions, the imperfect indicative is used in a present sense, in an unreal condition (either stated or understood)—here, 'I could be doing this, if I wanted to'—when there is an idea of potentiality or obligation clearly contained in the verb or verbal concept. The

# ADDITIONAL NOTES

usage is not found in Comedy, but begins with Lucilius and is regular down to late Latin; see L.-H., pp. 566 f., K. II. i, p. 173, Lebr. pp. 279 ff.

§ 30. 17. **persona**: 'character', in the action, looked at as a drama; cf. *Sull.* 68 'neque tamen istorum facinorum tantorum, tam atrocium crimen, iudices, P. Sullae persona suscipit'; cf. Fausset and Ramsay on *Clu.* 78. Reid, on *Sull.* 8, denies that in the best Latin the word is employed like our 'person': but it is very nearly that here.

§ 30. 22. **nullae sedes:** *nulla* certainly gives a better clausula; but the clausula in *nullo auctore emissae* is equally rare (cf. Zielinski, *Das Clauselgesetz in Ciceros Reden*, pp. 153 f.), and here *P*[1] has *missae*, which Havet would read (*Manuel de critique verbale*, 1179, p. 290).

§ 31. 4. **res est ... Clodia:** see Dorey, loc. cit., for the view that in reality Clodia's part in the case was only subsidiary.

§ 32. 18. **mea fides:** *fides* here is used of an advocate's duty towards his client; cf. *RA* 30 'qui libere dicat, qui cum fide defendat ... non deest profecto', *Clu.* 118 'a me ... omnia caute pedetemptimque dicentur, ut neque fides huius defensionis relicta ... esse videatur'. See *Thes. L.L.* s.v., col. 679. 50 ff.

§ 33. 23. **severe ... prisce ... austero more:** cf. *in Clod. et Cur.* frg. 20 (above, on 27. 10).

§ 33. 3. **minimum ... videbit:** there is an equally schoolboyish piece of wit in *in Clod. et Cur.* frg. 25 'sed, credo, postquam speculum tibi adlatum est, longe te a pulchris abesse sensisti' (!)

§ 33. 5. **quid tibi cum Caelio:** cf. *in Clod. et Cur.* frg. 20 (above, on 27. 10).

§ 34. 10. **tenuisse:** cf. Suet. *Cal.* 25. 1 'matrimonia contraxerit turpius an dimiserit an tenuerit, non est facile discernere'; it is difficult to decide whether *te* is subject or object to *tenuisse*, but the run of the sentence suggests that it is object.

The manner of this passage is closely similar to that of *in Clod. et Cur.* frg. 24 'tune, cum vincirentur pedes fasciis, cum calautica capiti accommodaretur, cum vix manicatam tunicam in lacertos induceres, cum strophio accurate praecingerere, in tam longo spatio numquam te Appi Claudi nepotem esse recordatus es ?'

§ 34. 16. **nonne ... ne ... quidem:** for this use of *ne ... quidem* cf. Madvig's edition of *de finibus*, Excursus III.

§ 35. 2. **videro:** for such tenses see Madvig, *Opuscula Academica*[2], pp. 463 ff.

§ 35. 12. Professor Watt points out that under the later *Lex Iulia de vi publica et privata* (the successor of the law under which Caelius was being tried), it was enacted 'hac lege in reum testimonium dicere ne liceto ... (quae) palam corpore quaestum faciet feceritve'

# ADDITIONAL NOTES

(*Digest* xxii. 5. 3. 5; Bruns–Gradenwitz, *Fontes iuris Romani antiqui*[7], p. 111). Cicero's branding of Clodia as a *meretrix* (hinted at here, explicit in 49) must have been something more damaging than mere abuse (cf. Dorey, loc. cit., p. 178, n. 3).

§ 36. 19. **in isto genere:** 'in that respect' (so *de domo* 14); cf. *de or.* ii. 17 'qui . . . in aliquo genere ('in some sort of way') aut inconcinnus aut multus est'. Sometimes a defining genitive is added, as in *Sest.* 90 'hoc in genere praesidi comparati', where see Holden; see also S.-M. on *de am.* 15 (p. 92).

**urbanissimus:** cf. *in Clod. et Cur.* frg. 22 'nam rusticos ei nos videri minus est mirandum, qui manicatam tunicam et mitram et purpureas fascias habere non possumus. tu vero festivus, tu elegans, tu solus urbanus, quem decet muliebris ornatus, quem incessus psaltriae, qui effeminare vultum, attenuare vocem, laevare corpus potes. o singulare prodigium atque monstrum! nonne te huius templi, non urbis, non vitae, non lucis pudet ?'

§ 36. 25. **aspexisti:** for this use of *aspicio*, see *Thes. L.L.* s.v., col. 832. 81 ff.; there is a good example in Terence, *HT* 773 f. 'sese ipse dicit tuam vidisse filiam; eius sibi complacitam formam, postquam aspexerit; hanc cupere uxorem'.

**candor:** it is much more likely that the word implies a clear complexion, rather than simply 'beauty' (cf., however, Porphyrion on Hor. *Epod.* 3. 9 'candoris nomine et Vergilius in significatione pulchritudinis semper utitur'). It is an unusual word in prose, when applied to a human being, and this appears to be the first occurrence of such a use in a prose author (unless *corpore niveum candorem* in *Rhet. ad Herenn.* iv. 44 is an example—Marx refers it to *Il.* x. 437, the description of Rhesus' horses). Livy has it of the white bodies of the Galatians (xxxviii. 21. 9), and Pliny uses it in two passages where he comments on the cosmetic qualities of asses' milk (*N.H.* xi. 238 'conferre aliquid et candori in mulierum cute existimatur', xxviii. 183 'cutem in facie erugari et tenerescere candore custodito lacte asinino putant'). But it is mainly a poetic use, just as the poets like using *candidus*.

§ 36. 27. **isdem:** to the passages quoted in my note, add Ovid, *Met.* xiv. 346 'venerat in silvas et filia Solis easdem', where *easdem* = 'at the same time'.

§ 37. 11. **nunc enim:** *enim* is presumably asseverative, as regularly in Plautus (cf. Sonnenschein on *Most.* 551).

§ 37. 14. **sceleste:** Professor Watt suggests that the meaning is 'unlucky', as often in Plautus (see Lindsay on *Capt.* 762; cf. *Most.* 563 f. 'ne ego sum miser, scelestus, natus dis inimicis omnibus'). In that case, Cicero is here contrasting (*a*) the hard-hearted father in Caecilius with (*b*) another who is compassionate; he then elaborates the pair in (*a*) 37. 15 ff. and (*b*) 38. 4 ff. If this is accepted, *aut illum* here would have to be emended to *an illum*, to provide the necessary disjunctive form of the sentence. The suggestion is very attractive.

§ 37. 16. egone ... velim: Professor Watt notes *ad Att.* xi. 7. 6 'o rem miseram! quid scribam ? aut quid velim ?'

§ 38. 1. maledica civitate: Gilliam (op. cit., p. 106) notes St. Jerome, *Epp.* 127. 3. 1 'difficile est in maledica civitate ... non aliquam sinistri rumoris fabulam trahere'. Cf. *Flacc.* 7 'et is est reus avaritiae, qui in uberrima re turpe compendium, in maledicentissima civitate, in suspiciosissimo negotio maledictum omne, non modo crimen, effugit ?', ibid. 68 'in tam suspiciosa ac maledica civitate locum sermoni obtrectatorum non reliquit'. It is a pity that we can never know a Roman jury's reaction to such Ciceronian gags.

§ 38. 4. patre: is this conjecture by Schwarz (*sic*: Clark misspells the name) really needed ? I cannot now see how *patri* would involve 'a difficult change of subject'; Professor Watt suggests that it can be taken as a *dativus iudicantis*, and it certainly provides a better contrast with *huic tristi ac derecto seni* above.

§ 39. 22. hac indole virtutis ac continentiae: cf. *Phil.* v. 47 'magna indoles virtutis ... exstincta est', *de off.* iii. 16 'iis omnes in quibus est virtutis indoles commoventur', *Epp. ad Brut.* ix (i. 3). 1 'Caesaris vero pueri mirifica indoles virtutis', Livy xxi. 4. 10 (of Hannibal) 'cum hac indole virtutum atque vitiorum triennio ... meruit', iii. 12. 3 'tantam indolem tam maturae virtutis'. *Indoles* implies 'natural gifts', 'endowments', often with the idea of 'promise' contained in it (cf. Paneg. Lat. iv. 16. 6 'ut iam infantulo indoles futuri roboris emicaret'): Servius, on *Aen.* x. 826 (Aeneas' pity for Lausus), comments 'indoles autem est proprie imago quaedam virtutis futurae'. It is even possible to speak of *indoles ingenii* (Plaut. *Mil.* 921 'novi indolem nostri ingeni', Cic. *Phil.* xi. 33 'summa in filio spes, summa ingeni indoles', Livy ix. 17. 10 'indoles eadem ... erat animi ingeniique').

*Ingenium*, though often apparently synonymous with *indoles*, has many more and wider aspects (e.g. in connexion with the intellect); its use with genitives such as *indoles* has in these passages is not 'classical' (e.g. Val. Max. viii. 14. ext. 5 'Theopompi magnae facundiae ingenium', cf. *Thes. L.L.* s.v., cols. 1525. 50, 1529. 44); Plautus, with his love of word-fun, has the remarkable phrase (*Stich.* 126) 'ingenium ingeni' (cf. *Trin.* 665 'pernovi ... ingenium tuom ingenuom')—but *ingenium indolis* would surely be impossible.

§ 39. 6. Camillos, Fabricios, Curios: cf. Milton, *Paradise Regained* ii. 445 (Jesus is speaking) 'Canst thou not remember / Quintius, Fabricius, Curius, Regulus ? / For I esteem those names of men so poor, / Who could do mighty things, and could contemn / Riches, though offered from the hand of kings'.

# ADDITIONAL NOTES

**§ 41. 19. dicendi facultate:** better, 'by their clever skill in argument'; Cicero means dialectic, for which the Academics were noted.

**§ 41. 23. vias . . . lubricas:** cf. *Flacc.* 105 'quem posthac tam amentem fore putatis qui non illam viam vitae, quam ante praecipitem et lubricam esse ducebat, huic planae et stabili praeponendam esse arbitretur ?', *rep.* i. 44 'nullum est enim genus illarum rerum publicarum quod non habeat iter ad finitimum quoddam malum praeceps ac lubricum'; Gilliam (op. cit., p. 104) notes St. Jerome, *Epp.* 7. 4. 1 'scitis ipsi lubricum adulescentiae iter, in quo et ego lapsus sum', which may be a reminiscence of the *pro Caelio*. Pliny, looking for a good school for a young boy, observes (*Epp.* iii. 3. 4) 'adest enim adulescenti nostro cum ceteris naturae fortunaeque dotibus eximia corporis pulchritudo, cui in hoc lubrico aetatis non praeceptor modo sed custos etiam rectorque quaerendus est'.

**§ 42. 2. propitios . . . iratos:** cf. Livy ix. 1. 11 'cum rerum humanarum maximum momentum sit, quam propitiis rem, quam adversis agant dis'. The implication is that of a contrast between bliss and misery; so *dis inimicis natus* is proverbial for 'being under a curse' (Plaut. *Mil.* 314, *Most.* 563; see Otto, *Sprichw.* p. 110); Seneca, in his mockery of Claudius, remarks (*Apocol.* 11) 'hunc nunc deum facere vultis ? videte corpus eius dis iratis natum'. See Mayor on Juvenal x. 129.

**§ 42. 3. frondibus:** 'branches' (see *Thes. L.L.* s.v., col. 1352. 46 ff.). Maas observes (*Archiv für lateinische Lexicographie* xii, p. 517) that this is probably the first occurrence of the plural form in prose (the plural, in the accusative, is regular in poetry from Ennius onwards; Virgil has *frondes* seventeen times, *frondem* once only).

**§ 46. 4. in hoc genere:** see on 36. 19.

**§ 49. 2. non nupta:** cf. my note on Virgil, *Aen.* iv. 550 f.; in Catullus 68. 6, *caelebs* may possibly be used of a widower.

**§ 49. 6. incessu:** cf. *in Clod. et Cur.* frg. 22 (above, on 36. 19).

**§ 51. 2. summorum facinorum:** Professor Watt has convinced me that my note is wrong; the phrase must certainly be taken with *crimina*.

**§ 55. 10. una vox:** Pluygers' conjecture is hard to resist; cf. *ad Att.* ii. 12. 2 'ubi sunt qui aiunt ζώσης φωνῆς ?': it is true, however, that in most of the examples of *viva vox* some such formula as *ut vulgo dicitur, ut aiunt* is added (see Otto, *Sprichw.* s.v. *vox*).

**§ 61. 9. pyxidem:** cf. Pliny, *N.H.* xxx. 43 'viperam mulier praegnans si transcenderit, abortum faciet, item amphisbaenam mortuam dumtaxat; nam vivam habentes in pyxide impune transeunt; etiam si mortua sit atque adservata, partus facilis praestat vel mortua'.

§ **61. 15. simultas . . . discidium:** see Dorey, loc. cit., p. 178, for a suggestion that Clodia had herself tired of Caelius and was no cast-off mistress.

§ **62. 4. quadrantaria:** cf. Athenaeus 596F ἑταίραν τὴν καλουμένην Δίδραχμον, Plaut. *Cist.* 407 '(amicae) diobolares'; see J. Colin, *Revue Belge de Philologie et d'Histoire*, xxxiii (1955), pp. 858 ff. With such phrases as *homo dipundiarius* cf. *OED*, s.v. *triobolar*, *triobolary*; so in the preface to the *Memoirs of the Life of Sir Stephen Fox* (published in 1717), the author says of his works that they 'have not met with so ill a reception . . . as to fling him into the list of *triobularian* scriblers'. (I owe this reference to Professor Mark Thomson.)

§ **62. 5. balneatori:** possibly another aspect of Cicero's witticism could be imagined from Martial iii. 93. 14. For the passage of Quintilian (ix. 4. 63 f.) quoted in my note, see some remarks by B. Axelson, *Der Mechanismus des Ovidischen Pentameterschlusses*, in *Ovidiana* (Paris, 1958), p. 131.

§ **63. 14. temere prosiluerunt:** there is a clear echo of this passage, and of 62. 23 above, in Dictys Cretensis iv. 11 'quos visos Ulixes, "non temere est", inquit, "quod hi turbati ac trepidi repente prosiluere".' How did the talented author of the *Ephemeris belli Troiani* happen to remember this scrap of Cicero ? It is tantalizing that the Tebtunis Papyrus has a lacuna here (see Eisenhut's edition, Teubner, 1958, p. 136); but it is clear, from a comparison with the versions of Malalas and Iohannes Antiochenus, that this is one of the passages where the Latin writer expanded his Greek original (see Ihm, *Hermes* xliv, 1909, p. 18; *Tebtunis Papyri*, Part II, p. 17).

§ **64. 23. fabella:** this diminutive form is used first by Cicero.

§ **64. 24. plurimarum fabularum poetriae:** a wiser translation of *fabularum* would have been 'comedies'. Giri is probably right in claiming that this is no proof that Clodia wrote verses or plays: Cicero chose to use *poetria* merely because he was having his fun with the idea of *fabulae* connected with Clodia's name (see *Rivista Indo-Greca-Italica* vi, 1922, p. 163, n. 3).

§ **65. 15. imploraret hominum fidem:** cf. Sen. *Epp.* 15. 7 'nemo statim Quiritium fidem implorat', where the context shows that such a cry would be highly emotional and made at a crisis. For the phrase, see *Thes. L.L.* s.v. *fides*, col. 666. 65 ff.; note the vivid lines of Caecilius, frg. 212, quoted in *de nat. deor.* i. 13, 'pro deum, popularium omnium, omnium adulescentium / clamo, postulo, obsecro, oro, ploro atque imploro fidem'.

§ **67. 12. equus Troianus:** Cicero's various allusions to the Wooden Horse show both his own versatility and the adaptability of the animal. In *Verr.* iv. 52, he brings it in to illustrate the misery caused by Verres when he stripped Haluntium of its silver

# ADDITIONAL NOTES

plate and Corinthian bronzes ('quem concursum in oppido factum putatis, quem clamorem, quem porro fletum mulierum ? qui videret, equum Troianum introductum, urbem captam diceret'). In *Mur.* 78, the Horse is a hideous peril which the unsleeping Cicero will himself avert; but in *Phil.* ii. 32 he counts it as a noble compliment to himself that Antony should think of him as one of the Liberators, stowed away in the patriotic beast. In *de or.* ii. 94, the Horse is made to serve a donnish piece of sly wit, with reference to Isocrates and his school ('ecce tibi est exortus Isocrates, magister istorum omnium, cuius e ludo tanquam ex equo Troiano meri principes exierunt'). And here in the *pro Caelio* Cicero, with a grin, introduces the creature to mock this Tale of a Bathtub. See my paper *Virgil and the Wooden Horse*, in *JRS* xlix (1959).

§ 67. 19. **alia fori . . . triclini:** Gilliam (op. cit., p. 105) quotes St. Jerome, *Epp.* 50. 5. 4 'tunc intelleget aliam vim fori esse, aiiam triclinii: non aeque inter fusa et calathos puellarum et inter eruditos viros de divinae legis dogmatibus disputari'.

§ 68. 28. **de cognatorum sententia:** for such family councils, cf. Varro, *RR* i. 2. 8 'quorum si alterutrum decolat et nihilominus quis vult colere, mente est captus adque adgnatos et gentiles est deducendus'; [Quintil.] *decl. min.* 356 (p. 388 R.) 'cum iam nec sumptibus nec inverecundiae finis imponi posset, habuisse cum cognatis consilium, quidnam se facere oporteret'.

§ 69. 11. **fabula:** cf. Sen. *Contr.* ii. 7. 9 'unus pudicitiae fructus est pudicam credi, et adversus omnes inlecebras atque omnia delenimenta muliebribus ingeniis est veluti solum firmamentum in nullam incidisse fabulam'.

§ 70. 25. **ad statum patriae:** *status* in such phrases = 'stability'; cf. *Sest.* 1 'qui auderent se et salutem suam in discrimen offerre pro statu civitatis et pro communi libertate' (so with *rei publicae*, *Flacc.* 3, *Sull.* 33, Matius ap. Cic. *ad Fam.* xi. 28. 6).

§ 71. 10. **Vetti nomen:** it is impossible to identify this Vettius; several persons of the name appear in this decade. Mr. J. P. V. D. Balsdon has reminded me that the Vettius of *in Vat.* 24 ff. had been used by Cicero as an informer in 63 B.C., and that he was not the obscure figure that my note on 71. 8 would suggest: he figured prominently in some bizarre events of 59 B.C., and was found mysteriously dead in prison (*in Vat.*, l.c., *ad Att.* ii. 24, *Sest.* 132, Suet. *Iul.* 20, Plutarch, *Lucull.* 42). Presumably it is he who is referred to as a disreputable friend of Catiline in *Comm. Pet. Cons.* 10. Then there was a Vettius from whom, or through whose agency, Cicero bought a *villa* that had belonged to Catulus (*ad Att.* iv. 5. 2, written in 56 B.C.); and in *ad Att.* vi. 1. 15 (50 B.C.) there is a contemptuous mention of a Vettius who was a *manceps*, in company with a cobbler (Syme, *Roman Revolution*, p. 91, n. 5, appears to identify these two men). In *ad Att*. ii. 4. 7, Cicero names a Vettius whose services should be used in connexion with the building (or repair ?) of a wall (59 B.C.)—presumably the *Chrysippus Vettius, Cyri architecti libertus*, named in *ad Fam*. vii. 14. 1 (written in 53 B.C.). There is no reason why the Vettius of *Cael*. 71 should not be yet another bearer of the name.

For the word-play in *vetus, Vetti* cf. H. Holst, *Die Wortspiele in Ciceros Reden* (Symbolae Osloenses, fasc. suppl. 1, Oslo, 1925), pp. 47 ff.

§ 76. 28. interpositus: 'intervening' is probably the sense, i.e. the tattle that intervened between the period of Caelius' blameless early youth (72) and the time when he 'surfaced'.

§ 76. 2. insequitur, revocat: these are true presents, referring to the fresh proceedings instituted by Caelius against Bestia.

§ 76. 10. refrenandi . . . incitandi: a favourite type of metaphor, e.g. *ad Att*. vi. 1. 12 'Cicerones pueri amant inter se, discunt, exercentur, sed alter, uti dixit Isocrates in Ephoro et Theopompo, frenis eget, alter calcaribus' (so *Brut*. 204, *de or*. iii. 36; cf. περὶ ὕψους 2). *Si quidem* (below) is probably causal, not as translated ad loc.

§ 77. 17. dies: cf. *ad Fam*. vi. 13. 2 'nam et res eum cotidie et dies et opinio hominum . . . mitiorem facit'; the poets use *longa dies* in this sense ('the passage of time'), e.g. Virg. *Aen*. v. 783 'quam nec longa dies pietas nec mitigat ulla'; cf. Landgraf in *Archiv für lateinische Lexicographie*, xiv, p. 63.

§ 77. 19. bonarum partium: Professor Watt notes *Epp. ad Brut*. 5 (ii. 5). 3 'qui vir, di boni, quam gravis, quam constans, quam bonarum in re publica partium'.

§ 78. 6. re . . . fide . . . spe . . . sede: for such assonances cf. Holst, op. cit., pp. 81 ff.

§ 79. 25. Professor Watt notes an accidental 'alcaic' in *Epp. ad Brut*. 24 (i. 16). 1 'quae morte qua non perniciosior'. The Emperor Marcus Aurelius was pleased with an accidental 'hendecasyllabic' in one of his letters to Fronto (ii. 5, p. 30 N.), 'nos istic vehementer aestuamus—habes et hendecasyllabum ingenuum. igitur priusquam poetari incipio, pausam tecum facio'.

(p. 141). Several passages in Cicero well illustrate not only the importance of voice and gesture in pleading (cf. *Orat*. 58 f., *de or*. iii. 220 ff.), but also the 'atmosphere' of a court. Thus, he observes (*Brut*. 200) that even a passer-by, if he has intelligence, can tell at a glance what kind of an orator is speaking: if he notices one of the *iudices* yawning, or talking to a colleague, or sending out to inquire the time (*mittentem ad horas*), he knows at once that the speaker is not one *qui possit animis iudicum admovere orationem tanquam fidibus manum*; but if the court is eager and rapt, hanging upon the orator's words like a bird hearing a decoy-note, if those present are gripped by deep emotion, then he will know, even if he does not hear a single word, that a true orator is speaking and that the proper function of oratory is being performed. And again (ibid. 290), Cicero depicts a crowded court, with the bench full and the clerks bustling about, masses of spectators (*corona multiplex*), all tense at the news that a famous orator is to speak: 'cum surgat is qui dicturus sit, significetur a corona silentium, deinde crebrae assensiones, multae admirationes, risus cum velit, cum velit fletus; ut qui haec procul videat, etiam si quid agatur nesciat, at placere tamen et in scaena esse Roscium intellegat'.

The reference to the great actor Roscius is significant (cf. *de or.* i. 130). Time and again Cicero stresses the way in which a great orator will 'get inside his part'; thus he makes Antonius say of Crassus (*de or.* ii. 188) 'tantum est flumen gravissimorum optimorumque verborum, ut mihi non solum tu incendere iudicem, sed ipse ardere videaris', and Antonius, speaking of himself, states (ibid. ii. 189) 'non mehercule unquam apud iudices aut dolorem aut misericordiam aut invidiam aut odium dicendo excitare volui, quin ipse in commovendis iudicibus eis ipsis sensibus, ad quos illos adducere vellem, permoverer'. Some orators did not even wait for the actual hearing to arouse their own emotions, as is shown by the story of Galba in *Brut.* 87 f.: this speaker, entrusted at short notice with the conduct of a trial concerning mass murders, worked at his case in private until the last possible moment, and then he emerged for the pleading *eo colore et eis oculis ut egisse causam, non commentatum putares*, with his clerks completely knocked up (*male mulcatos*) as a result of their efforts.

A good commentary on the whole subject may be seen in Cicero's treatment of the orator M. Calidius, whom he opposed in a case brought against Q. Gallius; Calidius had charged this man with attempting to poison him, and Cicero argued in rebuttal (*Brut.* 277 f.) that in spite of his allegations he had pleaded *tam solute, tam leniter, tam oscitanter*: 'tu istuc, M. Calidi, nisi fingeres, sic ageres? praesertim cum ista eloquentia alienorum hominum pericula defendere acerrime soleas, tuum neglegeres? ubi dolor? ubi ardor animi, qui etiam ex infantium ingeniis elicere voces et querelas solet? nulla perturbatio animi, nulla corporis, frons non percussa, non femur, pedis (quod minimum est) nulla supplosio. itaque tantum afuit ut inflammares nostros animos, somnum isto loco vix tenebamus. sic nos summi oratoris vel sanitate vel vitio pro argumento ad diluendum crimen usi sumus'. The last sentence is very significant. Such passages, and many others, help to show the immense personal power for good or ill that a republican orator could wield. It was the existence of such power that made Quintilian in a later age stress at every turn the ethical aspect of an orator's function: he must be, in old Cato's words, *vir bonus dicendi peritus* (Quintil. xii. 1. 1), or he will betray his trust. In a famous simile (*Aen.* i. 148 ff.), Virgil sums up the whole ethical issue:

> 'ac veluti magno in populo cum saepe coorta est
> seditio saevitque animis ignobile vulgus,
> iamque faces et saxa volant, furor arma ministrat:
> tum, *pietate gravem ac meritis* si forte virum quem
> conspexere, silent arrectisque auribus adstant;
> ille regit dictis animos et pectore mulcet.'

# INDEX NOMINVM

(An asterisk marks references to the Additional Notes)

Antonius, C., 15. 22, 74. 11; pp. vi, 158 f.
Asicius, P., 23. 6.

Baiae, 35. 10, 38. 11.

Caecilius, 37. 9.
Caelius, M. (*pater*), 3. 11, 13, 73. 2; p. v.
Calpurnius Bestia, 1. 13, 16. 26, 26. 16; pp. vii, 154 f.
Caninius Gallus, 15. 24.
Canopus, 35. 11.
Claudius, Appius (Caecus), 33. 2.
Claudius, Appius (Pulcher), *cons.* 143, 34. 19.
Clodius, P., 36. 16.
Clodius, P. (*subscriptor*), 27. 3; p. 155.
Clodius, Sex., 23. 3, 78. 3; p. 151.
Coponii, 24. 19.
Curius Dentatus, 39. 6.

Dictys Cretensis, 63. 14.*
Dio, 23. 3, 24. 19, 56. 5; p. 152.
Domitius Calvinus, 32. 7.

Ennius, 18. 27.

Fabius Maximus, 15. 24.
Fabricius Luscinus, 39. 6.
Fufius Calenus, 19. 23.
Furius Camillus, 39. 6.

Gellius Poplicola, 23. 2; p. 155.

Herennius Balbus, 25. 1; p. 156.

Interamnia, p. 146.

Lentulus Spinther, p. 152.
Licinius, P., 61. 6.
Lucceius, L., 51. 6.
Luperci, 26. 20 ff.
Lutatius Catulus, *cons.* 102, 78. 9.
Lutatius Catulus, *cons.* 78, 59. 20, 70. 26; cf. l. 7.

Metellus Celer, 34. 10; p. 119.
Mucius Scaevola, 9. 23.

Palla, 23. 2; p. 152.
Plotius Gallus, p. vii.
Pompeius Rufus, *praetor* 63, 73. 24; p. v.
Pompeius Rufus, *tribune* 52, p. ix.
Praetuttiani, 5. 1; p. 146.
Ptolemy Auletes, 23. 3, p. 152.

Scribonius Curio, 19. 12.
Sempronia Atratina, 23. 2; p. 155.
Sempronius Atratinus, 1. 13; pp. vii, 154 f.
Sergius Catilina, 10. 11, 12. 1, 13. 13, 14. 6.

Vettius, 71. 8; p. 172.

# INDEX VERBORVM

absolvere (c. abl.), 78. 26.
abs te, 50. 16.
accusatores, 3. 9.
ac mihi quidem videtur, 3. 7.*
actae, 35. 10.
aculeus, 29. 2.
adferre, 53. 21.
admirabilis, 13. 17.

adulescens, 2. 1.
adumbratus, 12. 4.
advocatus, 10. 14.
alia (for *cetera*), 30. 19.
ambitus, 16. 26.
amplificatio, 38. 13.
annus (for *unus annus*), 10. 12.
aqua Appia, 34. 25.

176

argumentum longius repetitum, 18. 27.
armarium, 52. 13.
aspicio, 36. 25.*
atrocitas, atrox vis, 1. 3.
auctoritas, 55. 5.
audacia, 1. 11.
audaciter, 13. 24.
aulaeum, 65. 23.
austerus, 33. 24.
autem (with rel. pron.), 3. 14.

balneae Seniae, 61. 8.
barba, barbula, 33. 25.
beneficium, 7. 7.
boni (party term), 14. 7.

candor, 36. 25.*
caput, 31. 25.
caput fortunaeque, 67. 27.
Catuli monumentum, 78. 9.
clausula, 65. 22.
cohibere bracchium, 11. 20.
condicio, 14. 3, 36. 5.
conficere tabulas, 17. 9.
coniuncta causa, 24. 16.
convicium, 6. 25.
credo, 36. 20.
crimen, 1. 10.
cuicuimodi, 24. 15.
culpare, 1. 15.
cupiditas, 16. 5.*
cupio, 68. 4.

de cognatorum sententia, 68. 28.
decurio, 5. 3.
deducere, 9. 24.
defervescere, 43. 21, 77. 16.
deformare, 3. 9.*
deliciae, 27. 1.
descendere, 2. 19.
describere, 50. 18.
dies deficiat, 29. 24.
dignitas, 8. 13.
dis inimicis natus, 42. 2.*
discidium, 31. 3.
disertus, 15. 18.
dissice, 37. 21.
dolet (impersonal), 37. 22.

equus Troianus, 67. 12; pp. 171 f.
exempla, 39. 6.
experiri, 20. 1.
expressus, 12. 4.
extremis digitis, 28. 11.

fabella, 63. 23.*
facilitas, 14. 2.
facinerosus, 13. 24.
fas, 27. 8.*
femina, 31. 5.
fidem implorare, 65. 15.*
fides, 32. 18.*
fons, 19. 19.
frater ('cousin'), 60. 24.
frons ('branch'), 42. 3.*
frugem bonam, 28. 14.
furere, 60. 24.
furor, 15. 19.

gratia, 3. 9.
gurges, 44. 6.

habere (= scire), 3. 16.*
haec (= hoc imperium), 39. 6.
horti. 36. 27.

iactura, 38. 27.
idem ('together'), 36. 27, 52. 12, 57. 20.
incessus, 49. 6.
indoles, ingenium, 39. 22.*
inimicitiae, 32. 16.
in isto genere, 36. 19.*
inquit, 62. 17, 68. 7.
in quo (= qua in re), 15. 17.
insula, 17. 12.

laboriosus, 1. 16.
laudatores, 5. 5.
lenis, levis, 25. 5.
lex Domitia, 19. 12.
lex Iulia municipalis, 5. 3.
lex Licinia de sodaliciis, 16. 26.
lex Lutatia de vi, 1. 7, 70. 24.
lex Metalli Vipascensis, 62. 3.
lex Plotia de vi, 1. 7.
liberalis, 6. 19.
libido, 1. 15.
longe alius, 67. 22.

loqui, 11. 29.
luctus, 4. 27.
ludi Megalenses, 1. 3; p. 151.
ludus aetatis, 28. 16, 42. 14.

maeror, 4. 27.
male audire, 38. 2.
maledictio, 6. 23.
matrona, 32. 10, 49. 6.
mea sententia puto, 39. 4.
meretricii amores, 48. 20.
meta, 75. 17.
mimus, 65. 21.
minutio, 38. 13.
miseratio, 79. 16.
modo (with adjectives), 33. 24.
mulier, 31. 5.
munire viam, 34. 26.

nam quod, 4. 23.
natus huic imperio, 59. 11.
navigia, 35. 11.
negotium, 1. 4.
ne ... quidem, 34. 16.
nobilis, 31. 5.
non (in questions), 33. 7.
notus, 3. 13.

obsequium, 13. 18.
omitto, 27. 27.
operam navare, 21. 17.
ornatus, 5. 7.

paenitere, 6. 19; p. 163.
partim, 43. 27.
patruus, 25. 10.
periculum, 16. 2.
persona, 30. 17.*
petulantia, 50. 25.
praegustatores, 58. 4.
praevaricatio, 24. 12.
precario, 27. 8.
primoribus labris, 28. 11.
prisce, 33. 23.
probatus suis, 5. 28.
profecto, 1. 2.
profundere, 28. 17.
protervitas, 29. 26.
prudentia, 19. 10.
purpura, 77. 15.

pusio, 36. 21.
putare, 76. 11.
pyxis, 61. 9.

quadrantaria permutatio, 62. 3.
quam velit, 63. 11.
-que (attached to prepositions),
    46. 5.
quidam (intensive), 26, 21.
quidem (adversative), 12. 5.
quid signi, 38. 26.
quotus quisque, 38. 27.

redundare, 57. 21.
religio, 22. 21, 54. 17.
reprehensio, 32. 16.
reverti, 6. 12.
rivolus, 19. 19.

sales, 67. 18.
scabillum, 65. 23.
scelestus, 37. 14; p. 168.
se ipse, 11. 23.
seiuncta causa, 24. 16.
sequester, 16. 26.
sermones, 49. 7.
si licet, 27. 8.*
sic agam, 36. 16.
sodalicium, 16. 26.
spes (as genitive form), 80. 29.
splendidus, 3. 11.
squalor, 4. 25.
status ('stability'), 70. 25.*
subscriptores, 3. 9.
subtilis, 25. 4.
sui ('one's own'), 5. 8.
symphoniaci, 35. 11.

tamen, 20. 24.
testimonium, 55. 7.
tirocinium, 11. 19 f., 46. 2.
tituli, 19. 23.
toga, 11. 20.

urbanitas, 6. 25.
ut ne, 8. 11.

vel dicam, 75. 23.
velut, 64. 23.
verbo, 56. 1.
versari, 25. 9.

# INDEX VERBORVM

versura, 17. 9.
via Appia, 34. 26.
videor mihi, 5. 7.
videro, 35. 2.
vidi (from *visere*) 27. 10.
viva vox, 55. 10.*

ἄτεχνοι πίστεις, 54. 12.
ἔντεχνοι πίστεις, 22. 26, 54. 12.
ἐπαναφορά, 13. 12.
ἐπανόρθωσις, 32. 16.
προσωποποιία, p. 90.

# INDEX RERVM

ablative (instrumental), after *comitatus*, etc., 34. 26.
abstract for concrete, 22. 21.
abuse, 6. 21.
anacoluthon, 9. 22.
antithesis, 13. 22, 38. 13.
assonance, 38. 27, 68. 28, 78. 5.

bath-fees, 62. 3.
beards, 33. 25.
bribery-clubs, 16. 26.

case of nouns when repeated from an oblique case, 32. 16; cf. 75. 23.
Christian writers and the *pro Caelio*, 22. 27.
clausulae, remarked upon by Quintilian, 31. 5, 33. 7, 34. 11, 62. 5.
cruelty to slaves, 58. 4.
curtain in Roman theatres, 65. 23.

*de-* compounds, 44. 10.
*diceretur* for *esset* in reported speech, 3. 12.

editing of a speech, 19. 23.

gardens, 36. 27.
genitive (qualitative), 64. 24, 77. 19.
gerund with direct object (after *ad*), 50. 26.
gerundive of intransitive verbs, 51. 8.
'grand style', p. 143.

homoeoptoton, 63. 14.

indicative, imperfect, implying potentiality or obligation, 30. 6.*
indicative in concessive clause, 25. 8.
invective *in Clodium et Curionem*. 27. 10.*

*locus de indulgentia*, p. 102; *de testibus*, 20. 2.

manumission of slaves, 68. 28.
mimes, 65. 21.

nicknames, 18. 6, 62. 3.

participle with *volo*, 8. 8.
party terms, 14. 7, 15. 19, 60. 24.
past tenses used of a general truth, 25. 8.*
*per-* compounds, 25. 2.
'plain style', 11. 20, 25. 4.
pleonasm, 7. 3, 14. 27, 39. 4.
pluperfect passive with *fueram*. 64. 8.
poisoning, 58. 4, 65. 21.
*praenomen* and *nomen* separated by pronoun or particle, 34. 18.
*praeteritio*, 53. 28.
pronoun, redundant, 10. 10.
prosopopoeia, p. 90.
proverbial expressions, 28. 11, 14, 34. 11, 42. 2*, 61. 16, 67. 12, 22.
purple, shades of, 77. 15.

quotations in Cicero, 18. 27, 37. 9.

# INDEX RERVM

rents at Rome, 17. 11.
repetition of words, 3. 16, 70. 24.

'saints' gallery', 39. 6; p. 169.
'stipulative' clauses, 8. 11.
subjunctive, imperfect, in apparent primary sequence, 62. 27; pluperfect, after *postquam*, 59. 12.

Trojan Horse, 67. 12.*

verse-rhythms in prose, 79. 25; p. 173.

wit, terms for, 6. 25, 67. 18.
witnesses, depositions of, 55. 7; interrogation of, 4. 25.